T
Wonder
SAFARIS

THE
Wonder
SAFARIS

African journeys
of miracles
and surprises

ADAM LEVIN

First published in 2003 by Struik Publishers
(a division of New Holland Publishing
(South Africa) (Pty) Ltd)
New Holland Publishing is a member of Johnnic Communications Ltd

London • Cape Town • Sydney • Auckland

Cornelis Struik House, 80 McKenzie Street, Cape Town 8001

ISBN 1 86872 885 4

1 3 5 7 9 10 8 6 4 2

Publishing Manager: Dominique le Roux
Managing Editor: Lesley Hay-Whitton
Designer: Sian Marshall
Editor: Michelle Coburn
Proofreader: Anna Tanneberger

Reproduction by Hirt & Carter Cape (Pty) Ltd
Printed and bound by Paarl Print, Oosterland Street, Paarl, South Africa

The photographs for this book were supplied by the following,
who made material available from their personal collections:

Peter Baasch: Sunset at Forodhani Gardens; Bwejuu Village; The Blue Room, Emerson's House.
Andrew Bannister: Front cover; Fish-seller; Voodoo priestess; Maman Hamisi.
Peter Blackwell/Struik Image Library: Back cover.
John Hodgkiss: Berber man smoking; Berber guides; Dinner-time.
James Ashley Stephenson: Modelling kanga cloths; Facade, Emerson & Green Hotel; Hadza and huts.
Photographer unknown: Postcard: La Grande Mosquée at Djenne.

Visit us at **www.struik.co.za**

Log on to our photographic website
www.imagesofafrica.co.za for an
African experience.

Acknowledgements

Many Thanks

To my parents, Lionel and Louella Levin, for introducing me to a wide world and respecting the unlikely choices that resulted. To Marilyn Hattingh for being such a good and grumpy editor. To my people: Roy Weisz, Katy Bauer, Alexandra Dodd, Albert Venter, Jan van Deventer, Carl Collison, Cathi Evans, Alli Levin, Rahla and Jason Xenopoulos, Hein Verwey, Marcos Teofilo, Martin di Martino, Petra Mason and Kenny Eddy for your unwavering friendship, humour and support. To Dominique le Roux, Michelle Coburn and Sian Marshall at Struik for your enthusiasm and belief. To Andrew Bannister, Peter Baasch, John Hodgkiss and James Stephenson for your camaraderie on these journeys, and to Emerson D. Skeens for believing in it all. May you all live long lives and have many wondrous journeys.

MOROCCO

*Ouarzazate

MALI   Tiguidit
                        *Agadez
St Louis*   NIGER
Dakar* SENEGAL   *Bandiagara
        Mopti* *Djenné
          *Bamako

CÔTE   KENYA
D'IVOIR   Kilifi*
                                       *Mombasa
Abidjan* Busua* Accra* Ouidah* Chem-chem* Pemba
                  Cotonou* BENIN   Arusha* Zanzibar
              GHANA TOGO
                                TANZANIA

                                          MOZAMBIQUE   Tamatave*
                                                       Antananarivo
                                                            *
                                                       MADAGASCAR

                              Bilene*
                    Johannesburg* Maputo

                    SOUTH
                    AFRICA

Contents

Preface

Wonder Full

I am growing weary of life in this jungle. This savage hunting for money and things. This relentless gathering in plastic supermarket packets. This drumming on dark disco floors. Perhaps it is time to walk again. To walk until my feet turn a tar road back to dirt. Till my garden grows wild as savannah and my dogs run free as wolves. Then one day perhaps, when the last wounded cries of burglar alarms are but whimpers, we will hold hands around a sulphurous neon blaze of cars, shoes and cheque books. We will roast our television sets and the frantic babbling of talk show hosts will fill the universe. But first we must learn to walk.

I've been thinking lately about something Einstein said: that the world is either all miracles or no miracles at all, depending on how you look at it. I know there are miracles all around me: on pavements, in shopping trolleys, outside nightclubs; or buried nearby in the lives of checkout girls, lovers and petrol pump attendants. But gradually, trapped in the sameness of this city, I have grown blind to their powers. Somewhere in the garish, deodorized supermarket of modern life, I have misplaced my miracle eye – and with it, my sense of wonder. My gut sags with the weight of urban sensory overload. My heart goes hungry. Again, I must learn to eat. Life.

Sometimes I feel myself drowning in this sea of convenience. Too much, too fast and all too available. And when I do stumble across a miracle, it is only because some silly, wayward cog has slipped out of place in the big, shiny machine. Magic does not flourish easily on the urban factory floor – it shrivels, blooming only in our accidents and mistakes. And it is only when we fuck up that we hear, ever so faintly and briefly, the primal, chaotic splutterings of the universe again. The wet gurgling of the womb. The ancient chatter of mermaids. The ever-cracking flames of immortality.

Lunatics can hear those sounds. In fact, I suspect they thump away in the ears of all those we cast off as naïve and helpless – those too old, too young or too poor to matter. And the further away from the world one wanders, of course, the louder those rhythms will become. Way out there, on bad roads, in broken towns and cruel states, there are deep souls who are very much alive. Because, for all the conveniences and technologies they lack, in the simple quietude of their lives they have remembered how to listen with open ears: how to tune their eardrums to the great primeval wireless broadcasting from the belly of the earth – neither missing a sound, nor distinguishing one from another. They hear the whole planet, I am told. And their palms are chafed with earth songs. And magic turns their eyes to light bulbs.

Listen, if you will. Listen to all the weird languages in the world being spoken at once. Just imagine opening your ears deep and wide enough to really hear that sound, and to hear rhythms that emerge from its chaos. There are some who believe the answers to all the riddles in the universe are written in those rhythms, and the more I learn, the more I am one of them.

Again, I must learn to listen. For with each day in this jungle, I grow deafer. I shuffle through the quick, glorious dance of evolution, and yet I fear I might be dying. For nowadays, I scarcely recognize those rhythms when I hear them. I have stopped speaking in miracles – stopped listening out for them – and so it's natural, I suppose, that they should cloister themselves behind the drab, ordered curtain of modern life.

I sense a shiver of anarchy surfing my spine. The nerves of some insane geography begin to tingle. I am hungry for miracles and surprises right now. I am starving for the taste of my own senses. Take me to my teachers. To those whose hearts still thump with exquisite beats of faith. Those whose beliefs have not yet vanished in the name of science and money and power. Those wayward and forgotten animists, for whom every atom in the universe is ripe with spirit and meaning. Tell me their tales. Fold my body through their gestures. Let me feel the shapes of their lives in my knees and elbows. The textures on my palms. And let me un-know what I know so well. So I, too, can be 'WonderFull'.

What a world we're making. A world that explains itself so eloquently, it has forgotten how to sense or feel. A world that stutters so on the grammar of true sensuality that nowadays, if I am to grease my miracle tongue, I must pay the price of long and hardy pilgrimage. I must wander widely, into faraway cracks of the earth; and deeply, immersing myself, shivering, into hostile, murky pools of otherness. I must forsake this urban desert and flee to some exotic, ramshackle metropolis, where I have a chance of reversing the cycle. Where my English might lose its currency, and the rich languages of miracles and surprises might bury themselves in my gums.

But where? I shuffle through the messy flip-charts of my memory. I run my fingers over the palms of my hands for clues. I search my palate by tongue. Already, there is so little left of the planet. As we speak, the fat merchants of the tourist trade are sweeping the earth, herding with them their droves of shallow holiday cattle, swathed in sunscreen and 'No Problem' T-shirts. No problem? Sure, no problem while the lost world still harbours miracle crannies for our refuge. No problem while there are still lands too thorny and remote for such lazy and mediocre beasts. But come quickly, for we must learn to wander. You know the deal in this cosmos: you wait too long, it disappears.

Introduction

A few years ago I began journeying into Africa, bringing home travel stories and profiles. With each trip, I grew more and more enchanted with the place. I wanted to explore further, not just to feed my ravenous curiosity, but also to find out what the word 'African' meant on my passport. To find out who and where I was.

I had journeyed many times – through South Africa, Mozambique, Kenya, Tanzania and Madagascar; travelling rough roads, stumbling across secrets and forgotten people – and yet somehow my experiences had remained fleeting and superficial. I wanted more. More ancient. More remote. Deeper. The miracles and surprises of this continent held me captive.

As the months passed, I felt further and further away from my life in Johannesburg. I wound my way through the mazes of lost towns, swapping stories for cigarettes, buying secrets, watching, thinking, laughing, dancing. I could scarcely believe this was the continent of my birth, for it seemed so very strange and rich. And yet this was just a tiny piece of the great African puzzle. The more I discovered, the more I realized that Africa was bigger and older and more complicated than I'd ever imagined.

For so long, it had been a blacked-out map to me – inaccessible but for the droning miserable accounts of coups or famine or disease. Even after Nelson Mandela's release from prison, the scope of African literature, music and information available here seemed to me pathetically inadequate. As if by conspiracy, Africa had been written out of the script. If I really wanted to know what was going on north of the Limpopo, I'd have no choice but to voyage into dusty obscurity and explore for myself.

It seemed an odd road to choose, urbane as I am. Middle-class; often impatient and fussy about insects and certain foods. More interested in cities and culture than in trees or reptiles. Diligent slave to fashion dictates and new music releases. If this was a post being advertised, I was the candidate least likely to succeed.

Only now, it was a little late for such considerations. I had already travelled roads far more interesting than Johannesburg's highways. I'd found weekly markets, bustling with goats and warriors, far more thrilling than my local supermarket; and sweated my way through village drumming sessions more primal and more frenetic than Johannesburg's nightclubs. To forsake the majesty of these landscapes and return to the safe, predictable life I'd known was an option too banal to contemplate.

Besides, the stories here were so much richer – Karen Blixen wasn't a bad hack, you know, but she wasn't Shakespeare either. Set against Africa's sweeping vistas, amid the old mysteries, simple stories wrote themselves into sweeping epics. Ordinary people, through the remoteness of circumstance, had lived extraordinary lives; and customs, in their obscurity, appeared strange and magical. It was a world that, as photographer Mirella Ricciardi expressed to me, ' ... was truly vanishing'.

For then, I decided, I was happy to live the life of a vagabond – travelling along these less-travelled roads, capturing the images as they sped out of sight and bringing them home in scruffy notebooks – coming and going, buying and selling, as African traders had done for centuries. A couple of weeks later, when photographer James Stephenson said he was travelling to Northern Tanzania to spend time with East Africa's last surviving hunter-gatherers, I saw no option but to accompany him.

The weeks I spent with the Hadzabe were a turning point for me, for not only was I in awe of this Stone Age society, I felt totally at ease with its people. Despite the millennia between our cultures, in their spontaneity, their creativity and their warmth, I felt closer to them than to most people in the cafés back home. We laughed together, and in the thick forest night, as we tracked down some savage beast, they held my hand as though I was one of them. Eerily, the shapes of identity began to blur. Was this what the word on my passport meant? Was this what it meant to be African?

Over the months that followed, I would ask myself these same questions many times. On the hard floor of a wooden *pirogue* in Mali, when the dry, colourless landscape had not changed for days. On the back of a motorbike taxi, on the smoggy, low-rise streets of Cotonou. In the frenzied throng of a two-am *bacheque* dance session in a nightclub in downtown Abidjan. In the shuttered, afternoon breeze of a ramshackle balcony in St Louis, a stone's throw from the Mauritanian border, I would ask, 'Is this who I am?' And sometimes it was, and sometimes it wasn't.

Only, at the same time, something else was happening to me. For each time I returned home I would ask myself these same questions. I'd stroll down my street in Johannesburg, hoping to relive the magic that walking had held in Stonetown, for instance. But instead of yelling shopkeepers and hustlers, there'd be cars and dogs and intercoms. Instead of a bowl of rice and coconut curry shared among many hands, there'd be single servings that one popped in the microwave. 'Is this me?' I'd ask. And sometimes it was, and sometimes it wasn't

Nowhere on this continent, however, had I been more aware of my whiteness. In Mombasa, Dar es Salaam or Antananarivo, I could rattle along in broken Swahili or Malagasy and forget the colour my skin, while at home I so often felt like a stranger, a settler – a white boy in a black land that seemed always to be slipping through my fingers. 'So what's South Africa like?' my chums in Mali or Senegal would ask. 'Strange,' I'd reply.

'But hasn't everything changed since Mandela?'

'No. Not really,' I'd tell them. 'It's still very strange.'

Indeed, much of my wandering has left me less resolved than had I stayed home. For with each answer, there have been more perplexing riddles. With each experience, more possibilities. With each platitude, more exceptions and surprises. And all along the way, the richness of these journeys has been written on my body – each bump, each bite, each smile and each street – so that even if I never was an African, my journeys have made me one.

Today, there are few places still sufficiently remote to be considered truly exotic. Yet, by chance and by cruel design, much of this continent has been forgotten by the world. The wretchedness of its roads; the tyranny of its distances; and the nastiness of its insects and governments, have always kept it outside the cosy cuddle of the global village. Its slowness, its brokenness, its poverty, have allowed only the most passionate of voyagers the privilege of penetrating its mysteries.

Yes, even today, amid the spaghetti bowl of satellite dishes, super-optic cables and information highways, you cannot see the Niger at dawn if you have not slept on the clay floor of a Peul hut the night before. And if you do not take the horrible dirt road to Busua on the Ghanaian coast, you will never meet Josephine Winston, posed against a tattered, pink wall, in curlers and a perfect shirtwaister dress, selling cigarettes with names like Embassy, Diplomat and Statesman. Neither will you hear the tales of the lost, white chiefs; Pan-African gurus; pale missionaries and ten-cent Rastas; nor sip sodas with the fat whores who fan themselves at half speed in the wet, rotten heat of a worn-out Sahelian town. And just in case you don't, I am writing down all their stories, and mine, in a hundred ragged notebooks, and you can read the highlights on the following pages.

NARRATIVES &
Travelogues

THE TEA SONGS OF
Senegal

According to Sahel tradition, the three glasses of mint tea should be drunk over a number of hours. The first glass, *lewul*, is so dark and so bitter, one can barely taste the mint leaves; the second, *taari*, is lighter and less so; the third, *salik*, is clear and sweet. To proceed to the third cup without drinking the others is a sacrilege of time-worn tradition.

Macuba

The day William Burroughs died, I moved into a grand weathered brothel on the edge of Dakar's Place D'Indépendance. Home was a large, perfectly square room, with a lazy ceiling fan, elegant Provençal shutters and a family of cockroaches. To recount the events of this, my first day in Dakar, still leaves me tingling with great joy, numb pain and disgust.

'Let me ask you one thing?' Macuba had asked. 'Just one?' I am not sure why I stopped. For the whole length of the Avenue Ponty, I had held my gaze slightly above the hateful cattle auction of perfume, *schwarmas* and underpants, but I allowed him to continue: 'Why do all the whites who come here go to see prostitutes?' he asked almost angrily.

It was an original opener to be sure; all the same, I figured that I'd forego any further bonding. I lowered my eyelids and kept walking, but unfortunately it was at that moment that he flashed a programme for the upcoming St Louis Music Festival on the Mauritanian border. By the time I creaked open my lids, I was like a lamb to the slaughter.

What transpired over the next eight hours was a tragic farce comprising a *djembe* drum, a bottle of Fanta Orange, one hundred French francs and an envelope of weak marijuana that I had never even requested. Tragic because Macuba was indeed a first-class Senegalese con-artist, and farcical because all along, there were prescient signs of the pending swindle which, given our heartfelt chats about goodness and honesty, I chose to ignore. Regardless, by three am I found myself one hundred francs poorer and taxiing across town, seeking the comfort of a Coca-Cola and then drowning in a puddle of broken promises. My first sip of Senegal's capital had been a bitter one.

I resolved not to look out for Macuba the next morning. I knew that everything we'd said was now cruelly void and that Dakar was a horrible place. I spent the day in a passive-aggressive trance, running through the previous night's events like a hamster on a wheel. By ten pm, when I heard a knock at my door, I had uttered but three phrases to the universe: '*Un café noir*', 'Taxi to Tahiti Plage' and 'Yes, it's very hot today'. I wrapped a mudcloth around me and opened the shutters. 'Telephone,' the receptionist grumbled.

'Telephone? But nobody knows I'm here,' I gasped – in English, by mistake. He looked at me quizzically. Macuba, I wondered. Does the tale continue? 'I'm coming,' I said, and shuffled along the terracotta tiles to the phone. 'Room ten?' the strange voice enquired. 'I have an apartment for you. Macuba said I should call. You look for apartment, no?'

'Yes.' I heaved. 'But where is Macuba? He was supposed to meet me last night. He has my money.'

'Oh, Macuba's not here,' the voice replied. 'But you can meet me at the Score supermarket and I will show you the apartment. We'll drink tea together. I am wearing white African clothes. My name is Ibrahim. Can you come now?'

I agreed, and dressed myself, amazed by the shameless endurance of the Senegalese hustle. Nowhere else would a thief leave a forwarding address.

Ibrahim

I grimaced through *lewul*, the first glass of tea, as I recounted my sorry tale to Ibrahim. His response shifted from utter denial of Macuba's wrong-doing to scolding me for having trusted someone so quickly. 'But Dakar is a small place,' he said. 'We will find him and he will find your money.'

I was dubious, yet somehow, with each glass of tea, the evening grew sweeter. 'You are a nice boy,' he said, after *taari*. 'Nice boy.' The words had all the warmth and sentimentality of a Yiddische Mama. When he said 'Hey man', however, it was Jimi Hendrix all the way. For, as I was soon to learn, Ibrahim was not only stuck in a horrible financial crisis here in the medina, but also in the year 1974.

We spoke of his family. They were *griots*: West Africa's legendary troubadour caste that I had long wanted to document. His grandfather had been a *griot* to the descendants of King Sundiata, he told me as we sipped on *salik*. We could explore all this and more together, he suggested. He placed his hand on my knee. 'You have taken a risk to be here,' he said. 'You have trusted me. This makes me very happy.'

For each place in the world, I imagine, there is a magic mode; a brief trance, wherein the elements of time, place and people transpire to bliss. In the Sahel that trance comprises the following elements: a night sky, a soft breeze, a courtyard, mint tea and marijuana. By no means, however, does this amount to a recipe for the trance, for without the blessing of the hand of chance, the moment is meaningless. Many times, I have drunk empty teas in shallow squares and waited pointlessly for the moments to dissolve into bliss. But as I have now learned, it is only when all present have sufficiently surrendered their wills, that the seconds become as perfect as circles. I've experienced this trance twice in the Sahel: once in a suburb of Bamako, amid the braying of goats and the nibbling of mosquitoes, and once tonight, with Ibrahim.

I have long believed the following, I told him: While those who seek always to control the universe shall receive few gifts from the hand of chance, those who risk the waves of experience, shall, in time, be vindicated. Only by risking like this might one truly sense the sacred textures of destiny – the timeless ebb and flow of existence. I smiled. 'Yes,' I said, carefully. 'I'm pleased to be here.' Perhaps we would pass more such nights together. One could never be sure.

The Surprise

I sauntered to a coffee stall the next evening and asked about the night's entertainment prospects. The tablecloth glowed pink plastic under the street lamps, and the clink of teaspoons in coffee glasses was warm and familiar. 'Do you know which bands are playing tonight?' I asked. The vendor was suddenly silent, then gestured awkwardly to a man sitting next to him. And it was after a frozen instant of silence that I recognized Macuba, grinning discreetly under the peak of a grey cap. I was astonished.

In a city of over a million people, we had met again – by chance or by cruel design, I couldn't be sure. I kept my calm and went over to speak to him.

Immediately, he launched into a barrage of explanations that made no sense, twisting puerile accusations from the petty details of the moment. I made myself very clear and he grudgingly agreed to repay me, but we would need to fetch the money in the medina. I nodded politely, saving my fury for the minute I had my cash in hand, and we climbed onto a *car rapide* and rattled off into the Dakar night, the chaotic beats of Mbalax clunking from the stereo.

The moments were strained with distrust and worry. He tried to soften me with conversation; I remained guarded. I considered what Ibrahim had said: that theft, when necessary for survival, was justifiable in such a poor country. 'Steal to feed your family if you need to,' he'd said. 'But steal for a living? Never. *That* is sinful.' The neon lights of bakeries and police stations flashed by, losing us, then finding us in a bar where Macuba played the drums from time to time. We sat on the balcony and I softened a little. 'You know, I thought you'd robbed me the other night,' I said. 'I can understand you thought that,' he replied. 'But we've been very honest with each other. We've spoken from the heart. And you know now that it was a misunderstanding.' I nodded. 'Anyway,' he said, 'I'll go inside and see the patron here. He owes some money.' I sat on the balcony and waited.

'He only has a two hundred franc note,' Macuba explained when he returned. 'So it's better we go to the city to get the money.'

'Don't worry,' I said shaking my head. I was growing weary of this soap opera and needed to be more authoritative in the exchange. 'I have a hundred francs here; give it to him and bring me the two hundred.' It was after ten minutes of waiting that my saliva turned bitter and began dripping down into my stomach like molten lead.

I stepped inside. The bar was red and empty, with an open window at the back. There had been no patron. No two hundred franc note. Simply another spectacle in the repertoire of a shameless trickster, polished off with an ingenious farewell. Rage. Humiliation. Despair. I had been robbed twice, in two days, by the same despicable thief. I slumped back to the brothel, sure that no-one would believe this sad mess and that now Macuba was gone forever. I lay awake, clenching the sheets in my fists – sleepless, for my faith in decency and reason had betrayed me.

Home

The next morning, I recounted my woes to Ibrahim. Again, he scolded me for my stupidity, then began to seethe. 'If I see Macuba again, I won't even give him a cigarette,' he promised feebly, then reached over and lit one of mine. 'You must come and stay with us,' he insisted. 'We will catch the thief and take him to the police. And we will go and meet the *griots*. Here, you are safe,' he continued. 'You are in the medina, with the family. Here we have *le Social Lee-veeng*!' The words carried the hollow idealism of African socialism. I looked around me. It was difficult to imagine this as my home. *Le Social Lee-veeng* comprised a tiny room, two red velvet chairs, a mattress and too many net curtains embossed with mustard-coloured, seventies motifs. On the turquoise wall, a photocopied image of the Grand Marabout, Cheikh Amadou Bamba, was framed in tinfoil, offset with a grey suit and a collection of Ibrahim's wife's handbags in red, black and gold.

Her name was Ahuma M'baye, and she and her four striking sisters had lived around this courtyard since their births, plaiting their hair, grinding the chillies and groundnuts for the daily meal, and swanning around in magnificent states of undress, shoulders glistening in the sunlight. Nowadays, Ahuma covered her stomach with floral cloth and left her breasts exposed. She neither carried her handbags nor plaited her hair, for she was within a fortnight of the birth of her first child. I simply could not impose. 'Hey man,' said Ibrahim. 'This is your home.'

I shook my head. Besides, I would have no privacy here. The striking family M'baye would be privy to my eating, my sleeping, my bathing, my thoughts. I had spent so many special evenings in such places – blurring the cruel boundaries of class, culture and distance, connecting and feeling free. But never had I surrendered the middle-class emergency pack in my wallet: just enough cab fare to get home – to a room of my own, where I might want to retreat into myself and refresh for the upcoming adventures. The truth was, to forsake the bourgeois spaciousness of my culture for the tight, clawing poverty of this community would require a giant leap of faith. I shivered at the thought, took a deep breath and leapt.

Ahuma

Moving in with a family was a flashback for me. The nagging, the worrying, the very politics of caring was a marathon trial. Given the now evident dangers of Dakar, I was also convinced to surrender my remaining liquid cash to Ahuma's grandmother for safekeeping – and with it my independence. I never saw the woman's face: I knew her only by the gesture of a locking key and the words 'the old one'. And every time I wanted to buy a cigarette, I would need to wait for 'the old one' to arrive and twist her wrist.

Furthermore, it had been agreed that I would buy enough rice, oil, sugar and Nescafé for the family; I would pay Ibrahim for the accommodation and for his services as a guide, and I would pay for nothing more. I would live as they lived, here among the goats, taxis and curious glances of the medina. But already, as I recovered from my sleepless night, I could feel my new home aching in my joints. To change my T-shirt, I had to move the two velvet chairs, open the cupboard to haul out my bags and then put everything back afterwards. Perfect neatness – not for neatness' sake, but out of necessity. It was neither the bush toilet nor the bucket shower that perturbed me, but deprived of the space, freedom and choice I had grown accustomed to, I felt imprisoned here. I simmered like a teenager, then approached Ibrahim.

I knew we had made a deal, I explained. Only now, after waking up in this strange place and making my calculations, I realized it would actually work out more expensive than a hotel. They were wonderful people but perhaps it would be better if I moved back to the Hotel Provençal and found the peace and quiet to write. Ibrahim was silent. 'I am a good Muslim,' he shivered. 'And if I had the means, you would live with us without paying. But as you know, I am a poor man. The money you gave us is no longer here. We have sent it to buy a goat for the baby's baptism. If you want, I will sell all my things and return your money and you can go and stay in your hotel and give your money to some rich Lebanese hotel owner.' He sat down, still breathing quickly. 'Or you can stay here and help us,' he said. 'It's up to you.'

My neck ached. I was amazed how quickly I'd implicated myself in this miserable drama. How what had been my own decisions a few hours ago now weighed so heavily on these other lives, so far away from mine. How responsibility had landed in my lap like a windswept potato crisp packet. I lit a cigarette and I stayed.

That evening, when Ibrahim went to pray, Ahuma brought me a cup of

Nescafé and we sat together. We spoke without language but with awkward smiles, the silence blurred only by the whimpering of the pink electric fan. I showed her some pictures of my friends in Johannesburg. She giggled warmly, without losing her composure. She humbled me. Even now in this rainless rainy season, she bore her grubby household chores and the heaviness of her pregnancy with grace and endurance. Indeed, as life in the medina grew more and more trying, it would be the goodness of her heart that kept me from fleeing.

Space

The following afternoon I met with a group of African academics in a marble-floored mansion with a view of Ngor beach, and a flushing toilet. I sat on it for a good half hour, savouring the trance of safety allowed by the smooth, plastic comfort of the seat. Most of those spread out on the divans were stationed abroad, it turned out, and were only here to discuss development issues at conferences. Nobody commented on the grubbiness of my T-shirt, but we spoke at length about the beauty of the antique Mauritanian carpet under the dining-room table. I sat on the edge of the divan, ashing my cigarette into my palm and I told them my bleakening tale.

'I've always wanted to make journeys through Africa,' Achim, the esteemed Cameroonian scholar, lamented – only lately he'd been living in Philadelphia. 'So you really don't have a shower?' Jean-Marc chuckled, stroking his beard. 'No,' I replied. 'But Ahuma brings me a bucket of water and a cup in the mornings and she lends me her flip-flops to negotiate the filth of the drains.' They all laughed. And in the accents that America, France and Canada had lent them, they encouraged me.

I returned to the medina late that evening, to find Ahuma swaying worriedly down the street. She smiled when she saw me, then lowered her eyes. She had been so concerned at my lateness, Ibrahim explained, she had walked up and down to the bus stop all afternoon, palm cradled stoically beneath her belly.

I felt embarrassed as we walked home, and a little suffocated, and when we arrived I noticed how awkwardly my big, white body fitted into the dark, narrow shapes of the place. My hips too wide. My gestures too grand. My glances too sweeping. And the stiffness I felt – in my elbows, my shoulders and my eyes – was the very African story of poverty, scripted grittily in nerve and muscle and sweat. Although with their mouths, today's academics could tell all about the pain of this continent, the aching of my joints tonight told a deeper story. For, of course, to know Africa intellectually is of limited value. For how can one know it without knowing the weight of the forces that grip it? The heaviness of its bars? The monotony of its rhythms? The cramped ache of its spaces? To shower bouquets of sympathy from safe balconies, I decided, was as empty and pointless as casting paper aeroplanes into a storm.

Sissoko

The *griots* have always occupied a paradoxical position in West African society. Though among the lowest of social castes, for centuries they have performed a key role as communicators – wailing flattery at chubby chiefs with their praise songs and travelling between villages, recounting their indispensable tales of origin and genealogy to the melodies of *khalams* or *koras*. So sweet and so soft are the sounds of these instruments, it is not uncommon for those listening to offer tears as an expression of gratitude.

In a part of the world where written literature is a new and tenuous innovation, these oral historians remain indispensable in small villages. Yet the *griots* are still feared, for their proximity to important people vests them with extraordinary powers for those of such a lowly caste. 'They know all the secrets,' Ibrahim tells me. 'All the history. Even the very old history.'

The genealogies they recount are especially important in West Africa, for here a name expresses not only who you are but also what you are allowed to do. Traditionally, it was only if you bore a name like Djom or Guisse that you might work as a weaver. Thiong, an ironmonger. N'dour or M'baye or Sissoko, a *griot*. And even today, amid the chaos of a developing economy, these roles still carry meaning. When Salif Keita, the great Malian musician, achieved his extraordinary success, he went to the *griot* families and wept. 'I am not a *griot*,' he said. 'I am from the royal line of Keitas. Forgive me for stealing your tradition.'

This morning we ride in a yellow taxi to the working-class suburb of Yoff, where we have arranged to meet a young, talented *griot* and *kora* player called Sissoko. I have waited many days for this privilege, nagging and insisting like a Dakar hawker, and finally it has been arranged. But there is tension in the car, for this morning Ibrahim asked me for money to pay for a pregnancy scan. I refused. 'But you have money,' he insisted. 'Give it to me. I will pay you later.'

I dared not part with another franc of my future. Already I had surrendered so much of myself. Whatever I had left, I would leave where it was – with the old one. 'You'll just have to sell the goat,' I suggested blankly. He was furious. 'You do not know my culture,' he seethed as the taxi rolled up to a grimy apartment block. 'I will never sell the goat.'

Yet as soon as we had climbed the stairs, passed the blocked toilets, yelling babies and steaming cooking pots, Ibrahim's face broke into a great smile. 'Hey man,' he said, proudly. 'You are going to hear the *griots* today. You will see, everything will be perfect.' And from the moment I saw Sissoko tuning his majestic *kora* on the roof of the building, I knew that he was right.

I could not have hoped for a more magnificent stage for this perform-ance. A roofless, concrete slab of a theatre. At one end, a low wall, plushly upholstered with bags of garbage; at the other, a neat line of front row seats: three plastic mats and some scraps of cardboard. And before it, the young master seated beneath a grand washing line of a stage curtain, hung with grand *boubous* and denim jeans. Sissoko nods at my arrival, but stays distant.

The *kora* was born here, long before *here* was Senegal. It has a calabash for a speaker and bears 17 strings fastened to a wooden mast. To pluck these strings is to weave droplets of water into music. And as Sissoko dips his fingers into the strains of the first ancient melody, I am cast off, breath-less, into a river of song. I sense a shiver of relief in my arms. Again, in the wake of an argument, I feel the coming of a trance. All morning I have felt trapped and angry and taken for granted, but now that I have flung up my huffy arms in the resignation of the moment, the moments are melting into bliss. The tea bubbles in an enamel pot, the flies dance, the sun burns an orange crust into the Dakar sky. 'I'm going to tell you a story,' he says. 'But it's a very long story.'

'I like long stories,' I smile, without opening my eyes. 'Hey man,' says Ibrahim, slapping my thigh. 'The *kora*!' I nod, but cannot look at him. I know he has paid dearly for the intimacy of this audience, and he has done it for me, but I cannot share the trance with him. The songs reach too deep to share.

Sundiata

Over the following hours Sissoko recounts, with great skill, the legend of King Sundiata, tinkering all the while on his magic *kora*. We drink *lewul* and he tells of the king's birth and how his mother summoned a scorpion to kill him while he was still a baby; how the scorpion bit him three times, but that Sundiata drew out the poison and kept it in the palm of his hand. Over *taari*, he tells how the woman summoned the bees to sting the boy, but that the bees were enchanted by the young savant and only frolicked with him. Ibrahim excuses himself, lays a scrap of cardboard at the eastern side of the roof, and speaks to Allah.

It is already dark when we drink *salik*, and Sissoko has recounted but a tiny chapter in this epic tale of strength against adversity. It has been an unforgettable afternoon, marred only slightly by Ibrahim's constant, thigh-slapping enthusiasm. 'But if this is all we ever learn about the *griots*,' I tell him, 'it is enough.'

Saturday Night

The following evening I stroll down to the Café d'Etudiants to hear some salsa. Like Joni Mitchell, I seem to always be in search of love or music, and yet I am so often a victim of creepy surprises. Yes, Macuba is seated, under that same grey cap, at the end of the bar.

He snatches a tale from thin air the moment he lays eyes on me. 'Where were you this morning?' he fumes. 'I was waiting here for you.'

'Where is my money?' I ask, raising my eyebrows.

'Didn't you get the message? I told Ibrahim I'd meet you here?'

'Where is my money?'

'Come, we will go and find it,' he huffs, heading off into the dark street.

'No!'

I hold Macuba's wrist firmly and yank him into the light. He pulls and I grab hold of him. 'Thief,' I yell, as loudly as I can, and it is at this moment that a stocky bouncer in a Nike T-shirt starts yelling too, and promptly escorts us to the police station. As we walk, I shiver, unsure if I am heading for a refund or a dope conviction. Lieutenant Diouf eyes us grumpily. He buttons up his beige jacket and opens his ledger. Macuba begins to speak and I bate my breath for the coming lies. He speaks in tedious detail, back-pedalling through the quick and sorry history of our friendship, recounting everything – from our conversations about goodness, to the two hundred francs – with calm and accuracy. I nod as he talks, surprised but relieved. It is only when he arrives at the great escape that instead of saying, 'I fled through the open window at the back of the red, empty bar,' he looks me in the eye, and says blankly: 'I just popped off to visit a friend.'

I am speechless. 'So, where's my money?' I spit. And Macuba dips into his filthy manipulating self and pulls out his trump-card. 'But you asked me to buy you marijuana with that money.'

Lieutenant Diouf sighs. 'I think you should explain this all to the captain on Monday,' he says. 'Give me your addresses and you can leave.' Macuba offers his, and it is then that I realize I haven't a clue where I live. 'And yours?' he asks curtly. There is a long silence, and eventually it is Macuba who states, 'Fifty-seventh Avenue, in the medina, with the family M'baye.' Lieutenant Diouf looks very puzzled and writes it down.

When I get home Ibrahim and Ahuma are sitting on the balmy pavement on a mat. I buy a big bottle of Coca-Cola and tell them every-thing. Ibrahim translates it into Wolof for Ahuma and she shivers at the violent bits. 'And what if you meet him again?' she asks nervously. 'Oh,' I sigh. 'I think I'll burst into tears,' and I fall asleep between them, on the pavement.

Ngor

On Monday morning, Macuba is nowhere. I meet with the captain and tell him the whole, horrible story, including the bit about the unwanted mari-juana and the escape at the end, and how pathetic it is that I have been fooled a third time by the same despicable thief. And he says he thinks it's quite pathetic too and goes off to look for Lieutenant Diouf to hear his side of the story, only to learn that Lieutenant Diouf's uncle died yesterday and he will only be returning to the office on Friday. I thank him stiffly and tell him that Thursday I will be flying out of this cruel, unjust country. Again I am angry. Again a fool. 'Well, if you ever come across the two hundred francs,' I express, 'you should put it in an envelope and give it all to the family M'baye.'

I stomp home to tell them the miserable news. But the household is tense this morning, for Ahuma needs to go to the hospital and there is no money for the trip. I ask that the old one turn her wrist for the last time, only her wrist has already turned, it appears, for the last of my money has gone for a pregnancy scan. I am enraged. Ibrahim says nothing with his mouth, but his eyes fix on me and say: a thief is not a thief if he steals to feed his family. I say nothing either, but my eyes say: a bourgeois tourist is not a tourist if he does not sneak a secret hundred dollar bill into the back of his wallet for emergencies. I bundle up a few of my things and walk out of the house. And had I not hopped on a boat for Ngor Island an hour later, I think my waters may have broken before Ahuma's did.

I would spend the last three days of my journey on Ngor, and I would spend them alone, in a big, soft hotel room all of my own – *Anti-Social Lee-veeng* if you like. I didn't care what it cost and I didn't care if it was un-African. For now, I would bath and shit and eat whenever I wanted to, for I had begun to lose everything in this mess.

Already from the boat, I could hear the plaiting of braids on the island. The kissing of white girls and their short-lease Rastafarian princes. The sales pitches for *djembe* drums. I'd been here before, though never quite here but in Kenya, Côte d'Ivoire or Mozambique, and I wanted no part of this generic beach scene. I wanted nothing but my aloneness. I lay on the beach until sundown, warding off potential chums with irate glances, and savouring the space around me. I stretched my legs, my arms, my eyes. Perhaps it was better this way? Perhaps I could dip in and out of every grubby city on this continent and would still always find myself, in my big, soft hotel room of a self? Perhaps I was made this way – simple as that? Perhaps places *made* you?

I thought of Ibrahim. If another place had made him, we might have been good friends. But given the hell of *here*, I could no longer hold him close to my heart, for with each franc he'd sucked from me, he'd let go of another part of himself, and still there were not enough francs to change anything about his wretched life. Of the goodness of his heart, I had little doubt. Yet, trapped in the clawing sadness of the medina, his hands, his thoughts, even his words were prisoners to the destitution that surrounded him. His heart, too, was no longer his own, for he had hired it out – with the rest of him – in a last, desperate plea to ward off the wolves at the door.

Given another place, we might even have been brothers and slithered together along the rollercoaster of life. But here, we had been brothers once only – for a few hours, in a courtyard where, in our mutual despair, we had let loose our fears and skipped together through a deep, perfect song of mint tea, soft breeze, night sky and marijuana. A tea song, I thought to myself. Bitter, sweet and timeless.

Tea for two, I figured. Tea for three or tea for ten. But never tea for one.

Paul

I strolled up to the beachside bar, bought a beer from the Rastafarians and savoured the last moments of my solitude. 'Staying on the island?' Paul asked, pulling up a chair. 'Yes,' I said. He lived here, he told me, and this was his favourite time of the day. For at dusk, when the bulk of the tourists climbed onto the last boat back for the mainland, so the people of Ngor became a family again. They did everything together here. They sang and played the drums together. Ate, swam and slept. '*Social Lee-veeng*?' I said brightly. 'Yes,' he chuckled.

I looked around me. They were indeed a family – waifs and strays really. Rebels, cripples and lost villagers who had drifted up on this island in search of freedom. And when the thumping of the *djembes* rang out in the denim sky, even the boy in the wheelchair tapped his fingers to the beat. I bought a plate of food and shared it with Paul. And when we finished, he told me something I will never forget. 'We saw you alone on the beach today,' he smiled. 'And we saw that you wanted to be alone, so we let you be. But that was today. You can try it again tomorrow but you haven't got a chance. Tomorrow, if you want to be alone, you'll have to lock yourself up in your hotel room and stay there, because if you come and lie on this beach, we will come and pester you. We will nag you for cigarettes and we'll think up a hundred other ways to irritate you. And d'you know why? Because we just don't like it. We're Africans, you see. And we might be really poor and fucked up and going nowhere. But we're a family. And we don't like *alone*.'

He laughed and I laughed. And the entire mottled clutch of beach boys who'd been eavesdropping laughed too. I thought about where I come from. The place and the people that made me. My Mom and Dad and everything they'd done for me. Food, shelter, swimming lessons. They had gone out and bought those awful plastic wings, and driven me to some blue swimming pool so I could learn to bob around on islands like this. How had they ever found the time? 'Fucking swimming lessons!' I cried. And some stoned islander smiled and gave me a thumbs up.

I could be a part of this family, I realized. I could stay right here on Ngor and share out my life like a box of cigarettes, but never without surrendering some of myself.

Ivory

On Thursday morning I returned to the medina, where the courtyard was heavy with waiting. Ahuma sat on a wooden bench, perspiring. 'Do you want to know what his name will be?' she asked. I nodded. 'Adama,' she replied carefully. 'And this is how we will repay you.'

It was not what I'd had in mind, but I knew it was a great honour and that it was all that was possible. I blushed. 'Hey man,' I said, putting my arm around Ibrahim's shoulder and savouring the tastes in my mouth: sweetness and bitterness, melting into salty tears. I packed my bags, and I thought again about what a name meant here. How a name told not only who you were, but what you did. And how it had nothing to do with where you did it. For though a place could shape you, and sometimes break you, it could never take your name away.

Ahuma came into the room to say her farewell. Again, it was just me and her and the pink fan, and silently she wound a small, yellowed ring off her hand. 'Ivory,' she said. And she placed it on my finger, with the softness of true gratitude and the warm, fragile, sadness of a goodbye.

Afterwards

I flew home to Johannesburg and wrote this all down, running the narrative through my head, like a *griot*. The piece was published and a year later I entered it in a journalism competition, and won second prize in the features category. The prize money amounted to a little over double the total that my wily Senegalese entrepreneurs had drained from me. Ultimately, some weird justice had prevailed. A child had been brought into this world and no-one had lost anything. I tried to call Ibrahim, but the lines to the medina were dead.

It was two years before I returned to Dakar to make a film about Senegalese Fashion Week. I could scarcely contain my excitement at the prospect of meeting Adama – my namesake, my crying, kicking bundle of human debt – and my heart beat quicker as the cab rattled past the Score supermarket, and along the broad tree-lined block.

Little had changed. The goats still nibbled on scraps of cardboard on the pavement. Women in soft, voluminous robes swayed gracefully along the dusty street. The house had grown vague in my memory and as I paced the block looking for it, I was ambushed by a group of local kids. A blur of tiny hands and voices surrounded me. I did not recognize any of them, but they must have known me because they led me to the familiar metal gate and creaked it open. 'Ahuma is dead,' one of them yelled. 'Ahuma is dead.'

The yard seemed emptier than before. There were three pairs of blue flip-flops lined on a mat, some water boiling on a small fire. And it was Ahuma's beautiful sister who walked gravely towards me. 'Yes it is true,' she said. 'Ahuma died when we took her to the hospital to have the baby.'

'But how?'

'Oh, complications, you know. They couldn't really explain.'

'And the baby?'

'The baby also.'

I held her hand. I had worn the ivory ring especially for my return, and she noticed it. Tears welled in me and we stood silently for a few moments in the muddy yard. I felt so angry. She had been a solid sunbeam of good-ness in this fog of thieves and now she was gone. The goodness shone a little out of the faces of her sister and her nieces, but not quite as strongly as it had in her.

'And what of Ibrahim?' I asked.

He went back to the bush,' she explained. 'He said the city was eating him up. We don't hear from him, for a year now.'

I folded my arms and took one last look around the yard, knowing I would never return. I walked back through the gate. There had been so many twists in this tale, and it had all come to so little. An empty yard, a dead mother, a child that was never born. Only the gentle melodies of the *kora* might fill the void.

For days I had avoided Avenue Ponty, taking longer routes so as not to tempt fate. But tonight it didn't matter anymore. Now that so much had been lost, I cared less about who approached me. I walked past the packs of growling hyenas on the sidewalk. Rabid, desperate, untruthful, compromised. 'Hey!' The voice came from nowhere. 'Aren't you the American from the hotel?'

My heart slowed. It was Macuba. 'I met you at the hotel this morning?' he grinned, his eyes wide and shifting. He had no recollection of who I was, and yet he was attempting to lure me into some con, regardless. I froze. I could say nothing, for there was nothing to say. I simply turned away and walked off slowly among the restless throngs cluttering the broken pavement. And I walked and walked, until I felt full enough to carry on.

HANGING WITH THE
Hadzabe

The Hadzabe have no leaders, no possessions and no sense of time or space. They are also East Africa's last surviving hunter-gatherers.

Chem-chem

In the purple shadows of the Ngorongoro Crater, a stone's throw from where Mary Leakey stumbled across the three-million-year-old footprints of our ancient hominid relatives, the earth tumbles abruptly to the south, creaking out into the vast, craggy haze of heat and dust that is Central Tanzania. For most of the year, the plains crack with thirst and the lakes shrivel into bleak, silvery pads of spilt salt. Why anyone would want to haul a Land Rover through the agony of these roads is beyond me. But for the oasis of Chem-chem.

In Chem-chem, I am lost in time. Just as the afternoon sun makes green-gold umbrellas of the acacia trees, a monitor lizard, the size of a small crocodile, emerges silently from the rushes. There is the ancient trickle of an icy spring; the neon turquoise flash of a Kingfisher; the lazy sway of the vine curtains, festooned from the muscular boughs of primeval fig trees. Had a Tyrannosaurus Rex come sauntering through the marshland at this moment, I'd have barely blinked in surprise.

A few decades ago, this Garden of Eden was thick with game. The Hadzabe people who lived here, I imagine, had little trouble sustaining an enviable lifestyle of hunting, gathering, sharing, chilling out, getting stoned and chatting away in *clicklout*. The grocery cupboard was well stashed and the tedious concepts of time, a cash economy, the nuclear family and the Victorian work ethic had yet to complicate the simple bliss of existence. Kinda like Adam and Eve, I guess. Pre-apple.

Today Eden is not what it used to be. Like the !Kung and Khwe of the Kalahari, and the Native American Indians and Australian Aborigines before them, the Hadzabe have begun surrendering their lands and their lifestyle to the pressures of more developed societies. Today, sombre Barabaig pastoralists herd their cattle along the paths of Chem-chem. Wasukuma, Iraqw, Niramba, Wachuga and many more tribespeople have brought their hoes and their animals to this green garden. And so the remaining warm-blooded ingredients of a good Hadzabe lunch have fled to the dry thorny forests below the Rift Valley Escarpment and in the Yaeda Valley. Without a history of aggression, the Hadzabe simply retreated into the forest to hunt.

Today fewer than two thousand Hadzabe survive. With the Wadorobo and a few small groups of Pygmies, they comprise Africa's last surviving hunter-gatherers (those in the Kalahari are no longer able to live a traditional lifestyle). Despite various efforts to conserve the Hadzabe's way of life, many believe that within a couple of generations it may vanish from the face of the earth. Of course, the mere thought of such ethnocide is a ghastly indictment on contemporary humanity. Imagine, just as we save the black rhino, a group of human beings slips into extinction, right under our noses! But besides anything else, the Hadzabe are a pretty cool crowd.

Njegela

One afternoon, I make my way through Chem-chem with James Stephenson, a New York-based writer and photographer who spent a month here the previous year. We walk smack into Njegela and his charming wife, Mtenda, whose dainty hand he has recently secured for the price of two baboons.

Njegela is thirty-something; Mtenda is in her late teens – neither of them knows for sure. Both wear chunky strings of plastic beads, melted down from found plates and cups for which they had no use. On each cheek, Mtenda bears a symbolic scar and through a layer of grime, I can make out the words 'Fuji Photo' on Njegela's T-shirt. But as I am soon to learn, with Njegela it is always a Kodak moment.

Free from the dull treadmill of materialism, the Hadzabe enjoy a sense of spontaneity long forgotten by our civilizations. Njegela sits cross-legged next to me, takes my hand and begins to teach me a song. '*Dinako akwe chaba e*,' he chants, his voice a deep, timeless drum. '*Tatatao ao baa ko.*'

We proceed to the campsite, where Mzee Mahmoud, the Swahili

cook, hovers anxiously in front of the meal he has prepared. '*Bwana*, I learnt to cook in Nairobi,' he proudly told me. '1964!' As citizens of a pre-agricultural society, I figure, our guests might forgive the sogginess of his vegetables. Mzee Mahmoud grins stiffly as we sit down to dine. In the eyes of most Tanzanians, the Hadzabe rank just above undomesticated animals on the social scale.

As it turns out, Njegela and Mtenda devour three helpings each. Afterwards, Mtenda glances curiously at the pot, and when accommodated, licks it clean. I reach for a cigarette, only to find that the few half-full boxes that were lying about have been emptied: Njegela has wrapped all the cigarettes in newspaper and stuffed them in his pockets. To the Hadzabe, the notion of personal ownership is culturally incomprehensible. Take off your T-shirt and it's history.

Often, travellers to the less-developed world complain of a persistent nagging and begging on the part of the locals. In such cases I would hesitate to recommend a holiday in these parts. Aside from their bows and arrows, the Hadzabe own nothing and share everything. Occasionally, when a Hadza is taken on as a labourer, his entire clan pitches up on pay-day; by the next morning, the earnest payee is penniless. Predictably, the concept of fixed employment enjoys limited appeal.

Njegela eyes a pair of my sneakers. I have another pair of shoes with me and his are wearing through. Still, this pair was an indulgence from Diesel and I retain a shiver of nausea at the thought of their price tag. I grin politely at Njegela and roll on some Tabard. Mtenda is transfixed. Mosquito medicine, I explain. She reaches out both arms in excitement, strips off and rubs the remaining contents of the bottle all over her. A rare night's rest for the malaria carriers.

After dinner, Njegela escorts us up the hill to where a clan of Hadzabe has recently set up camp. Mtenda cannot contain her glee. 'We're going to the camp of the Hadzabe,' she yells every few metres; no matter how quickly I trundle through the thorns, I lag pitifully behind. 'Forgot to tell you,' James shouts from up front. 'They walk kinda fast.'

Suddenly, Mtenda is silent. She points to where a few small fires are burning on the hilltop. 'Hadzabe!' she exclaims. The journey has taken little more than fifteen minutes and yet, with these last few steps, we traverse millennia. As we venture into the flicker of firelight, I psych myself up for a chatty, alfresco evening with a Late Palaeolithic theme.

Part of the problem in assisting the Hadzabe, the chubby Spanish priest in a nearby mission explains, is that their society lacks structure and organization. Elders enjoy some respect. However, unbound by the duties of sedentary life, the Hadzabe have no use for leaders or hierarchies.

'If we want to offer them something,' Padri Miguel shrugs, throwing up his arms, 'who would we give it to? It's just *take, take, take* with the Hadzabe. The way they live, it's as though they speak another language. We can't even start a dialogue with them.'

There are few people who still live in harmony with nature. Their numbers are so minuscule, we easily forget how fundamentally their lifestyle differs from ours. Yet, until very recently, this same way of life comprised our most persistent and successful adaptation to our environment. Peer back over the three million years of human evolution, and ninety-nine percent of our time on the planet has been spent hunting and gathering, relying on our cunning, co-operation and intelligence, in a state defined by social and political fluidity.

While developed societies thrive on order and regimentation, for the Hadzabe and others like them, looseness remains critical to survival. And so it is tonight, that we make our way democratically from fire to fire, discussing our arrival with every man, woman and child, dishing out cigarettes en route, like a mobile vending machine.

One Hadzabe elder named Salibongo is anxious about our visit. It takes a certain breed of wayward twentieth century voyager to come in quest of Stone Age society. Undoubtedly, many visitors to Hadzaland have been as obscure and unconventional as the Hadzabe themselves. Recently, the story goes, a middle-aged German man apparently popped into the camp, stripped naked and made himself at home. He had come to die in Africa. One night, after trying to ensconce himself between a sleeping couple, he was asked to leave. He refused.

In the ensuing soap opera, one Hadzabe man was injured with the tip of an arrow and a local farmer was summoned with his shotgun, after which the deranged creep was seen fleeing naked into the bush. I nod sympathetically at Salibongo, trying my best to not look like a psychopathic rapist.

Eventually, after a long clickety debate and the gift of a couple of blankets, everyone is assured of our good intentions. Salibongo invites us to dance. We hop frenetically in a circle. Clueless, I gasp, *'Dinako akwe chaba e,'* and hope for the best, after which everyone is so relaxed, we are invited to dinner. 'How kind,' I gush, glancing at the large tortoise crackling among the flames. 'I'd adore to. But we've had such a lovely dinner down at the camp.'

Land

The Hadzabe will eat anything that moves – elephant, giraffe, lion, you name it. While women gather wild fruits and berries, the men hunt with their bows and arrows, the tips of which are smeared with a poison so toxic it will kill you within minutes of entering your bloodstream. Only nowadays, there are fewer and fewer animals to hunt.

In this region, vast tracts of land have been set aside in the name of wildlife conservation. The legendary Ngorongoro Crater and Serengeti reserves nearby need no introduction as prime international game-viewing destinations. Other lands in the area are controlled by hunting companies who generate substantial revenue for the Tanzanian government. According to legislation, any Hadzabe found hunting in these areas must be arrested and charged with poaching.

A few years ago, Danieli Taiwashi, a respected Hadzabe elder, died in prison. Allegations of torture were substantiated when other Hadzabe were released from prison, showing broken joints on their limbs.

According to the German-based organization Friends of Peoples Close to Nature (FPCN), which represents small groups of aboriginal people everywhere from East Africa to the Amazon and the Philippines, Hadzabe have not only been stalked and killed by white trophy hunters, but, in extreme cases, hung in trees as wildlife bait. For any government, FPCN is a fairly radical thorn to have in one's side. Innocuous as it may sound to be 'working for the rights of aboriginal peoples', anyone with a self-determination agenda within a national state will inspire a messy hotbed of moral and ethical dispute.

To complicate matters, Tanzania comprises one hundred and twenty tribes. And although the relative harmony among them remains one of the few achievements of Julius Nyerere's rule, in the east the country borders on Rwanda, Burundi and Zaïre. Decades ago, Nyerere called on the

Hadzabe to come out of the bush, roll up their sleeves and muck in for a doomed bout of African socialism. For the most part, the Hadzabe declined the invitation. Others, however, proceeded to participate in what must be one of history's odder experiments in tribal harmony.

In this region, and throughout Tanzania, Nyerere created a series of Ujamaa (or Socialist) villages. The idea was to resettle individuals from various tribes and force them to live together. Step into Qangndeng, the Ujamaa village on the edge of Chem-chem, and you're strolling through a bizarre ethnography textbook. There are low Iraqw huts, grassy Tatok shelters, brick huts with Islamic doors. Only the homes have been built so far apart from each other, one can't be sure whether Qangndeng is a village at all. Today as many as fifty tribes live in this province. Given this multicultural muddle, the likelihood of a small, cash-strapped group of hunter-gatherers securing sovereignty seems thin. Yet for FPCN, sovereignty is the only solution.

Not only does the organization condemn policing, legal, military and educational activity on Hadzabe lands, it is categorically opposed to any development project advocating Westernization or civilization, and all missionary work. Nowadays, Hartmut Heller, a self-appointed champion of the Hadzabe cause, concedes his pleasure when he hears the news of burnt-down churches.

Heller first came to Hadzaland some twenty years ago. He lived with the Hadzabe on and off for six years. 'And the longer I stayed,' he recalls, 'the more fascinated I became with their way of life.' From Heller's point of view, any compromises the Hadzabe might make with 'the rotten civilized world' are as good as suicide. Given that the idea of permitting them to hunt in the game reserves has been rejected on the grounds that it sets a precedent for all tribes, the only possible solution would be the redefinition of traditional Hadzabe hunting grounds, now long settled by other tribes.

The Market

One morning at around six am I get a lift to the Hadzabe camp. Zaïrian *Soukous* music blares from the car radio. As I open the door a wizened, topless grandmother begins to dance. She rolls a joint, lights it and passes it around the circle. Everyone, including her four-year-old granddaughter, takes a puff. Then everyone coughs like a steam engine, especially Njegela.

The next morning, Njegela and two friends arrive at our camp. Gradually they work their way through a box of watercolours. They paint cows and baboons and trees and people, and when they have filled two sketchpads, they begin to paint on their sandals. By afternoon, the visiting clan has swelled to fifteen and I am feeling twitchy – a full day wasted. I yawn. I look around me, only to register that I am the only person remotely bothered by this. With Mzee Mahmoud at the fire, there is no need to hunt or gather. There is no need to do anything. Guilt, it appears, is a product of more complicated societies. I resolve to do something useful, and for the next half hour, sit carefully carving a ganja pipe from a piece of carrot. When finished, I pass it proudly to Njegela, who looks at me quizzically, then takes a large bite out of it.

Where I come from, it is hard to comprehend the isolation that persists on this continent. Most of my Hadzabe friends had seen neither a town nor a television. Nor had they any sense of time or geography. Furthermore, they are the only Africans I have met who have no idea who Nelson Mandela is.

In recent years, the Tanzanian government has made sustained efforts to acculturate the Hadzabe. This scheme has included kidnapping Hadzabe children and taking them to a boarding school in the nearby town of Endamaka, where they are prohibited from speaking their language and forced to learn Swahili. According to Heller, many Hadzabe girls have been raped by the teachers in this school. Often, the children escape, living alone in the bush until they find a clan to join. As the Hadzabe reject no-one, any clan will do. One such returnee, Ishingo, accompanies me to the vast mirage of a market that emerges on the fifth day of each month in the clearing outside Chem-chem.

What was barren, scrubby path yesterday, today is a highway of cattle, bicycles and people. Already, the event is one of the more multicultural bashes I've attended. There are Barabaig warriors, naked but for their jewellery, scarifications and blood-red cloths, some of which are accessorized with plastic hairbrushes dangling from metal chains. A Sukuma man wears a small goat around his neck. Another carries his snuff in a film container, plugged neatly into a stretched earlobe. A black-veiled Iraqw woman brushes past me, carrying her morning's shopping: a briquette of cow-dung charcoal and the head of a goat.

As we walk, a brown-toothed minstrel appears. He weaves a haunting Swahili ballad on a violin he has made from calfskin and impala tendons. On the hide, the words 'Welcome My Music' have been scrawled in blue ballpoint pen. His song carries us to market. At the edge of the clearing, a freshly slaughtered cow twitches in a puddle of blood. The aisles of this primal supermarket stretch way out to the horizon. There are spiky sandals for sale, cut from old car tyres. Mounds of overpriced second-hand clothing, Mike Tyson T-shirts, grass mats, carcasses, beads, and a spattering of cheap manufactured goods. Wary as they are of the crowd, most of the Hadzabe hover in the bushes around the market.

Ishingo refuses to go near the Tatok cattle auction, but time and time again, escorts me past a stand where a few tacky gold watches dangle from a piece of string. 'Okay,' I concede. 'I get your beaded buckskin bag; you get the watch.' Ishingo is delighted. Though he has no idea how to tell the time, he straps the deal proudly to his wrist. He looks kind of dull trotting off with the Taiwan special instead of the bag, but then again, who am I to style Tanzania? I plonk in the shade of a baobab tree and down a vile mugful of home-brewed beer.

Nguruwe

Later that evening, the minstrel returns to our camp with a friend. The friend has drunk far too much vile beer and proceeds to complement the ensuing recital with a wild, Presleyesque routine of pelvic thrusts. We sing, we dance, we laugh, we trance and all of a sudden, we hear a series of shrieks and grunts from somewhere in the thick, dark swamp. Njegela leaps to his feet and grabs a spear. Ishingo takes my hand. Perhaps if I'd understood the word *nguruwe* at this stage, I'd have chosen to stay behind. Given my poor Swahili, I find myself tiptoeing terrified through the swamp.

We clamber over fallen trees, wade thigh-deep in mud. The shrieking gets louder. A few moments ago, I felt fully connected with my Hadzabe friends but now, in the primal thick of the hunt, there are again millennia between us. In a flash, all three Hadzabe scramble up a tree. James and I are left staring at each other. We are bleak with fright.

Ishingo leaps from the tree. A scramble, a last crazed grunt, then silence. Carefully, I sweep a torchbeam across the dead *nguruwe*, the spear impaled tidily in its chest. Wild pig is one of the more dangerous animals to hunt. When cornered, it often panics and attacks. With its thick, sharp tusks, it is perfectly capable of goring a messy hole through your shin and maiming or killing you. Ishingo looks like he's just run a marathon. He removes the spear, then takes my hand and fastens it around a stiff, warm leg. It is time to bring home the bacon.

It would probably have been easier to drag a grand piano through the swamp than this pig. We haul her across ditches, through thorns and through slush, but dearly departed remains downright uncooperative. She weighs a ton. She slips by her tail. She gets her head lodged in the roots of a tree. I try not to connect with the task at hand.

On dry ground, Ishingo hacks the animal apart with a *panga*. He skewers the bloody chunks onto a stake, and we trudge up the hill to the Hadzabe camp. It is now one am and a tad too reminiscent of *Lord of the Flies*. We wake the clan, who are truly delighted and feast until it is almost daybreak. I can neither speak nor eat. My Diesels, I notice, are stained with pig's blood.

Ishingo

A few days later, on my last day in Chem-chem, I bump into Ishingo, who looks utterly miserable. He reaches into his shorts pocket and hauls out the now strapless watch. Yesterday, he explains, he went hunting; when he flexed his bow, the cheap strap shattered and most of the pieces were lost in the surrounding scrub. It is a month until the next market.

Trivial as the incident seems, it is a poignant metaphor for the bigger problems the Hadzabe are facing. Even time, the most fundamental cog in the development machine, somehow proves incompatible with their lifestyle. Too rigid perhaps, or just too foreign. 'Shida,' Ishingo says gloomily. Problem. I offer him a blue Woolies T-shirt, which he happily pulls over his vest. He has no cupboard, I remember.

In modern times, the world has found a variety of uses for leftover hunter-gatherers. Time and again, they have taken up urban positions as bums, criminals or alcoholics. The freedom and fluidity they have known has stood them in poor stead for the contemporary urban experience, it appears. Without structure and without the hard realities of the bush to balance things out, their innate decadence seems to engulf them. Time and again, they have been marginalized, misunderstood and humiliated. It is as though we cannot find a place for them in our world.

Ishingo and I sit together for a long time. James, by this stage, has thrown himself fully into the experience. He has bought spears and provisions at the market and has embarked on a ten-day hunting safari with Njegela and friends. A part of me longs to be with them. After all, as Padri Miguel snorts, 'It's not a bad life, is it? I know a lot of people who wouldn't mind living like the Hadzabe do.'

Perhaps. No mortgage. No bosses. Fresh food and loads of leisure time. Provided, of course, Hartmut or some magician can pull off a miracle deal with the rotten civilized world.

So what are you going to do?' I ask Ishingo. 'Do you want to go back to school?' It strikes me that for all the opinions I've heard, I still haven't really ascertained what the Hadzabe want for themselves. Do they want to be saved? Perhaps, given the naïve, powerless vacuum they live in, clarity is an unreasonable assumption to make. But Ishingo manages something of an answer.

'*Ndio*,' he says finally. Yes.

'And after you've been to school?'

'Well, I'll come back here,' he says.

'And hunt in the forest?'

'*Ndio*,' he says, nodding profusely.

'But Ishingo, there aren't enough animals left, are there?'

He sighs, and it is as though all the riddles of humanity, conservation and development are written into that sigh. And all the tragedy and inevitability too.

'So what are you going to do?' I ask again.

'*Shida*,' he says, gazing clueless into the future. We shake hands warmly and we part and I watch as he trots off among the acacia trees, until he is only a faint blue speck of Woolies cotton against the green.

SLOWBOAT ON THE Niger

There are bats over Bamako. Hundreds of them, spinning across the mighty Niger River to feed. Along its banks, the capital's administrative buildings stand guard like medieval fortresses, crenellations poking the heavens like fat, ochre fingers. Even by day, these concrete caricatures of ancient Sudanese architecture seem steeped in mystery, but as a yellow moon creeps over the escarpment and the wails of the *griots* meander from a thousand roadside radios, the buildings silhouetted so eerily against the dusk sky, this might as well be Gotham City.

Mali is poised for romance. Its glorious past, wretched Sahelian climate and sheer remoteness all make for one of Africa's most alluring and adventurous destinations. And to journey along the Niger from Bamako, tracing the dusty footprints of the Ghana, Songhai and Mali empires, has long been a dream voyage for me.

Before the continents split, some believe, the Niger was one with the Amazon. If so, the destinies of these great rivers are astounding in their contrast: while one floods its way through the planet's thickest rainforest, the other splutters for breath, keeping at bay the ever-encroaching sands of the world's largest desert.

Each year, as the Sahara claws its way further into the savannah lands, or Sahel, so the Niger becomes more vital for Mali's survival. Over the next few weeks, whether by taxi, *pirogue* or blistered foot, I will rarely move more than a few metres from its banks.

All over Mali, the reminders of desertification are frightening. In grimy village markets, jiffy bags of water and sparse bundles of firewood are sold at a premium. As for the wooden doors and shutters one sees all over Africa: here they are metal – once grey metal perhaps, but now so sandblasted by the annual harmattan winds, they seem to have lost their greyness. Yes, travel north of Bamako – to the ancient cities of Djenne, Gao or Timbuktu – and the trees too have lost their greenness, the sky its blueness. Here, there is only one colour: earth.

Tonight, we stretch out on mattresses in a courtyard in the capital, puffing on weak marijuana and planning a journey. A white goat brays; the mosquitoes nibble. The conversation is predictable: Mamadou, our dread-locked Malian guide, is fantasizing about life in Europe and nagging about visas. Raphael, a French student, and I do our very best to convince him (and ourselves) that Africa is where it's at – that the developed world is chock with lonely, selfish individuals living meaningless lives, and that it hasn't a patch on Africa's warmth, culture or sense of community. Only Mamadou, who is running as fast as he can from the conservatism in his home village, doesn't believe a word we say. He twiddles his dreads and nods politely.

Ironically, had we been skinning up a few centuries earlier, our roles might have been reversed. For, between the third and sixteenth centuries, this was a land of wealth, culture and learning. Mali's location along the Niger made it a lucrative crossroads between the agricultural, forest states of the coast and the desert empires of the interior.

It wasn't until 1324, however, that Mansa Musa, the great Malian emperor, made his legendary pilgrimage to Mecca and captured the world's attention. Musa's arrival was anything but low-key: sixty thousand courtiers in tow, five thousand camels and enough gold to have Europe and the Middle East drooling for decades. Had he known that less than a century later the first Portuguese ships would arrive to commence their plunder of West Africa, he might have gone a little lighter on the gold.

Today, Mali is one of the world's five poorest nations. In Bamako, cripples crawl through the filth of the Grand Marché and children beg for pens and aspirins. Everything here is three times broken; twice mended; often garish. In a *banco* bar in Quinzambougou, I hear the voices of the Wassoulou women blaring from a television set. For years, I have listened to their songs on Women of Mali compilations, and pictured them in Bogolan robes and *banco* villages. To see them tonight, in frilly, pink chintz dresses, pouring their music into scratchy mikes, on a stage set straight out of *Love Boat*, leaves me tingling with wonder and sadness.

Yes, Mali is tinged with sorrow. Images of glories past spin a hollow dance amid the broken Renaults, tacky bistros and shrivelled vegetables of the modern state. But as I am soon to learn, this tale of loss has as much to do with the shifting needs of humanity as with the shifting sands of the Sahara.

Two days after our discussion in Bamako, we travel by bus to Mopti, the largest town on the Niger delta. As we rattle along the dike to its entrance, Mopti glows magically in the early light. Its main mosque (like most mosques in the Sahel) is as fanciful as a sand castle. Crooked cross-beams poke through its *banco* walls like porcupine quills, each phallic crenellation topped with a traditional ostrich egg. Even in the cool dawn, Mopti heaves with heatstroke.

I step into the blue, neon-lit reception of the Bar Mali, where a ceiling fan spins lazily through the cobwebs. Here, even the plump whores propped at the foot of the staircase wave their straw fans at half-speed, and it is only Solou, the young Ivorian gold dealer lodging upstairs, who seems to have any energy.

Outside, the weekly market is stretching and yawning. Peul traders set up their sad stalls of tiny tomatoes, onions and sachets of Maggi or coarse salt, bound with rubber bands.

Impossible as it may seem, five hundred years ago salt was so essential for rearing livestock here, that pastoralists traded it ounce for ounce with gold. Vast slabs of the stuff were dragged on camelback across the dunes from Taoudeni in the extreme north of the country. Mali's control of these caravan routes was critical to its power.

This morning I buy a senseless sachet for fifty CFA francs (five US cents). Doubtless, it has arrived by truck from Bamako – no, salt isn't what it used to be here, and neither is the Sahara. Since the fundamentalist attacks in Algeria, even the most romantic overlanders have forsaken the treacherous crossing. Mali's once strategic position is meaningless.

A market woman yells for my attention. Like many here, she is Peul. Some say the Peul came from Egypt originally, some say they have Jewish roots. Either way, they are now scattered from northern Nigeria all the way to Guinea, and the chunky gold earrings, sinuous braids and head-scarves the women wear seem appropriate for West Africa's gypsies. She grumbles a greeting, dunks her baguette into a cup of sticky Nescafé, and grins, her single tooth just off-centre from the gold ring clasped to the septum of her nose.

It's not long before I find what I'm looking for. Wandering through Mopti, I hear the singing of the *griots* in a courtyard. I follow the sound. For centuries, the *griots* have lived like this, travelling between villages and recounting ancient tales of origin and genealogy to the soft melodies of *koras* or *balafons*. They have always been of the lowest social castes, only now many of these ancient troubadours been reduced to buskers; to bumming a cigarette for a tune on a one-stringed guitar.

The courtyard rings with the thumping of *djembes*; under a tree, a *griot* in a tired La Coste shirt blows into a wooden flute rigged up to a small amp. This is a Peul wedding and I am welcome on condition that I dance with the women. They sway sultrily, floral scarves suspended from their fingertips, their gazes long and fearless.

I proceed to the harbour where I view what will be our home for the next few days. Six metres long and a metre wide, it is by no means a pleasure cruiser. There is a clay urn at the stern where meals are prepared and a hole, further back, for a toilet.

What with the motley clutch of voyagers we have gathered along the way, we are now seven. Raphael, the gold dealer; Julien, a student from Montpelier who looks like Jesus of Montreal; and the crew. I smile anxiously, heartened only slightly by the straw canopy that has been fastened to the centre of the boat. Sekou, the boatman, has agreed to buy the rice and the tea. We'll buy the fish, we'll pay eighty thousand CFA francs (sixty US dollars) and we'll leave tomorrow. We shake hands – his, I notice, has six fingers on it. 'Yes, the water is high enough for us to paddle to Djenne,' he affirms. As it turns out, he is a liar.

I do know there are easier ways to get to Djenne – near the harbour, there are French tourists climbing into air-conditioned 4x4s, embarking on convenient five-hour journeys. But given the town's legendary status in the Sahel since the thirteenth century, I figure that this is a little too banal a means of arrival. So we cast off as promised, to the frantic waving of hands and an Alpha Blondy song, courtesy of Sekou's ghetto blaster.

Pole by tedious pole, the *pirogue* creeps forward. I gaze along the impossible flatness of the river banks, broken only occasionally by the toothpick silhouettes of a farmer or a pack mule. This is the Bani, a tributary of the Niger and, as I am soon to discover, it is too low for swimming, let alone paddling. We will not be gliding to Djenne. We will continue at this plodding pace, upstream through the slow, emptiness of this landscape, just as traders and scholars and worshippers have done for centuries.

It is night by the time we arrive at the village where we will sleep. A young girl drags a baby to view the strange, pale *toubabs* who have arrived. The child takes one look at Raphael and bursts into tears.

We eat in the darkness which, considering the crispy bits in my stew, is not a bad thing. Later, I try to forget the hardness of the clay floor on which I'm sleeping. 'Suppose most people in Mali have never sat on an upholstered seat in their lives,' Raphael remarks, cheerfully. It does little for the aching of my joints, but Sekou has switched to Radio Mali and through my mosquito net the sky is bursting with stars.

The next morning the floor of the boat seems harder; the canopy smaller; the poling slower. We take turns at it: balancing at the boat's narrow stern, then lunging the poles into the muddy river bed and dragging our beloved home forward, like a ten-ton sled. Only today, like most days, there are no clouds in the sky, and the heat is unbearable. We crouch under the canopy and nibble on sweet tubers called Tiger Nuts, as the crew poles on. We grow more and more irritated with Mamadou, who, it transpires, has no idea of a guide's function and is enjoying a paid holiday with his new white friends. Only his new white friends are simmering with fury. I snuggle down on a bag of rice and hook my left leg onto a beam in the canopy. There is no room for my right leg. I fantasize about throwing Mamadou to the crocodiles.

The next day, we drink pink baobab tea to ease the tedium. We pass a yawning hippo and some white egrets. I climb ashore and walk along the bank. Though I must clamber often through the eroded cracks in the earth, I keep an easy pace with the boat. I pass among the straw beehive huts of a Bozo fishing village, where I enquire about fish. There are no fish today, they tell me. There are four chickens and they aren't parting with them. Later, we eat rice with Maggi. It is only the prospect of seeing Djenne that keeps me in vaguely good spirits.

Unquestionably, Djenne is the most beautiful town in the Sahel. Its Grand Mosque is as significant to this part of the world as the Taj Mahal is to India. Holding five thousand worshippers – almost half the town's population – it is the largest and most important example of

Sudanese architecture in existence. Each year, after the rainy season, the townsfolk dutifully clamber up the walls to replaster the outer layer of *banco*. Like all of Djenne, however, the mosque plays tricks on the eye. Ancient as its style may be, it was only constructed in 1905. Only a single neon tube and a couple of bullhorns for the *muezzin* place the building in the twenty-first century. Otherwise, like all of Djenne, it is timeless. And this afternoon, as the last rays of sun trace its sinuous curves, the hellish days on the *pirogue* all seem worthwhile.

Protected by UNESCO, Djenne is built entirely from *banco*. There isn't a single vertical line in the town; every wall and every doorway carries the organic charge of the hands that shaped it. Even the post office is as hand-sketched as a comic strip. Step inside the houses, and a maze of rooms and staircases signals a sophistication unusual in African architecture.

Though Mali's literacy rate is around thirty percent, in Djenne everyone can read. Children scurry through the streets carrying dusty tablets scribbled with Koranic verses in vegetable ink. That survival – let alone civilization – has been achieved in the harshness of this climate, is astonishing. Later, I eat chicken and chips at Ali Baba's restaurant – tonight, as every night, it is the only dish on the menu. And as I fall asleep on a rooftop, under a feeble blanket of clouds blown north from the Atlantic, I sense the sacredness of this place.

It is decided the next morning: Mamadou must go. He takes the news amicably enough, until the final parting at the junction town of Sevare, where he grabs Raphael's wrist aggressively. They scuffle. '*Merde!*' Mamadou spits out the word, turns and storms off back to Bamako.

Later, en route to Bandiagara, Raphael and I wonder what we're doing here. It is surely indulgent to be holidaying in one of the world's poorest countries; and inevitable perhaps, that beneath the chummy surface, much of the brief, superficial contact between tourists and locals should be strained, exploitative and forgettable. This time, even the ritual exchange of false addresses has been waived.

By the time we reach Bandiagara, we are not in the mood to meet anyone, but we proceed, with resignation, to Antonio's campsite. There is so little in Bandiagara, but go to Antonio and there are chairs in the shade, recordings of Malian jazz, live at Montreux and, amazingly, espresso. 'I've lived in Europe for a while,' he remarks. 'But I chose to come back home to the Dogon country. It's calmer here and people share more.'

'I'm proud to be a Malian,' he says later. He takes a stick and pokes it into the soft earth. 'In a few years, this stick could be half-buried in sand,' he says. 'And a few years later it could be totally buried, so it must stand tall. It's the same with Mali. Here, we must stand tall and proud.' Antonio asks nothing of us – not even our addresses.

The next morning, we cover the arduous twenty-kilometre stretch to Djuigibombo. I stagger into the village, dragging my mosquito net behind me like a tattered wedding dress, and head for the chief's house. I am caked with dust and wearing only a pair of green underpants, so it is with some shock that I behold five perfectly charming English girls, on their summer hols, swatting the flies with scraps of cardboard.

'We're taking the horse and cart,' Anastasia says.

'Good plan,' I nod.

We walk again, this time to the edge of the plateau, where the scorched earth collapses some eight hundred metres into the fertile plain which is Dogon country. For centuries, the steepness of this descent has defined Dogon culture – protecting their animist belief systems from Islamization and inspiring the region's unique architecture. Throughout West Africa, Dogon culture is reputed to be as ancient, and truly African.

As we clamber down the rocky staircase, we sight our first Dogon dwellings, perched, like earthenware telephone booths, along the immense cliff-face. Among them are the crude Dogon ladders I've seen mounted so senselessly in African Art stores. How cute, I'd figured, they make ladders! Little did I realize that traditionally, the Dogon live at a ninety-degree angle.

Higher still on the cliffs, are the tiny caves of the now-extinct Tellem, or Pygmies, who, legend has it, ascended to their primeval penthouses on baobab vines. Today, why anyone would choose to live like this seems senseless but centuries ago the Bandiagara plains were dangerous jungle. This dizzy vertical existence, which meant hauling up sacks of millet to store in their granaries, was their only shot at protection.

Today, the villages have slunk down into the valleys. And in each village, we sleep on cane stretchers at the chief's house. It's easy enough to recognize the chief's house, for there is always a collection of stuffed cane rats' bodies, dangling from the crossbeams, their skulls buried in the *banco* walls to form a mosaic. Tonight the village is called Telli and the chief is the size of an ox. He dresses up in old Dogon gear and storms about busily, challenging one of us to an arm wrestle every now and then. He grins at the terror of our refusals.

Down on the plain we walk a few kilometres each day, from village to village, staying within the shade of the cliffs. The walking is gentle, through millet fields and onion terraces. We swim in a cool waterfall and clamber among the precarious ghost towns that cling to the rocks, stumbling over goat droppings and broken bits of pottery. We fall asleep under the baobabs at Kani Kombole and it is at four am, when the sky blanches with lightning, that we scurry into a hut, and through the doorway I watch the rain falling, like tears for Mali.

In the morning, we heave our way back up the cliff. Below, a road is being built, I notice. And so as we rattle back to Bandiagara by horse and cart, I wonder how long before aluminium ladders become vogue in the Dogon.

I had decided, on the advice of many a weary traveller, not to continue from here to Timbuktu. In 1828, when the French traveller, René Caille, arrived in the desert town, he wrote, 'I found it neither as big nor as populated as I had expected ... a jumble of badly built houses, ruled over by a heavy silence.' Today, Timbuktu remains unexceptional and inaccessible – fourteen days on the river, just to nip into the post office and get a Timbuktu stamp on my postcards? No thanks. But by chance, the weekly bus to Bamako is departing in a few hours. It is to be the worst journey of my memory.

It is an orange school bus, designed to seat twenty. Today, there are forty of us crammed like beasts among the little seats. Mine, in fact, is not a seat, but a wedge of plastic between two seats. Behind me, a man in a grey suit clutches a live chicken, its beak poised within millimetres of my spine. With each bump in the road, I picture myself pecked to death.

Just how I survived seventeen hours of this, I cannot recall. I know that I groaned loudly each time I saw a spacious Land Rover whiz by; that I cursed the woman sitting next to me for having had so many children; and that at one point, I dragged the bus driver to the police. And much as the Malian passengers encouraged me, they knew it was of little sense, for over the centuries, they had grown accustomed to the harshness of life here.

The discomforts, the slowness – even the dryness they had come to endure with a rare dignity. And for me, it is this brave stoicism that defines

Mali. Grand satin *boubous* in urban slums. The sweet songs of a *griot* during the power cuts – rich, ancient traditions facing today's ravages of poverty and obscurity, like proud sticks in an ever-deepening sea of sand.

THE SLIPPERY
Coast

Dona Maria is mopping up her stew with some bread in the dining-room of the Pensão Central, a boarding-house in downtown Maputo. She's the only person in the room with her back to the TV. The others – four hundred or so students from rural Mozambique and East Africa – glance at the evening news and chat while they eat, but Dona Maria mops on stoically. Her white hair is pulled sensibly into an Alice band, her daily black frock safe under a napkin. Gruff as her tone may be when she barks her staff around the kitchen, when she looks up to bid me *boa noite*, her eyes are warm and smiley.

Back in 1973, when Mozambique won its independence from Portugal, most whites scurried home. After four hundred years, they left in a matter of weeks, causing as much damage as possible before they left. They pushed cranes into the harbour and poured concrete down the elevator shafts of the city's grand modern apartment blocks. But a handful of colonists stayed. And as Dona Maria mops up her stew, I witness her fierce streak of resignation.

Pensão Central, the boarding-house she runs, is situated on one of Maputo's broad, dirty boulevards. It's a cheap, badly-lit dive, smelling of soap and mothballs. But what it lacks in hot water and toilet paper, it makes up for in tatty, art deco charm.

Outside, students lick watery soft-serves under a neon sign and trashy *putas* in miniskirts giggle at their patrons cruising by. On a balmy evening like this, two US dollars will get you a quick bonk across the street, and far less will get you a beer.

Kanda finds the whole scene distasteful. 'Prostitution is so exposed here,' he says. 'Sure we have this in Liberia, but it's much more discreet.'

Kanda is on holiday here – or so he claims. He has come to check out Southern Africa. His distance stems from the fact that he speaks no Portuguese and cannot relate to the local students. After all, *he* works in a bank in Liberia. So Kanda just hangs out, hair writhed back with glycerine, snaky eyes gazing across the street. I fob him off. I must pack for Bilene.

A man in dark glasses with a clipboard tugs at my sleeve. He drags me through the crowd and into the office. Ticket for Bilene, he explains. I pay and he tugs me onto the bus. Sacks of fish, chickens and too many people sardine me in next to an over-friendly *skabanga* in seventies shades and a tatty women's blazer. If the bus had any windows, I'd feel claustrophobic.

The *skabanga* speaks German. He pulls a tired textbook from his bag to prove it. A year in Leipzig, I understand. Viva Karl Marx? Yes. *Fantastisch.*

It is a tedious hour at the bus station, but once moving, we are quickly into the countryside. No-one travelled this road a couple of years ago, but since peace came to Mozambique, Maputo is no longer the walled Berlin it once was. A fair number of cars bump along the north road now. Skeletal homes crop out of the tall grass at the roadside, only the bricks having survived the plundering of the RENAMO rebels.

The *skabanga* edges behind my back to roll a joint. There goes page three of the German textbook. The President used to smoke, he explains, so the drug laws were very strict here. But the new president's a Christian, so *nicht problem* now. Even *mit polizei, nicht problem.* No sooner has he lit up, than the entire bus spins around in noisy protest, chickens and all. '*Cigaro,*' he pleads, stubbing the joint out on his shoe.

Bilene must have been fabulous in its day. Set on an azure lagoon, fringed with palms and littered with flamingoes, it begs memories of Laurentinos cruising their Chevvies up from Lourenço Marques for glam weekends of sand, sun and seafood. But two decades of war cut the town off from the world. The large homes on the hill are empty now and the monumental Harbour Restaurant built under the promenade has misted up windows and serves only fish and coffee, sometimes only coffee. Parque Flores, a nearby resort, is literally a wreck. Aside from a couple of French tourists and perhaps a hundred locals in the vicinity, Bilene is a ghost resort.

For seven years, the channel linking the lagoon and the sea has been blocked. Parque Flores was flooded as a result and today it is a surreal shrine to the town's neglect: filthy bungalows and a beach bar knee-deep in sand and broken concrete furniture.

For a snack, one's best bet in Bilene is Estrela, a recently revamped restaurant on the promenade. Franco, a local Portuguese guy, fills me in on who's who. The men huddled around the tables are the few die-hard whites and Indians who remained here throughout the war, he explains. Whenever the rebels came to town on looting sprees, the locals rowed across the lagoon and hid in the bushes until it was safe to return. Today, they're buying plastic outdoor furniture, renovating chalets and sipping coffee till boom-time.

Meanwhile, the lagoon silvers and the coloured lights come on at the empty Harbour Restaurant. Later, Franco surprises me with a visit. As the sole inhabitant of thirty tired pink and blue cottages at the beachfront, I am easy to locate. 'I hope you don't mind,' he says. 'But I have to smoke something here. The others don't know about it.'

'Hashish?' I enquire.

'No, not *hesh*,' he says, scratching at his crotch. He rolls up a bank note, takes a small tinfoil sheet from his pocket and holds a lighter beneath it. 'Heroin,' he splutters, exhaling.

Three hits and he's tripping, spewing out local history. 'Everything in Bilene was in order before,' he says, still scratching. 'I'm telling you, every-thing was very nice. Then there was war and everything was broken. But now everyone from Maputo wants to come back here. I'm telling you, it's like a hundred dogs to one bone.'

I venture out onto the porch, pondering the town's history. The horrors of war are now almost invisible, but its effects – neglect and alienation – are still everywhere. A camping site has been set up and the channel to the sea opened, leaving most of Bilene smelling of algae. But the hundred dogs must be out of town this week – either that, or hiding in the bushes.

After three days in Bilene, Maputo seems like civilization. Dona Maria's just back from the cathedral and Kanda's hanging out in a West African robe. 'How's your holiday?' I ask.

'Well, I'm here twelve days and I still haven't found what I'm looking for. I'm looking for a certain liquid,' he says. 'And I can't find it. Maybe you can help me.'

'Maybe.'

'Come up to my room for a minute.'

He's concerned I may be some sort of agent, but I point out the matted state of my hair, which reassures him. It's a dingy single room. Laid out on the dresser are a hairbrush, some oils and a soft-porn rag. Kanda scribbles the words on a piece of paper. Bisodic Test Mercury Monography Liquid. 'This is what I'm looking for.'

He then produces from his luggage a rectangular wooden box, covered in tinfoil. I have a little of this liquid,' he says. 'But I need one litre.' He opens the box, pulls a grimy black slip of paper from the top and starts rubbing some liquid on it.

Gradually, President Jackson's head emerges on the black slip, then the number twenty in the corner. 'I have five hundred thousand US dollars here,' he says. 'The liquid costs twenty-seven thousand dollars a litre. If I can find someone with the liquid, I will give them a hundred and fifty thousand dollars as I don't have much time. I met an Italian who could get it, but he wanted half the money. Take this twenty-dollar note and go and change it. You'll see, it's genuine. Perhaps you can find the liquid?'

I take the note to exchange it, but change my mind. I walk along the Avenida Twenty-four Julho, past the deco buildings parked like distressed pink ships on the pavement, past the Communist slogans and graffiti. On the surface, this is the same tattered town I romanced three years ago. Destitute, yet rich in its café society, street culture and the open-heartedness of its people.

Dona Maria, for instance, seemed more than a survivor to me, bashing pots around that kitchen decades after her family had fled. Perhaps there were others like her, discarded across Africa, still traipsing past the *putas* each night on their way to church.

But a darker side of Maputo was emerging for me. Here, where spices, ivory and slaves have been traded since the sixteenth century, substances are changing hands and deals are spinning across prego rolls. Whatever colonial rule, war and socialism did to this society, deep in the cracks, it remains a seedy, free port on the slippery coast of the Indian Ocean.

'Where did you get this note?' I ask Kanda. He's silent, thoughtful, then abrupt. 'When the US sends this money to Liberia, they send it reserved, so that no-one but the government can use it. But that liquid takes the reservation stamp off. So you see, I really need that liquid.'

I don't know where those dollars were headed and I don't know where they came from but I'm sure there are many notes slipping down the drainpipes of Africa. I'd heard many stories of milk money going on whisky, but here twenty dollars of it was in my hand. This note was part of the reason Africa starves, part of the reason the kids on Maputo's streets don't have homes to go to. 'Is this Aid money?' I ask Kanda.

He just laughs, snaky eyes glinting in the neon, and changes the subject. 'Do you want an ice cream, white boy?'

'Yeah sure. Chocolate.'

WHISKY Screaming

You'll know you've hit Ghana after the Côte d'Ivoire, 'cos there's a chubby border guard who slaps you on the back, takes a peek at your passport photo and packs up laughing. No bribes. No tooth-pulling bureaucracy. In fact, by the time I haggle my way into a rusty, two-tone taxi, she is still rolling on the floor hooting – but as I am soon to learn, after gold and cocoa, laughter is Ghana's chief national product.

The Coast

Having spent a couple of months in West Africa, I am now quite accustomed to annoyances in the name of gifts and favours, but here things are different. Ghanaians will pester you alright – but to ask your name, to tell you a joke, or get your address. How many times, tip-toeing through some peeling town on the country's blowy Atlantic coastline, have I sensed the curling of small fingers around my wrist, only to behold some wide-eyed ten-year-old, armed presumptuously with a pen and a scruffy exercise book? Too many times, I fear. 'I sold you the packet of headache pills in Busua,' I read, opening my mail a few months later. 'Perhaps you remember me?' Well I don't, for friendliness is an epidemic in Ghana.

I am here with a harrowing agenda. Over the coming weeks I am to clamber sickly through the dungeons of derelict, windswept castles, where the stink of death tells the tale of ten million souls dragged down to this coast in leg-irons, and shipped off to cotton-picking misery across the ocean – well those who survived at least, for a third of West African slaves perished en route.

Not all these slaves came from Ghana: all along Africa's sensuous western bulge – from Goree Island in Senegal, through the Gambia, Sierra Leone, Benin and Nigeria – there are monuments to this hideous chapter in human history. But Ghana is an unusually cheap and peaceful destination for these parts, and despite the dizzying rhythms of local intonation,

English is its national language. As such, the country has proved the Soul Mecca of choice for the prodigal sons and daughters of the black diaspora.

Spend a little time in Accra, the country's wheezing, low-rise capital, and you'll meet Jamaican musicians, South London restaurateurs and visiting professors from the University of Chicago. At Jarro's rooftop restaurant downtown, George tucks his dreadlocks into a regal, purple knit-cap and reminisces about life in Kingston. On the notice-board, a map of revisionist African history advertises Dr Hamet Mautlana's courses in Afrocentric consciousness. However, when I contact Mautlana, he has an American accent and tries to enlist me as a salesman for his tapes and calendars.

As I weave my way among the coconut palms in towns like Winneba, Elmina and Cape Coast, I meet many ordinary, middle-class African-Americans, here to spill tears and burrow for their roots. Whether or not their ancestors ever set foot here is indeterminate and irrelevant: any roots will do. These are symbolic journeys, and the castles, parked like sad, ghostly ships along the rocky coast, are perfect stages for the bellowing of catharses and confrontations. Here, the slave confronts his master; the colonized, her colonizer; the oppressed, his oppressor. Fabulous vacation for a white South African still wrestling with the chains of *Apartheid* guilt, don't you think?

Yes and no, for unfortunately, there are some snags in the symbolism. Firstly, the slave trade was as complex as it was ghastly. Not only were there existing, messy webs of power and injustice in West Africa at the time; the whole horrible affair could never have happened without the co-operation of swarthy, local henchmen. So while some rotted in fetid hulls somewhere in the Atlantic, others fattened themselves on the spoils of a booming industry. Today, therefore, one can never be sure just who is the long-lost brother and who the long-lost traitor; and somewhere beneath the chummy donning of ceremonial names and *kente* cloths, the currents of betrayal run deep.

Secondly, looking at the slave trade from this side of the ocean has all the absurdity of glaring into a void. Like the shiploads of gold and ivory before them, the captured slaves left only holes in the land, and outside these dank, echoing chambers, physical traces of the trade are rare. 'It's the Americans who get all upset, darling,' a Ghanaian colleague in Accra comments bluntly. 'We escaped.'

Thirdly – and most importantly – this is Ghana, remember. And even when I do claw through my dead, white overcoat of guilt to scratch some genuine sadness, I don't have a hope of staying sad for very long. In most cases, barely have I carried my sorrow across the drawbridge, when I find myself wrist-deep in the local handshake ritual, and sooner or later, throat-deep in chuckles.

Francis Taylor

In the fishing village of Dixcove, I climb the hill to Fort Metal Cross where Kwesi Ansah, the shirtless local guide, walks me along the slave route. Dixcove looks picturesque enough from up here – what with the bright fishing boats pulling in and grey chorus lines of vultures arranged along peeling pastel roofs – but from up close, this is a poor and grubby place, with little income other than what the boats pull in. Now I am here, in my white coat, to interrogate the past with this ramshackle present. But just how much responsibility this long-forgotten fort holds for the village's stagnation is dubious.

'The Gate of No-Return,' Ansah thunders, gesturing at the grey Atlantic through a gap in the massive, stone walls. 'When our brothers and sisters passed through this gate, they knew they would never return to the blessed soil of the African continent.' His tone may be fire-and-brimstone, his grammar plucked from a colonial textbook, but Ansah has the grave delivery of a seasoned Shakespeare player: 'Very bad things have happened in these rooms,' he bellows. 'Things that must never happen again.'

I shed no tears but my gut buckles with horror. As we walk, I imagine myself as a villager tilling soil for a forest chief in this region, sometime between the fourteenth and eighteenth centuries. Given what the twenty-first century calls 'my individuality', I have little doubt I'd have been singled out and offered to the British or the Portuguese for a handful of beads – for in these conservative societies, the undesirables were always the first to be sold. Given my limited threshold for suffering and authority, I'd probably have been tortured and died, right here at Fort Metal Cross.

And yet, my coat is too thick to really feel a sadness. Guilt, yes. Dead, passive, stupid guilt that gets me nowhere, but no sadness. 'I'm not English, incidentally,' I mention to Ansah, as I leave. 'I'm South African.' Only he doesn't hear me.

Outside, it is one Francis Taylor who plants his arm on my shoulder. 'I'm goin' over to Busua,' he says, his voice gravelly as a Vegas pimp's. 'D'you want a ride?' I accept, and Francis rattles me along what Ghanaians call a road to the neighbouring village, a long-time favourite for long-haired overlanders.

Ghana never did much for Francis Taylor it turns out – indeed, he'd have probably been better off today had his ancestors passed through the hellish gate up on the hill. But Francis isn't the kind of guy to wait for hand-outs. 'Ain't no system gonna help me,' he rasps. 'So I stick with the Francis Taylor system. Dat's what I got.'

Recently, a couple of American businessmen swung through Busua. Kinda got sold on the Francis Taylor system, it turns out. Liked his daredevil ways. His crazy outlaw energy. Figured if anyone could get things done around here, Francis could, and so they gave him a share in a business. As we pull up to it, I decipher the words 'Alaska Beach Bar & Pub' painted on a wooden board. 'Alaska?' The very word drips in the humid afternoon. Francis packs up laughing. 'Yeah, it's a stupid name,' he wheezes. 'But dese guys, dey from Alaska.'

He pours some gin and tonic into a couple of chipped glasses and we sit a while with his wife Mary. 'They call this the Gulf o' Whisky,' Francis says gravely. 'Because it's full of spirits – the spirits of dem slaves who died in there. Jesus Christ! I can cry like a baby when I'm inside them slave castles. Those sick bastards. Whippin' 'em. Rapin' de women. Draggin' them across the ocean. Sometimes, you can hear the spirits out in the gulf you know? You can hear 'em screamin'. But what you gonna do about it? Nothin' you can do. And so you do the best you can.'

I scratch beneath my coat. Sorrow – not so much for what has passed, but for what is here and what's still to come. For Francis and Mary and the gooey *kenkey* porridge they eat, day in, day out. For the slavery of having no choices. And yet, as I am to discover, there is something definitively Ghanaian in this blend of doomed resignation and wily pragmatism. This is, after all, a country where one of the national heroes is a man who broke the cocoa embargo by swallowing a pip on board ship, then stealing ashore, squatting and depositing it in the fertile, tropical soil.

Another time, when President Jerry Rawlings got angry about something, the papers ran the headline: Rawlings is Mad.

'Whole country laughed at the same time,' Francis tells me. And we laugh. It is a special rattling laugh that you only hear in Ghana. And in that safe, rattling noise, we forget for a while. Francis forgets the sound of whisky screaming. Forgets he's too smart to be stuck here in Busua. That there's no power supply. That there aren't enough tourists to go around. And I forget my overcoat.

Richard

I stroll along the shore and it is Richard who talks me into a quick drumming class on the verandah of his hut. Some white American girls, who are planning to set up a Rasta commune nearby, have moved in with him. They all have long hair and long dresses, and one of them paces up and down reading the Bible. Jesus was a Rastafarian, she tells me. 'Moses too. Those are dreadlocks, man!'

I do my best to convince Richard that I have no rhythm but he will hear none of it, and so the ancient ceremonial pounding of the *djembes* commences to a forced and clumsy beat. The setting is blissful, but for the piles of black rocks held in place with chicken wire and arranged in bizarre, neat rows along the beach. 'We call that Money Fence,' Richard chuckles. 'Cost them fifteen thousand dollars to build it. There are children without porridge in this village but they build this stupid fence. They think they gonna hold the sea back, that the tourists gonna come and lie on this beach. But the sea is comin', my friend. Sea is comin' fast. You see that?' He points to a speck of sand out in the bay, crowned with a pair of palm trees. It looks like a Bugs Bunny antenna bobbing up and down in the waves. 'Well, ten years ago, that was a farm.'

He slaps the cowhide with his palms. 'Sahara is coming too,' he says. His words carry the charge of a mantra. 'Centuries ago, my people came here from Mali – from the great Songhai empire. Sahara was chasin' them down. Desert was gettin' bigger. And every year since, they just keep comin'. Now they try holdin' back the desert. Try holdin' down the sea. But it's no use. Sahara is comin', my friend. Sea is comin'. Gonna swallow us up.'

Fail as I do to wrap my hands around the rhythm from Burkina Faso, I succeed in deepening my understanding of global warming, the desertification of West Africa and the consequent land and population pressures. Richard is right: the town is slipping into the ocean, and when it does, he'll just pack up his drums and move on. He tried to leave before. Stowed away twice to Texas when he was a boy. Both times, they found him, hiding hungry in the ship's hull, and they sent him back. Didn't need any more slaves. Had enough of 'em puffing on crack vials in their inner cities. And so Richard is as stuck and free and helpless as the palm trees out in the bay.

Jesus

I check in at Sister Elizabeth's Place – a concrete shell behind a tin shack which has the words 'Busua Disco Church' painted above the door. There is a very pregnant goat tied to a tree in the yard, and my room has neither windows nor a door, but Sister Elizabeth is a kind and pious woman who boils up dirt-cheap lobsters for her guests and sits quietly in the evenings, planning her Sunday sermon in the light of a paraffin lamp.

She used to be a nurse in Accra, she tells me, gently lowering her eyeglasses, but when her mother died she came home to Busua and began letting rooms in the family house. 'Had to build up something,' she says. 'So as the children got something when I'm gone.' Here, where there is so little else, I notice, humanity shines so brightly.

Tricky as it is to see the scars of the slave trade in Ghana, the vestiges of the successive bouts of imperialism for which it paved the way are everywhere – lots of Jesus here, and lots of England. At the end of Busua's main street, there is a pink house with grey shutters. On its porch stands a middle-aged woman in a perfect shirtwaister dress. 'And what is your name?' I ask. She extends her hand. 'Josephine Winston,' she says, in the Queen's English. She adjusts her curlers and arranges her income in a stainless steel basin: a few packets of cigarettes with names like Club, Diplomat and Embassy – yes, even the brand names are stuck in a reverie of 1950s England.

It was in the year 1957 that a young man called Kwame Nkrumah secured what was then The Gold Coast's independence from Britain, plucking a name for the new country from West African history books. But while the ancient Ghana empire covered an area the size of the USA, Africa's first post-colonial state was small and far less powerful. Nkrumah was a great leader, but he was also an idealist, and within a decade his economic strategies were in ruins and he'd been overthrown in a bloodless coup. Since then, Ghanaians have endured more coups, shortages and dramatic swings in ideology. And though, since 1980, the country has shown one of the region's better growth rates, most Ghanaians have yet to feel the benefits.

When the Soviet doctrines lost favour here, however, missionaries made new inroads along the Ghanaian coast – sneaking unnoticed among the animist population with all the zeal of their slave-trading forefathers. Today, if it's not Christ the Redeemer Beauty Salon, it's Blessed Assurance Auto Spares, The Lord is My Shepherd Ice Cream Parlour or the Busua Disco Church. 'Why Disco?' I ask Elizabeth. 'Wait,' she says. 'You'll hear on Sunday morning.' And yes, it is very early on Sunday when the wailing of synthesizers confirms my suspicions.

Indeed, no matter where I lay my head in Ghana, I am never far from the call of evangelism. In the village of Elmina, the imposing white mass of St George's Castle – the oldest European building in West Africa – seems of far less consequence to me than the pale-faced Baptists who check in next door to me at the Soviet-style Nyansapow Motel. The next morning, I wander unsuspectingly downstairs in my dressing-gown, only to behold a dining-room thick with Ghanaians, and my two neighbours, palms clasped to a couple of bowed scalps. It is time, I decide, to move on.

A little later, I squeeze into a crowded *tro-tro* headed for Accra. The sound of the tyres over potholes drowns out the faint, forgotten screams out in the bay. However, I have only just observed that the man next to me has Clark Gable's smile, when he breaks the hypnotic thump with the rustling sound of a Bible in a plastic packet, and proceeds to yell verses from the New Testament for the following two hours. 'And how are you today?' he asks, when he finally sits down. 'Irritated,' I grumble, glaring directly ahead of me. 'You could have asked for a show of hands before you launched into that.'

'But it's not my word,' he replies. 'It's the Word of God.' We argue like this for a while, though never do I allow him the satisfaction of meeting my gaze. He tells me how primitive his parents were: 'savage idol-worshippers who slept with each other out of wedlock'. And with each exchange, I detest him more – his second-hand moralism obliterating the history and holy sensuality of this continent, as we speak. But in a weird way, I'm enjoying the chance to play the primitive. 'So what's wrong with sex?' I ask. 'Don't you enjoy it?'

'Oh yes,' he replies, merrily. 'My wife and I have sex all the time. It's marvellous.' I'm surprised by his answer – so much so, I allow my lips to curl into a weak smile. 'Sex is fine. But what of sodomites?' he thunders. 'How can you condone sinners like that?'

'Well actually, I'm gay,' I smile, looking him in the eye for the first time. He pulls a very ugly face, like he's just found a rat's leg in groundnut stew. 'You're joking.'

'No I'm not joking. Oh, come on. Haven't you ever tried it?'

'Well of course not,' he gasps, moving away a little. 'How could I? It's so...' He scours the bus for the word. 'It's so dirty!'

'No, it isn't,' I reply, deadpan. 'Not if you clean properly.'

Perhaps this isn't the best moment to be launching West Africa's gay liberation struggle. But somehow, very gradually, our mutual candour gives way to a fragile connection, and eventually I can't prevent myself from grinning, for rarely have I enjoyed such raw honesty with someone so utterly different from me. And by the time the bus wedges itself into the spluttering throngs of Datsuns on Accra's Ring Road, he's given up preaching and is rustling in his plastic packet for a pen and scruffy exercise book.

Kokomlemle

You'll know it's another busy day at the Kokomlemle Guest House, 'cos Jennifer, the buxom manageress, is lounging on a vinyl chaise longue waiting for her man to come by. Or *a* man, shall we say. Downstairs in the bar, there's groundnut stew in black, earthenware bowls and a beer advertisement that looks like a Tretchikoff print. And then there's Patrick, the Australian musicologist who lives at the back. Patrick withdrew all his savings and came to Ghana to record the region's music. Only Patrick hasn't found what he's looking for. 'It's Jesus' fault,' he seethes. 'The churches are demonizing traditional music. They're teaching them Gospel and R&B.'

Patrick hates Jesus. Hates Accra. Doesn't think there's anything groovy about the yellow neon light glowing in its twenty-four-hour restaurants. Doesn't go and watch the High-Life bands churning out their infectious jazzy riffs most nights of the week. Doesn't even notice the quaintness of businessmen climbing into taxis in their golden, hand-woven *kente* togas anymore. 'I'll tell you a story,' Patrick says, and he does.

'Guy came 'round here a few months ago. Had some eye disease. Needed money for an operation. Told him I didn't have any money left.

Didn't have any music either. But I did have an idea. There is a rather busy church in the next street you see. And I'd seen BMWs and Toyotas parked outside it. 'They're good Christians,' I told the guy. 'And I'm sure they'd be happy to help you out.

'Come Sunday, we arrived at the church together. But these good Christians took one look at my grubby companion and refused to allow him inside. We argued and finally they let him stay. After the sermon I stood up and explained his situation. There was a long silence. No-one had any idea what to say or do. Until someone started yelling. Then they all started yelling. After that, all I remember is lying in the dust outside and looking up at two massive bouncers. They didn't throw him out. But they didn't pay for the eye operation either. I paid for it in the end.'

It seems strange to me – an Australian, here to save Ghanaians from the greed of Western capitalism. To salvage ancient traditions from the trash heap in the name of something called World Music. And yet, I understand Patrick's sense of urgency, for a diverse world is a richer world.

In a restaurant downtown, facial scarifications peek through the waitress' make-up, but not through her daughter's. And indeed, every-where I go in Accra, the spectre of consumerism proclaims a new and brazen form of slavery.

Bush

'I'm Bushman,' he says, as he passes me on the dingy staircase at the Kokomlemle. 'Primitive Bushman.'

'That's a hell of a name,' I gasp.

'Yeah, some American woman called me that once. Didn't mean it in a very nice way. But I kinda liked it. So I had my passport changed. Made up the Primitive part myself.'

I'm not sure how I'll feel calling him Primitive Bushman in public, but I like him already. Kinda name that gets beneath your coat, if you know what I mean. Gets under your skin, even. He is somewhere in his forties – I can tell by the grey strands in his stringy, dreadlocked beard – and he runs a second-hand book stall among the curio hustlers at Labadi beach, Accra's only faint acknowledgement of being on the coast. But the man's name is the only provocative thing about him. Gentle. Modest. Poor as a cotton-picking slave.

We spend many days talking together. And he never asks me for anything. Used to be a preacher, Bushman. Used to do the *tro-tro* circuit actually. Only now he's a Rastafarian. One day, he takes me to where he lives. A forgotten ice-cream factory down at the seaside, a stone's throw from Christiansborg Castle, which is now the seat of government. There's no power at Bushman's place. No door either. 'I went to school with President Rawlings,' he says, looking along the shore at the castle. 'Always knew he'd be a leader. Had that about him. Saw him once, on a festival day. Smiled, but I don't think he saw me. Never saw him again. Strange really, we're neighbours, aren't we?'

The silence wafts off into the sea. 'You know,' he says after a while, 'they call this the Gulf of Whisky.'

'Yeah, I know they do. I think I heard the spirits screaming out in Busua once. Got through this weird, white skin of mine, that noise. Heard it for days afterwards. Strange thing though, afterwards I started hearing other noises. Rattling sounds that I'd never heard anywhere else. Deep, rattling sounds coming from the treetops. Kind of like the forests were laughing. Do you think that's possible, Bushman?'

He fiddles with his beard and smiles softly. 'Yes, I've heard that noise,' he says. 'Let's go to Labadi.' And we squeeze into a *tro-tro* headed for Accra's favourite beach. Bush sells second-hand paperbacks here from a makeshift little stand. He reads a lot and sells a few. Next to him Ali, a blue-robed Tuareg, sells beautiful *tafiliste* boxes – camel leather stretched over wood and tooled meticulously with traditional Tuareg designs.

Though the Tuaregs have a reputation as fierce desert nomads, Ali has a rare gentleness. He holds my hand as he speaks to me, and offers to take me to the compound where the Tuaregs are crafting their *tafiliste*. We proceed to a narrow alleyway nearby, where a group of Tuaregs are crouched over a variety of pieces, fiddling endlessly with their richly-hued *cheches*. 'We make some here,' Ali explains, 'but most I bring from my home in Mali.'

Each spring, he explains, he makes the treacherous solo journey to Gao in the Sahara. 'I go alone,' he prides. 'I go by Peugeot to Burkina Faso, and collect my camels, then I start my journey. I cross the borders at night, so the police won't find me. I drink the camel's milk. It takes me three weeks.' He holds my hand. 'You should come with me sometime.'

'Perhaps,' I smile. Of course, I am burning with enthusiasm for such a journey. The fact that such ancient trade routes persist thrills and delights me, but for now we return to Labadi, which, today being Sunday, is evolving into a great thumping beach party. There are reggae rhythms, and some crude Jamaican dance-hall music thumping out on *djembes.* 'You know what?' says Bushman. 'I'd like you to meet my girlfriend. Patricia.'

Trish

We all meet later at an outdoor restaurant. It is a beautiful evening, far too warm for a coat, and the sky is buzzy with the sound of traffic and saxophones. Patricia has a shock of red hair and thick glasses. She is as dirt poor as Bushman is, only a few years older. They both order drinks and say they aren't hungry. Patricia has lived most of her life in Canada, she tells me. A good wife to a civil servant in Ottawa. Had everything they needed. Did all the cocktail parties, till a couple of years ago, when she couldn't take it anymore. So she gave up everything and came to Africa as a volunteer. Met Bushman here. Calls him Bush. Calls her Trish. Smiles easily, Trish does. Laughs a lot too. 'Yeah,' she says. 'Learned that over here.'

THE MADNESS OF
Madagascar

'Some day, when I am old and worn and there is nothing new to see, I shall go back to the palm-fringed lagoons, the sun-drenched rolling moors, the pink villages and the purple peaks of Madagascar.'
EA Powell, *Beyond the Utmost Purple Rim*, 1925.

Madagascar is a bit of a shock. The pavements look Provençal, the houses look Nepalese and the language is a runaway train. In the countryside, yellow mafana blossoms tingle in your mouth like space dust, baobabs flower and silky lemurs leap out of eucalyptus trees to gobble sweet bananas from your hand. The rice is pink here; the earth, red and sacred.

In Tana, the capital, rustbucket Peugeots rattle up cobbled streets at forty-degree angles – streets that, for the most part, have no names. The locals eat crusty baguettes for breakfast, dance with their ancestors' bones and manage to drop the name of the nation's most famous king, Andrianimponimerinatsimitoviaminandriampanjaka, in a single breath. In an over-travelled world that suffocates on pretty palms and McDonald's patties, Madagascar is a strange, magical gust of oxygen.

Today is Independence Day, so Tana is doubly chaotic. A muddy park has become a fairground, and a game, something like *fish-pond*, is stirring a delighted frenzy. The MC yells persistently over the PA system, but the speakers are so wasted, the runaway train sounds like it's hit gravel. Some people are winning bottles of Coke or sets of orange Tupperware here, but first prize still shudders on the counter. Yes, today, someone lucky will be going home with a live turkey. That's if it doesn't drop dead from fright.

In the Zoma, the city's sprawling, central market, the traders haggle under a sea of white umbrellas. Their ancestors peer out of their faces: Indonesians, Africans, Polynesians. Actually, my guide looks kinda

Hawaiian. There are French sneakers for sale. Raffia mats, grated vegetables and *koba*, a pink, oily nut cake, which has been wrapped in black banana leaves and sliced as thin as salami. *Koba* tastes like wet cardboard. There is much, much more: spring rolls, tree ferns, bootlegged cassettes and patterned paper lanterns. By nightfall, these will all be alight and dangling from the fingers of a thousand children, so that from a distance, the streets will seem strung with Christmas lights. Steep streets, these. From the pretty rose garden at Tohatohabaton' Antaninarenina, the suburb of Ambondrona looks like a wall of houses. One out of ten for city planning, Tana. Nine for romance.

Even through today's hurricane of jubilation, sweet-faced cordiality is next to godliness. 'Be polite!' a street urchin reprimands me when I brush him off with an emphatic, 'No.'

'No' is not a good word to pack for this destination. Traditionally, when Malagasy mean 'no', they'll say 'yes' and then string you along politely till you suss the scene. Even in the stuffy Hotel Colbert, where professionalism demands a measure of Western decisiveness, the trouble with 'no' persists. 'Will you change my traveller's cheques here?' The cashier cringes. Smiles profusely. Eventually, spits out a strained negative amid a shuffle of eager nods.

I'm not quite sure why, but I've wanted to come here for a long time. Strange things have happened since the island broke off from Africa some one hundred and sixty million years ago. There are eight hundred species of orchid here, most of them endemic. Fifty species of lemur, all endemic. Africa may have one kind of baobab, 'Mad-land' has eight. In the rain-forests of Andasibe one morning, we track down the largest living lemurs, the *Indri indris*. There are only a few of them in the world and they only live here; they're painted like panda bears and they swing at whim among the treetops, waking every insect in the forest with their climbing soprano shrieks. Even a chameleon, the size of your thumbnail, bats a slow, prehistoric eyelid in affirmation.

East of here, the country's best road squiggles down to the seedy port of Tamatave like a strand of wet tagliatelle. I'd throw-up with car sickness if I wasn't so damn smitten with the geometry of the rice paddies, the quaintness of the double-storey mud huts and the grace of the Travellers' Palms, propping up the horizon like half-plucked feather dusters. I don't know this landscape: it is neither African, Asian nor Oceanian. A continent rather than an island, perhaps. A nowhereland, flickering in the yellow light of rusty Citroën headlamps. Even the CD compilations have titles like *A World Apart, A World Out of Time* and *Island of Ghosts.*

One afternoon in Tana, I meet with Christian Chadefaux, editor of one of the country's three daily newspapers. Chadefaux's lived here for forty-five years, worked in media for thirty-five, and he has the same moustache as the guy on the Gauloises packet. Because he wasn't born here, Christian's a *zanatany,* or a child of the land, and though he'll never be considered a real Malagasy, he's closer to the thick of things than if he were a *vaza,* or tourist, which is what I am.

Being a *vaza* does have its advantages of course. At Le Caveau night-club, a burly doorman brushes aside the queue and lets the *vazas* in for free. Between the Madonna tracks, jarring Malagasy dance rhythms will move you, groove you, then lose you. Across town at Le Restaurant, a grand, refurbished Tana villa, *vazas* dine on duck breasts in vanilla with sautéed vegetables for five dollars. Between courses, a stiff waiter rolls up the crumbs from your tablecloth with an antique, silver roller. For the same price, *vazas* rent basic cottages on balmy Île Sainte Marie, a lobster's throw from a still, perfect sea. So being a *vaza* is pretty cool really, you just don't get in on the secrets.

'Mentality here is as strange and insular as the ecosystems,' Chadefaux tells me. 'And just as the plants and animals have been protected in reserves, so the Malagasy have fortressed themselves against the outside world.'

Granted, hospitality has warmed since the mid 1800s when Queen Ranavalona I martyred the country's Christians and systematically rid the land of all foreigners, yet the island retains its isolation. Air Madagascar, which monopolizes the skyways, has only one 747; foreigners may not buy land here; and when I ask a local doctor if he feels African, I wait sixty seconds for a tentative nod. Then again, he may mean 'no'.

Effectively, despite sixty years of French colonial rule, seventeen years of Marxism and ten of reform, Madagascar remains an enigma, clinging to its mysteries, its traditions and its secrets with smiling tenacity. At the end of the twentieth century, Dama Moahomey still picks sweetly on his *valiha* and sings, 'Who really knows the true Malagasy?' Last year in Tana for instance, the Ruva, the ancient wooden palace you could see from most parts of the city, went up in flames. Chadefaux tells me the fire was an accident – a little fire to warm the guards in the cool highlands night, which got out of hand. There were no fire extinguishers around and getting a fire engine up that hill in a hurry is beyond a joke, so the world's second largest wooden structure simply burned to ashes. My Malagasy guide's face stiffens when he hears this explanation. 'Impossible,' says Vivi. 'How dare anyone suggest that?'

That something so tragic could be dismissed as an accident was quite beyond him. 'Political opposition,' he whispers. After all, the night the Ruva burned, Vivi cried for hours. If you think the lingo's tricky here, you should try the animist belief systems buried under Malagasy culture. The island writhes in superstitions; swims in red herrings. Eighteen tribes. Each with its own complex systems of taboos or *fadys*. For the Antandroy, it's *fady* to mention your father by name. For pregnant Skalava women, it's *fady* to eat fish; the Betsimisaraka won't work on Tuesdays or Thursdays. It's all a bit much for a simple *vaza* on a two-week break, so, of course, you'd be forgiven for switching off and shopping for checked raffia hand-bags. Then again, you could start with the dead.

Ancestors are important in most of Africa; here they're everything. In the newspapers, death notices state matter-of-factly that so-and-so has passed onto another world. And among the Betsileo and Imerina people, death is not so much a good-bye as an *au revoir*: a couple of years down the road, the embalmed, 'biltongy' corpse will be dug up for a *famadihana* celebration of drink, dance and celebration. And though the more urbane Malagasy aren't so keen on digging up granny and fox-trotting her round the village these days, the custom persists.

One night, hoping to get a grip on the spiritual underworld, I venture outside the city to the home of a legendary sorcerer. But as it turns out, Xhi is not your standard local mystic. His hair is plaited – to separate his thoughts – and he's strapped a seashell to his forehead, as the old Merina chiefs did. Xhi's world-view, is, shall we say, original.

Madagascar is the foot of God, I learn. For some very good reason I now forget, the toes broke off to form the Comoro Islands. The Shiloh-Christ is still on his way, you understand, and the people in Sri Lanka are blue, because they correspond to a certain phase of the moon. When Xhi learns I'm Jewish he is truly moved, and beseeches me, on departure, to send him the words of *Hava Nagila* by post. By this stage, even Vivi is retreating into rationalism. The land sings with legend.

When a Malagasy tourist drowned at a lodge, word got around that *lolos*, or ghosts, had caused his death. And though a post mortem revealed a coincidental brain haemorrhage as the actual cause of death, a national newspaper still wrote it down to *lolos*.

Nowhere have I been more aware of such an erratic tussle between past and present, truth and fable, worldliness and die-hard parochialism. In Tana, one city block boasts the Sauna Finlandais, the Patisserie Suisse and the La Hutte Canadienne, yet most Malagasy haven't even seen Madagascar – the French, you understand, were far more adept at *café au lait* than at road-building. For *vazas*, the upshot of all this is a reasonably priced domestic air network and regional variety that is as culturally astonishing as it is environmentally rich.

From Tana, you could head south-west to Tulear, and explore the mysteries of the spiny desert; south to the white beaches of Fort Dauphin; north to the charming port of Diego Suarez; or north-west to the hideously commercial island of Nosy Be. You could also wind your way east to the lush Cyclone Coast, as I did.

Cyclones only occur here in February, but when they do, commuters use taxi boats to plough their way down a six hundred-kilometre ribbon of lakes and canals called the Panagalanes. The boats are as narrow as gondolas, but longer. They are heavy with locals, chickens and sacks of rice. We pass a clutter of fishermen's shacks perched on a toothpick of an island, and we forge on to Antaninofy, which is plonk in the middle of nowhere. Clamber up to the restaurant here and the view of the middle of nowhere is quite sublime. You'd almost expect the Swiss Family Robinson to come trotting out of the jungle with orchids behind their ears. Instead, a coy waitress bears a tray of chicken, roasted in dijon mustard, and a salad of tart, pickled raffia hearts. It's a short crawl from here to a hammock. And from the hammock, I gaze out over the water at the darkening sandbank on the horizon – the last long, narrow smudge of sand between me and Australia.

North along the coast to Tamatave. Lazy and respectable as it is on the surface, come nightfall, this port grooves. You could sneak into a sidestreet, and gobble food at the Restaurant Vietnamien. You could dance at Queens Club, where the balcony is chock with long-limbed whores. Palm fronds frame a turquoise sky as the sailors roll in on red rickshas, though sadly, as Justine tells me, there are never enough sailors to go around.

Justine is a roughed-up Janet Jackson clone. She rolls up the sleeves of her black lummie and dishes me her take on local politics. 'Country's full of resources,' she snaps. 'So why are we so poor?' She pauses, then loops a long, red fingernail around her ear. 'Mentality.' Well yes, and corruption and under-development and the north-south divide, Justine. But we don't get into that. Business slips into the conversation; I slip into a red ricksha and rattle over to Stones, where retro night is in progress.

A video camera is propped on the deejay box. It has been linked to a screen. And the blurry strobe-lit view of revellers swinging their hips to an odd French version of 'Oh What a Night' remains, for me, the evening's defining image. It is some relief, the next morning, to find myself on Île Sainte Marie. Actually, I'd be relieved to find myself here any morning of the week, bumping along the little island's only road in a minibus. Postcards pass by the windows. Ramshackle Creole houses peek from behind yellow hedges in weathered pinks or greens. Coconut palms creak into still coves, and somewhere beneath the surface, a dark, anarchic edge of pirate history whispers through. The odd blonde fringe. A cemetery with skulls and crossbones carved into the tombstones.

The next morning I bike the hilly, eighteen-kilometre stretch to town and I count the cars that pass me – all two of them. I should fly back to Tana this afternoon, and yet, if you put me under a straw hat and left me here, I would dream of orchids and clear, spicy soup. Hammocks and bright, recycled tin Citroëns. Sweet *a cappella* melodies. Double-storey mud huts with tottering wooden balconies. Lemurs, ghosts and angel smiles.

Nomads
CLAPPING

Among the last nomads of southern Morocco, the clues to identity remain only in the varied rhythms of human hands, clapped out at night, over wood fires. But each year, fewer and fewer nomads scour these rugged moonscapes in search of grazing for their goats. I hoped to know some of them. To feel the rhythm of their identity between my palms, before it is all clapped out into the desert silence.

I cannot imagine the Sahara. In the blue-black night, the bus flick-knifes its way through the High Atlas passes like a frozen roller-coaster. The snowy summit of Jebel Toukbal gleams blue-white in the moonlight, and the paraffin flames of gnarled, wooden villages flicker among the massive cracks in the stone. I try to sketch a dune with my finger, but I can't. The desert is unimaginable.

Only a mountain range this fierce could hold back the eternity of sand that lies to its south. North of here, the terrain rolls into generous pastures that reach all the way to the Mediterranean. But crack your way south and the land shatters into black, stone plateaux, scrub and finally fine, reddish sand, where the earthy, fortified shapes of the architecture proclaim a land that is unmistakably African.

Just fifty years ago, this parched, forgotten moonscape still shivered on the knife-edge of clan rivalries, but since the *gendarmes* pacified the region, the fortress-like kasbahs perched on rocky outcrops are of little use to the population, most of whom now make their homes in boxy villages nearby. Though some kasbahs have been restored for tourists, most of these legendary mud towns are crumbling. So, too, with the people of these lands. Each year, fewer nomads bundle their scratchy, woollen tents onto their camels' backs to wander. Not that long ago, they carried their identities in the shapes of fine silver pendants: a crescent moon, an arched cross – fragments of place in the vast, placeless, sea of sand that stretches south to the Sahel and east all the way to the pyramids. Today, however, there is no need for these desert passports, and the clues to identity remain only in the varied rhythms of human hands. Clap me a place. Clap me Ouarzazate or M'hammid. And I will know who you are.

Three rivers ferry the last trickles of melted Atlas snow down to the desert's edge. Our route clings precariously to the Draa, tracking its course through dramatic gorges and verdant oases. At Tamenougalte, I clamber up to the kasbah: massive blocks of earth, straw and stone, now crumbling seamlessly back into the earth. A few families still scrape a living here, lending it the ambience of a half-let, biblical tenement block.

South. South to the perilous and unmarked Algerian border. A cramped and weary Peugeot station wagon rattles along the corrugated track. The land is turning to grey scrub, and the sun is setting. The driver places an Oudaden cassette in the stereo, and haunting, ancient Berber chants fill the pink, shivering sky. Against the car window, I sketch out the steep, pointed shape of a dune on the horizon.

The following morning, an ominous sign appears at the roadside: two wild-haired Berbers digging a blue Renault from a pile of fine, orange sand. We push. We laugh. I feel like an extra in a French comedy. And then I trace the shapes before me: a sea of upturned felt hats; giant, twisting whale-backs; curves and fine, pointed peaks. The ancient, deafening beauty of the dunes envelops me. We sleep, and wake to catch the silver yellow streaks of rising sun across the dunes. Later, I watch the wind chiselling delicate contours along their rims. I sense a rare stillness and solitude.

We arrive at a brown woollen tent. Moments after our arrival, a French hippie comes stumbling out of the tent, hazed out on hashish and isolation. 'Dédé,' he announces from under a sandy hat. 'And welcome to the Sahara,' he adds.

Dédé has been here for three weeks, he explains. 'Here' is pretty much nowhere, except for five tiny, struggling thorn trees poking out of the sand. They have been wrapped in barbed wire to keep them from the busy jaws of the camels, and they don't seem to be growing much. Dédé lights a hash joint. 'The desert is immense and it is growing,' he says. 'We must learn to hold it back. We can do this, but we need to come here and plant trees.

As they grow, so we will turn the desert back to green.' He grins and everyone nods politely.

I hear the thundering of hoofs across the sand: the wild-haired Berbers are running two camels across the camp. It is time to meet Kassim.

Kassim has a monster-sized head, big black eyes, and smells like the toilet at the Hotel Kawakib. I clamber aboard. He bolts. I grip the metal bar of the saddle. No problem. Uphill, I'm swaying backwards like a crazed belly dancer; downhill, I'm lunging into the fly-infested fuzz at the back of Kassim's neck. You get used to it, they tell me, but I don't.

I rock back and forth. The trails of dunes rise, then dip back into the stony plain. I pull my *chech* up over my nose when the wind sandblasts me. 'What do you think of Dédé's project?' I ask A'di. 'Isn't it amazing?'

'Pah,' A'di snorts. 'Those poor trees. They'll never grow.'

A'di speaks very little on our journey. Here, in the vast emptiness of the desert, its people have mastered a beautiful economy in their speech and gestures. A'di speaks carefully, pausing to capture the stillness of the dunes. Here, nothing trivial or superfluous is permitted. Even as we eat in the evening, the movement of hands around a communal plate of couscous is gentle and unhurried. And as we eat, I feel my way through the careful, measured pace of these lives.

The following morning I get off and trudge a while, and just when I can bear the monotony no longer, A'di points to a lone acacia tree at the edge of the plain. Beneath it, the emblematic shape of a tent, and some distant wandering cousins of his.

The mother is yelling. 'Brrk! Jkk! Frr-rt!' She whips her black, silver-trimmed *haik* over her face, leaving only a single green eye exposed. It must see everything, that eye. Father has gone to market for a few days and the daughters sit suspiciously around the fire. If we didn't have a few kilos of couscous in tow, I'm sure they'd yell us to Timbuktu.

This group lives as a family — nowadays, it takes a social structure as tight as this to clasp together the last shreds of tradition. And still it seems futile.

The eldest son, Zakariah, who has Down's Syndrome, scurries around herding his goats. We mustn't photograph them, he gestures frantically. No problem, man. No goat photos. His two brothers, around eighteen and twenty, sit elegantly on a purple blanket. One of them has a whacked-out tape recorder in a plastic packet. He is always rustling in that packet, snapping in hopelessly stretched *rai* cassettes, which peter out after a few moments. Batteries? First store on the left, I presume.

I ask if he has ever been in a car. No, but he was in a truck once. Is he married? Yes. That's his wife over there. Should a passing group happen to fancy one of his sisters, they'll simply leave a camel in trade and forge on with her. This must make for some anxiety, being a sister – which might be why the glances coming from the fireside are so very suspicious.

I never imagined the Sahara's last nomads to look like this. I pictured proud robed warriors, cross-legged aside a stark, sculptural tent. But this tent is not wool: it is a makeshift quilt of garish textiles and plastic bags. There is litter everywhere. A bicycle for fetching water, nine kilometres away. They have been here for three days. No-one sleeps indoors – as the bits of bedding strewn randomly around a hundred-metre radius will testify – and no-one baths much. Once a month, perhaps, should they pass an oasis.

I peek inside the tent. It's the cupboard in my granny's spare bedroom. Packets and packets and boxes and bags. A life in packets. A lifestyle in decline: since trucks began crossing the Sahara, the nomadic trade routes have lost their value. This family has only six camels. They are the last people, living the finale of an ancient lifestyle in a lost landscape. Rarely have I felt so far away.

At night, the men and women eat separately: couscous, soaked in sour dromedary milk. Suddenly, an eerie sound meanders from the darkness. It is Zakariah, whacking a tambourine and baying at the moon. I tap out his rhythm between my palms. Tap-tap tap-tap-tap-tap tap. The mother yells. A daughter rushes out and scolds him. But minutes later, he is at it again.

His agonized cry cuts through me. The last, tenuous link to a forgotten world. His brothers hush him silent. There is the rustle of plastic, the snap of the lid, and gradually, as the stretched, stuck sounds of *rai* musicians from another place fill the sky, I know that a rhythm has been broken.

Portraits

Emerson's
EMPIRE

It's dinner-time at Emerson's Rooftop Restaurant in Stonetown, Zanzibar. Emerson, who feels a single name boosts his celebrity status, is grinning broadly in his silk shirt and *kofia*. He circles the space and descends cross-legged at each of the low tables to connect with his hotel guests. Every now and then, and with no warning, he drifts off into the balmy magic of the moment. The panorama of Stonetown, Zanzibar's capital, is yellowing fast around us and the Indian Ocean is still and silver. But just when you're ready to say 'pinch me', Emerson's mad, contagious chuckle rings out in the sunset sky. 'It's theatre!' he beams wryly, when he joins me. 'All part of this mad, Bohemian fantasy I'm living.'

This particular fantasy was unleashed in 1989, when Emerson came to Zanzibar on his travels. A few years previously, he'd trashed his job as a child psychologist in New York and had come to teach English to school-children in Kenya. It was, he recalls, the warmth and hospitality of the Zanzibari people that convinced him to make a second move and make this island his home, playground and dream lab. In 1991, he opened Emerson's House, a twelve-roomed hotel squeezed into one of Stonetown's plank-narrow alleys.

By this stage, the fine line between visionary and lunatic was already a well-trodden path for Emerson. As a child, he'd alarmed the neighbours in his native Virginia by building an African-style mud hut in his parents' backyard and performing all sorts of personalized rituals there.

Later on, his penthouse in Greenwich Village became a famed stop on the map of heli-tourists who would hover to ogle the naked adults wandering around its roof garden.

Today, his modest East African empire, consisting of a restaurant, two hotels and another on the way, is no less imaginative, and yet steeped all the more passionately in romance.

Let's face it: the man has flair. He also has one of the better antiques collections in the region. As a result, Emerson's House is a dreamy cornucopia of swing benches, Bombay tables and witty retro-kitsch. In the lobby, a lit-up Taj Mahal shares space with bits of coral, an antique brass scale and an Indonesian Buddha. In the dining room, an early twentieth-century Venetian chandelier hangs above a divan, replete with soft, appliquéd cushions and an inlaid backgammon board. Indeed, the groups of objects seem less like decorated still-lives and more like stage sets, lying in wait for some Bohemian Rhapsody to commence.

Emerson's own bedroom is the size of a standard school hall. At one end, a carved four-poster bed pokes out behind towers of books; at the other, a low, tiled Arab bath practically hangs over the town.

'My restaurant is the second highest point in Stonetown,' he tells me mischievously. The highest, the House of Wonders, was so named as the tallest building in East Africa in its day, and the sultans decreed that no building should surpass its height. Given this fact, Emerson does occupy a rather prestigious rank in what he calls the local 'higherarchy'; yet more importantly, perhaps, he is also the hub of the local grapevine network. 'Anything happened in East Africa this week?' I pry. 'Well,' he muses, 'there is something quite juicy I've just heard which concerns a rather important member of the British Royal Family, but I've been sworn to deepest secrecy.'

Though I have no success squeezing the secret out of Emerson, I do catch glimpses of him, laughing and rattling away in Swahili with his staff. But this level of intimacy with the locals has earned him a measure of scepticism on the part of some expats and hotel guests. 'A con man,' spits a blonde, Italian socialite, when I encounter her on the other side of the island. 'A friend of mine recommended his hotel and I can't understand why. I had to check out early. The place is so odd, so impractical and so claustrophobic.'

Although I'd swap claustrophobic for intimate, the rest is accurate. For most guests, however, the quirks simply fold in with the hotel's charm. '*Fawlty Towers*, dubbed into Swahili,' an ex-employee quips fondly. 'As for Emerson, think what you will, but because he understands Swahili culture, he actually gets things done here – no mean feat in Zanzibar.'

'Take the tale of Emerson's stick,' she instructs. 'One day I needed to do the hotel's banking which is a notoriously tedious undertaking. I was advised to take Emerson's walking stick with me and place it in the corner of the bank, which I did. It seemed ridiculous, but it worked like a dream. I was served immediately.'

It transpires that a long time before, Emerson had marched into the bank wielding the stick above his head and thundering his instructions like a madman. He'd elicited roars of applause and consequent prompt service from the banking staff. Ever since, the stick had served as short-hand for the episode.

Jean de Villiers, a South African dive instructor and close friend of Emerson's, tells how he returned to Zanzibar to find his entire savings account dry. It turned out that Emerson had convinced the bank manager to release De Villiers' savings for the urgent construction of a new roof. He paid De Villiers back of course, and the incident didn't prevent them from going into business together on Emerson's latest dream-coming-true, Chole Island.

A few kilometres from Mafia Islands on the southern Tanzanian coast, Chole has been an important stop on the spice routes for centuries. Today, the town on the island is in ruins and abandoned as haunted by the superstitious locals. In a triumph over bureaucracy, Emerson managed to lease the island from the Tanzanian government and planned to open a small resort.

One can rest assured that Emerson tackles such projects more sensitively than most. After all, it was he who got signs put up all over Zanzibar to sensitize G-stringed, coral-snatching tourists to the modesty of local culture and the fragility of the ecosystems. And though his laissez-faire sensuality paints a portrait of a decadent, one senses a deep awareness of what he's doing here.

Emerson still has a home in New York where he spends time during the East African monsoon. But sitting here, sipping lazily on a G&T, the Emperor seems right at home in Africa – not just because he gulps down its pleasures so heartily, but because his reverence for its traditions runs so deep.

'Just look at these appliquéd cushions,' he says. 'For centuries, the Zanzibaris had rich patrons and developed a unique and highly sophisticated culture. What am I doing here? I'm facilitating a renaissance of that marvellous culture. So, I'm a Renaissance Man, I suppose.'

He slips into chuckles. 'A sort of modern day Cosmo de Medici, you might say.' Toss in a little Blixen, some Byron and a twist of Tarzan, and you have the picture.

The Emperor
AND THE VEILS

Never tear the veil, for you will both expose its secrets and destroy the magnificence of its dance. But gaze carefully as it shimmers in the tropic sunlight, and you will gradually come to see through it.

A few months after publishing *Emerson's Empire*, I received a letter of thanks from the Emperor himself. He was delighted with the piece – impressed with the accuracy of the portrait I'd sketched after such a brief, superficial meeting and tickled by its notes of send-up.

I thought of him often in the months that followed. He was a fantasist to be sure – and a brave one – and somehow, through a mixture of chance and lunatic design, he had engineered a most ancient and outrageous fantasy existence for himself out there on his fabulous Indian Ocean outpost. He had dared himself the most absurd of dreams, and now, having made them real, he seemed to revel in their absurdity.

Like all Africa's expatriates, he enjoyed a certain freedom. Not fully accountable to either local society or to those back home, he skipped happily over the standard fences of sanity and convention, chuckling mischievously as he went. While fraying khaki shorts and washed-out tropic-print shirts with buttons missing sufficed for the day's business meetings, evenings elicited an extravaganza of embroidered *kofias* and pink or yellow silk *kurtas* he'd had made in Rajasthan. For sheer theatricality, he was something of a genius. His life held resonances of Scheherazade's stories in *One thousand and One Nights*, he liked to say, and much of the time, it did. He had made some truly bold choices over the previous half-century, and I wondered, at times, if I would ever have the desire or conviction to make similar ones for myself.

Weeks passed and I grew bored with my life in Johannesburg. I remembered the evening I'd spent on the rooftop of his hotel – sprawled out on Persian rugs and appliquéd pillows, nibbling on fried breadfruit, captive in the sheer ecstasy of the moment. I remembered conversations about ancient, faraway things that, from that vantage point, seemed to be so close by – trade routes, *dhows*, explorers, slaves. Arabia. I remembered the silver stillness of the ocean at sunset, the cries of gulls in the sunset sky, and I picked up a pen and dared myself a little. 'Dear Emerson,' I wrote. 'I am pleased you enjoyed the piece. Do you have a job for me? I'd be happy to come and work in exchange for room and board.' The response was short and swift. 'Dear Adam,' he wrote, 'come at once.'

The vision delighted me – a sun-tanned, carefree *moi*, shaking up cocktails at the hotel's rooftop bar and chit-chatting with sun-tanned Italian holidaymakers. Little did I realize how much more complex, deep and layered my sojourn in Zanzibar was to prove.

A couple of weeks later, my plane skidded down late in the sticky thick of an East African evening. Immediately, I was drenched in the magic of the place: the coughing of mopeds; the distant, melancholy wail of cassette recorders; the drunk, butter-soft caress of the evening breeze. As always, the smells and the music came from nowhere and everywhere at once. I wound my way to Hurumzi Street, expecting to find the Emperor as I had last seen him, lost in long trains of giggles amid the decadent splendour of the rooftop. Two boys were sitting outside the building when I arrived, twiddling the evening between their thumbs. 'Babu is not here,' they explained. 'He has left for Kajificheni Street.' And one of them offered to walk me through the peeling, crocheted maze of streets to find him.

As we walked, I lost myself and found some of the magic that walking holds here. Through my flip-flops, I felt the heat of the day still baking in the stone tiles of the alleyways. We came to an ornate, wooden door on Kajificheni Street and knocked. '*Mzee!*' the boy yelled excitedly, 'I bring you friend.' A few moments later, I heard a shuffle somewhere in the house, but the door remained shut. And then from nowhere: 'Oh wonderful. You've made it!' The words ricocheted across the street and back. I recognized the voice but had no idea where it was coming from. 'Hello,' he giggled. 'I'm up here!'

The boy nudged me and gestured towards the sky. I craned my neck and peered up along the facade, past four layers of carved wooden balconies. Sure enough, there, above the top one, the Emperor's face peered down like a curious ornament atop an intricate, teak wedding cake. The light was dim but I could just make out the trademark glasses, moustache and cheeky, upturned nose. 'Good evening,' I yelled back.

'Well, I'm sure you've had a long journey,' he said. 'Why don't you go and get some rest and come and see me in the morning? Sheha will walk you back.' He smiled and vanished into his 'tree-house', and the boy walked me back along the same route to where we'd started.

Daze

I awoke the next morning in a daze. The generator had died during the night – in honour of my arrival, I imagine – and I had been escorted to my room by the flicker of a paraffin lamp. I felt deeply happy when I woke up, for I had no idea where I was. I brushed open the mosquito nets and cut a slow path through the string of rooms on this side of the house. The first would be my bedroom, the next my study. There was a red velvet sofa, caked with dust, and a Bombay side table, inlaid with cracked, green tiles. In one corner, a stack of disassembled wooden beds stood waiting for attention. A couple of dead bulbs dangled from the ceiling, which reached right up to heaven. Grandeur – as faded as a pair of eighteenth-century Levis. Fuck the dust, I felt like a Sheikh.

I pulled back the netting at the window and gazed down at the narrow mess of the street. Like most streets in the town, Hurumzi was closed to cars, but made a magnificent stage for the daily street parade. A lost flip-flop lay tanning on a browned, tin portico. A white-whiskered *mzee* was dozing in a cracked plantation chair, scratching lazily at his crotch. On a raised slab of pavement, the brightly veiled forms of women were exquisite against a pitted turquoise wall. One of them was painting henna designs on her feet, another arranging her tomatoes like strings of red beads. There were bicycles too. Chickens, mopeds and skinny white cats, all shuffling along to the shrill melodies of children, as they hop-scotched among the ragged paving stones.

I made my way down the grand teak staircase to the second floor, which seemed to function as a lobby. The Emperor had stationed himself on a wooden bench at the back of the room, and along its walls, a motley collection of souls sat waiting on mismatched antique chairs. Some were employees, to be sure, but some were simply pilgrims who would arrive each morning to seek help or advice from Babu, or Grandfather, as he was fondly known.

Babu didn't acknowledge my arrival. He simply rattled away in his loud, Virginia-accented Swahili, yelling or shaking his fist for emphasis, or clapping his hand on the knee of whichever subject was in the hot-seat. Sometimes he burst into demented, childlike shrieks of laughter that echoed across the room. Other times, he simply froze, raising his head and casting his pale blue gaze out into the middle distance. He'd hold it just there, for far longer than was comfortable, like some obscure, benevolent leader posing for an oil portrait.

He ruled by temperature, it appeared, regulating his exchanges like a human thermostat. Warm, then cold, then warm. He was a master of proximity and it unnerved me, and so did the laughter. But the pilgrims sat patiently through all this and so did I.

After around forty minutes I advanced to the high bench of consultation. He smiled, asked a few trivial questions about my journey, and then froze. The silence hung heavily in the grand, vaulted hallway. I braved a couple of anecdotes, but to no avail. He scarcely budged. 'You're making me nervous,' he said eventually.

'I think you should go and walk today. Tomorrow we will discuss the details. Go and walk. Walk through the town. Lose yourself. Find yourself. Walk off where you've come from. Walk it out!' He giggled, delighted with the melodrama of his tone.

I nodded and left, but I felt uncomfortable. How could I sponge away at his generous pool of hospitality without knowing what was expected of me in return? What was my job to be? What was the deal? The least he could do was inform me.

And so I walked. I followed the town's maze of narrow alleyways, losing, then finding myself in small, palm-treed squares where old men sat on wooden *barazas*, sipping tiny, bitter cups of coffee. I gazed in at little stores, at spicy doughnuts, sweating behind steamy panes of glass. I twisted, turned, felt out the angles of the labyrinth in my joints. I spoke to no-one.

He was right. I needed to acclimatize – if not geographically, then culturally. I needed to feel the rhythms of walking in my feet. Re-tune my ears to the sounds of the circling crows and the wailing of *muezzins* at dawn. Adjust my taste buds to the aroma of cardamon in my coffee and feel the pitted coral walls against my fingers. It was an appropriate initiation, I suppose, and yet the following morning, I had grown so anxious about the mystery of my intended vocation, I rose at seven to secure a good place in the queue.

I spoke frankly with him. 'Emerson,' I said, 'I am delighted to be here and I'm grateful for your hospitality, but I'd love to know what I'm going to be doing.' Again, he froze. Ol' blue ones suspended in the middle distance. 'Very well,' he said. 'Come to my rooftop tomorrow morning and we will discuss it all. Can you be there by six?'

I nodded, excused myself and left. What on earth was I getting myself into? Surely, it was simple enough to outline an arrangement up-front, before I had accumulated any serious debt to him? He was playing me like a violin and the sonata was growing resentful. By evening I felt so tortured, I dragged myself to a filthy bar, The New Happy Saloon and Pub, and drank far too many Safari lagers with a clutch of cane-soaked whores and smack-sniffing lay-abouts. And the next morning, as I trudged along the alleyways to his house, I was both tired and hung over.

The ground floor of Emerson's house summed up his aesthetics perfectly. A rather grand teak reception desk was stationed in the centre of the room, atop a plush wall-to-wall carpet of wood shavings. There were a couple of clear-glass mosque lamps stashed beneath the stairwell; some rare, original Tinga-Tinga paintings and more disassembled beds. Everything here was either still under construction or already in ruins, it appeared.

I groaned my way up the four flights of stairs to his teahouse, where Babu sat motionless on a teak bench, his tanned belly protruding over a cerise sheet of cloth, eyes half shut. I furnished him with details of the previous day's activities and he nodded. The morning mists hung heavily over the panorama of the town. He spoke little, but sipped away on a chipped cup of muddy coffee.

Gradually, a sliver of sunlight cracked through the clouds, painting splashes of rich golden light across the crumbling capital. Out on the horizon, a batch of concrete, Soviet-built apartment blocks glistened with mould. 'You know what Livingstone said about this place?' he asked, without looking at me. 'Yes,' I replied smartly. 'In Zanzibar, nothing is as it seems.' He smiled, satisfied, but kept on gazing.

The quote was a cryptic reference to something, I realized. The true purpose of my journey here? Or of his? Or of everything here perhaps? 'Nothing is as it seems.' I buried the words deep in me. In my quest for explanation right then, this was as good as it was going to get. Emerson stubbed an unlit Dunhill Red on the wooden table-top – a hangover from his days of unfiltered cigarettes. 'Take a note,' he said. He spoke slowly and carefully, as if he had rehearsed the words many times in his head. He paused lengthily, to search for the perfect adjective, or to build suspense. And I scribbled down a few paragraphs about the town's architectural history. I was unsure why I was doing so, but was delighted to be doing something. 'Well,' he said after a while, 'that's enough for today, I think. Tomorrow then?'

We had connected well that morning, and I felt better. Yet still, I realized, he had skilfully skirted the nature and conditions of my employ. Surely he had not lured me all the way here for this? Couldn't he just write it all down himself? He was clearly such a fine orator, there was no need for much editing skill on my part? What was my title? Typist to the Emperor? Secretary? Scribe? It seemed far less glamorous than cocktail barman, and as I trampled back down the stairs, I sought solace in Livingstone's observation. Perhaps my job, my very presence here was something other than it seemed.

Secrets

The following morning, I slipped quickly into the maze of streets and began to walk. My lostness frightened me, and yet I knew how important it was for my initiation. It would be weeks before I could tell one crumpled palace from another, for just when I thought I recognized a route, it fizzled into an alleyway or found me in some vacant lot, where the tropic rot had gobbled another building, and spat up piles of weeds and rubble in its wake.

Half a century previously, these buildings had been the homes to a wealthy and cultured elite. But with the People's Revolution in the 1960s, these fabled Arab dynasties had fled back to Oman, leaving their palaces and their treasures to the hordes of jubilant, looting peasants. Gradually, the peasants had moved into their homes, bringing with them their goats, chickens and wood fires. They had no interest in maintaining the buildings, and so many had crumbled over the years.

On some walls, the scars of alcoves and archways sketched out the histories of these long-collapsed courts. High up on one of them, a forlorn, brass teapot sat smartly on a shelf, testament to the memory of a gracious third-floor salon. The ghosts of grandeur and sophistication hovered eerily among the skull-like chunks of coral rag.

Declared a World Heritage site, the little town contained some seventeen hundred buildings of architectural merit. Most of them had been built in the nineteenth century during the great boom of the clove trade. The architectural style was unique and eclectic. While the carved wooden doors and stained glass shuttered windows were Indian, the style of construction was Arab and the building materials were local.

The palaces had been built very close to one another to provide shade from the sweltering tropic sun. Constructed from coral rag – the very bedrock of the island – their thick porous walls kept their interiors cool and dark in the daytime. Due to an absence of substantial trees, however, mangrove poles had been used as supports between floors. And though this had been structurally successful, it had limited most buildings' width. And so while often surrounded by flaking grandeur, one was never very far from a cupped ear, pressed up curiously against a wooden door or window frame.

I walked on, remembering the Emperor's instruction. I noticed a tailor's store, the size of a cupboard, raised above the stony dust of the street. Inside it, an old man in a yellowed *kanzu* rattled away on a Victorian sewing machine, his fabrics stashed loosely in blue plastic bags on the shelf above him. It seemed too tiny a space for a world, yet a perfectly adequate stage on which to play out his monotonous cameo each morning, in the tin-can musical of Mkunazini Street.

A black-veiled woman buzzed by on a moped, her secrets stashed behind a pair of fake Gucci sunglasses. A boy with a Bart Simpson haircut spun past on a makeshift skateboard, and skinny cats stalked about in tattered white coats, sniffing through burnt-out rubbish cans for leftovers. I looked carefully as I went, opening and shutting my eyelids, training my pupils to see more clearly, to transcend their own exotic gaze. Guiding my feet in the patterns of the labyrinth.

I walked alone as much as possible but it was difficult, for most times, moments into my stride, some bright-eyed local boy would slip in along-side my gait and begin asking questions. Where do you come from? Do you like Zanzibar? Are you on holiday? The content mattered little, but the combination of walking and company was sacred here. As I was learning, the motion of stepped feet carried with it far more than transportation.

Indeed, in this busybody of a town, one dared not breathe a sentence while still standing still, for it would ricochet through the delta of plank-thin alleyways, like a paper aeroplane aimed perfectly into the ears of the streets. Here, each mildewed cornerstone was a telegraph pole. Each glassless window, a live microphone. And so it was only motion that offered any respite from the incessant broadcast. So you walked, and as you walked, you talked. Secrecy danced to the shared rhythm of stepping feet.

Of course the odd few walked words were sure to drift up on the shore of some inquisitive ear, but mercifully the sentence rarely arrived complete or in its original order. A name might catch on a washing line; a scandalous phrase could dangle from an awning. And so, while true privacy remained a preposterous luxury, one might always enjoy the privilege of titillating the neighbourhood with gusts of jumbled utterances.

Over the years, these games of misunderstanding had evolved into a rich and engaging tradition, and much time was spent piecing together the possible meanings of these snippets as you stumbled across them.

Had you seen Yalma hurrying through the streets to Saida's house, for instance, you'd be sure she had a couple of names and places buried in her basket, and sure too that Saida would reach into her bottom drawer and dig out a gossipy titbit from her collection. And then, as they whiled away the afternoon painting henna designs on their feet, they would giggle and shuffle the words around like the pieces of a jigsaw puzzle. Here, where an immense oral tradition far outweighed any written one, people wrote their own tales, sculpting the banal details of their daily lives into meandering intrigues.

So, too, with the news of the planet. Here, so far away from the world, one could never be sure of the accuracy of the facts one learnt. There were phrases missing, absent contexts and agendas. Who knows? A paragraph may have lodged in the branches of a baobab tree up north, an opinion held up at a border post. And so, as Yalma and Saida dipped their sticks into the pot of henna and doodled away at their ankles, they'd piece together their world view with due irreverence.

Powerless as this made them feel at times, they'd become skilled in the poetry of the act. The sheer engagement of piecing together a picture was far more entertaining than a single, unquestionable truth. And as these stories passed from mouth to ear, they shrank and twisted and blossomed. Such was the language of the labyrinth.

～

In the weeks that followed, I grew familiar with my morning routine. The Emperor's tales were most captivating. Intended as a brochure for hotel guests, they explained the history of his palaces in great detail. 'There are many different stories about these buildings,' he'd commenced, striking an appropriately mysterious tone. 'And all are true and none is true ...'

The stories were anything but dry. There were tales of lovers passing notes between balconies on lengths of string. Of wicked neighbours laying planks across the alleyways and scampering through the windows of rubble-filled rooms to search for treasures rumoured to have been left behind by the fleeing aristocrats. Of jealous servants. Of gifts and bargains. Each room, each object, was steeped in a tale of wiliness and passion.

The Emperor was something of a self-made architect, I gathered. Some afternoons, I'd stumble across him yelling out orders in the hallway of another building, or marching about inspecting the teak inlay he had devised for the pigmented, concrete floor, or the lattice-work that was replacing the walls. For while obliged to preserve the grand peeling facades of the buildings, the rest was all romance and fantasy. He had studied the local building methods, and from there had improvised boldly. The resulting hybrid of style was not only Indian, Arab and African, but Emersonian.

There were deep shady divans and alcoves; carved wooden bridges trimmed with bougainvillaea; sunken baths poised over perfect vistas of the town. One room – The Ballroom, as it was called – stretched the entire length of a building, with a grand marquee of a bed at one end and a tiled octagonal bath at the other. The distance from bed to bath was so impressive, one might have asked room service for a bicycle.

Each room had a colour scheme: peacock blue; Maharajah pink; emerald. And the tones were picked up in the floors, tiles and trimmings. Each room housed an antique four- or two-poster Zanzibari bed, trimmed with grand, satin-edged mosquito nets. Then a writing desk, a plantation chair perhaps, or some elaborate Venetian chandelier left over from the days of the sultanate. The Lavender Suite had a portrait of Queen

Elizabeth over the dresser and was recommended to gay guests.

It was atop each palace, however, that the Emperor perched his most sumptuous and public keynote – a raised teak deck, trimmed with simple balustrades and topped with neat tin roofs, to which sheets of translucent voile were attached. From all over the town, you could look up and see these veils, billowing in the evening breeze, like opaque territorial flags.

Some mornings, he dictated letters to great friends. His eccentric East African inns had established a worldwide fan base over the past decade and he kept irregular contact with many of these people. His letters were heartfelt, but cunning. He'd mention this countess or that, suggest projects for funding and shoot off strategic invitations to the island. It amazed me that such an influential clique was accessible from this remote outpost. But this was only due to great patience on my part: if there was power, and if the printer, fax machine and phone lines were functioning, these missives were whisked off around the globe to senators, CEOs, celebrities and minor British royals. And as the weeks passed, I grew to know him better.

Because I never saw the replies to the letters, I knew only half of the stories, and even these halves were unreliable. But gradually, I had begun piecing together a portrait of my host. If there was information missing, I silently surmised. I, too, was learning the language of the labyrinth. The poetry of the place was scribbling itself in my mouth.

As the weeks passed, his moods grew more consistent, but still, he fiddled unpredictably with the thermostat. He was warm, then detached. Familiar, then suddenly formal. A mad African despot, then a fine Southern gentleman. I felt manipulated at times, and deeply gratified at others.

In this court, I realized, a twentieth-century notion like salaried employment was a crass anachronism. I was required to perform a minimum of duties, and beyond those, I was best occupied picking through the mysterious tapestry of local culture, reading in the town's dusty archives, or making art of some sort, so that late in the day, as the restaurant slipped into the wide saffron sea of dusk, I might have some interesting observations to feed into the gin-soaked sunset chatter. Details of East Africa's Islamization in the ninth century, perhaps. A charmed life? Perhaps, but the doors of such liberty hinged on a far stricter code of etiquette than I was used to.

I had grown up loosely, in the detribalized muddle of a middle-class nuclear family. Suddenly, I was required to behave with all the refinement and decorum of a seasoned courtesan. Shock tactics drew nothing more than a yawn in this court. Platitudes elicited stiff silences. And though mischief and eccentricity would always be praised, vulgarity and affectations elicited nothing but a raised and chilling eyebrow.

One evening, I paid Babu a visit at his teahouse. There were other guests present, sipping expensive Martinis in cheap tin cups, and the conversation swung to one of Babu's pet subjects: the American Civil War. He began spouting dates like an adding machine unhinged, stabbing the sky with a stiff index finger, stubbing Dunhills on the table like a drill. Each time I stretched my jaws to speak, he cut me off like a carving knife. Why was I even present, I wondered. To listen? To scribble this all down? By the end of the evening, I had not managed a full sentence.

A few days later, we met for a sunset drink on his rooftop. He circulated among the guests as usual, chit-chatting, cross-legged on the rich, burgundy rugs. I was deep in discussion with a guest on the subject of human relations. The warmth of community. The magic of time shared with others. I had not noticed Babu, seated with a nearby couple, but out of the corner of my eye I caught him turn his head and interject. 'That's all we have,' he boomed. 'Nothing! Nothing else is permanent. That's all we have.' Rarely had I seen his face so serious. And it was only a few moments later that his eyes lit up and the corners of his mouth crept ever so slightly upwards.

~

If one thing was becoming clear, it was this: out here, under this wide tropical sky, there was sufficient space for the most unconventional behaviour and arrangements. Be they friendships across class barriers, or passionate affairs, the town had learnt to accommodate them. For while these relationships were generally public knowledge, provided the translucent veils of secrecy that hung over them were not tampered with, they could survive years, or even decades. Husbands had husbands and wives had wives. Young girls had sugar mommies and dreadlocked young men had pale two-week wives. And those wily and wealthy enough kept harems or built empires.

Living out here, in one of the poorest countries on earth, Western formality seemed a perverted luxury. It mattered little how things were done, (indeed as far as Emerson was concerned, the more imaginative and outrageous the means the better), but it mattered deeply that things were done with a greater good in mind. Motive meant more than method, out here where method was so unreliable.

In a strange way, the remoteness and inefficiencies of the island worked to everyone's advantage, for they preserved a far more gracious and archaic existence than is common anywhere anymore. Bad cars meant walking. Bad television meant more time spent with people, and bad phone lines meant cordial, old-fashioned visitations. And bad governments meant empire-building. And indeed, for all the inconveniences and inefficiencies he grimaced through daily, it was unlikely Babu would have ever assumed the rank of emperor in Virginia.

The empire was modest enough, I'd discovered. A handful of grand coral mansions scattered about the island in varying states of repair; a couple of busy though oddly-run hotels and, word had it, a sizeable collection of antiques stashed quietly somewhere in East Africa. He had also managed to lease an entire island from the Tanzanian government. Tarzan in the Jungle, he'd giggled. Hammocks in the mango trees. Sunset *dhow* cruises. And while I never heard him quite utter the phrase 'my people' about the island's thousand inhabitants, the sentiment was surely there.

Yet even this – what seemed like an absurd anachronistic stretch of imperialism – had more to do with securing funding for a clinic and employment-generating projects. And, as I was learning, this strange mix of benevolence and devilish nerve was to emerge as the trademark of this unlikely East African crusade.

Ultimately, however, what qualified this as an empire had less to do with its scale than with its subjects and the way he dealt with them. For Babu, as I was observing, was capable of such unsolicited grandiosity, he could have been the emperor of a postage stamp.

It was a handy tip for any aspirant megalomaniac: Be an emperor, and the empire will follow.

The Veils

When the dust of two months was written on my skin, I swung open the toothless wooden shutters one morning and peered out over the muddy maze of Hurumzi Street. The entire town was draped in veils: translucent sheets of purple and orange gossamer strung up haphazardly from palm to pole to palm, in among the sagging washing lines and mangled telephone vines. They shimmered in the golden tropic light. Billowed, flapped, clung to the pitted coral walls, fluttered in doorways and window frames, draped themselves over every human form, male or female. Only the scampering children escaped their silky reach.

Weeks of patient observation had stretched open my eyelids to their existence. If I stood still and half closed my eyes, I could see right through them. They seemed pointless to me at that moment – for how feebly they obscured the goings on behind them. But perhaps, I wondered, their presence had less to do with concealing anything than with staging a show of secrecy for all to see – a grand spectacle of privacy, if you will.

This was a small, tightly-knit community, forgotten for decades by the world. With a population that was almost one hundred percent Muslim, there were strict religious ethics to follow, codes of modesty and consideration to observe; but this being tropical Africa, there were also earthly desires and passions to accommodate. Only the veils allowed for this tacit co-existence. Respect the curtains of secrecy and you can behave pretty much as you wish, but tear the veils and you tear at the very fabric of the community. 'Remember the golden rule here,' Babu had instructed me wickedly one morning. 'Never blow your hypocrisy.'

Indeed, if by ignorance, carelessness or even chance, you caught at one of the silky threads and it pulled, your foolish treason would not go unnoticed. Gradually, you would feel blinded, deafened, numbed, and until the vile gash had healed, the town would stone you with its silence. Little wonder that islanders went about so slowly, always taking care not to brush too sharply against the dancing sheets of silk.

Come late afternoon, the veils shone all the more brightly in the pink haze of the setting sun, for this was the hour of veiled passion, the haunting pre-dusk siesta that permitted the lovers of the town to steal about the maze – glancing over their shoulders at each blind corner – and into the arms of their illegitimate beloveds. At a time when there should only have been cicadas chirping, the streets of the town rang out with the urgent creaking of mattress springs – a symphony of illicit passion so deafening you could have heard it on the mainland. But here, the sound simply didn't exist. The fragile, squeaking noise of human fallibility had been veiled out of earshot.

In another place, I might have written these off as cruel curtains of hypocrisy, but here the language of the veils was written so deeply into the cultural heart, they were sacred and indispensable. To tear one was to tear the skin of the town to expose its raw, fleshy secrets to the hot, humiliating glare of the public eye. Observe all you will, the silent vow ran. Cup your ear to the scandalous whisperings of the town or run your fingertips along the contours of its secrets, but never rip the cloth that holds them. Tear the veils and you will both reveal their secrets and destroy the magnificence of their dance. But gaze patiently at them as they shimmer in the tropical sunlight, and you will gradually come to see through them.

In the days that followed, I watched the cloths fluttering in the gentle breeze. Slowly and carefully, I began to know their undulating grace. I was learning their language – their codes of privacy and translucent revelation. Nothing was as it seemed.

A few weeks later, a group of us gathered on the hotel's rooftop to watch for the new moon that would signal the jubilant end of the month-long Ramadan fast. As the date had fallen, by chance, on New Year's Eve, we were poised on a knife's edge of suspense: should a sliver of moon fail to crack through the indigo curtain of sky, we'd be restricted to a quick, clipped glass of celebration. If it succeeded, we'd explode into celebration.

In hope, a couple of friends and I had dressed ourselves in some rather outrageous costumes. Cheap thin polyester veils from the market place; yellow, purple and green, draped over the tackiest ladies' underwear, all synthetic bows and lace. With Gucci rip-offs perched proudly on our noses, the look was most Muslim *moderne*.

But Babu had another costume in mind. And at around quarter to seven, he motioned me downstairs with his index finger. He hurried into a room on the third floor, where the hotel's ornate satin-trimmed mosquito nets seemed always to be in a process of manufacture. Babu was stationed shirtless in the centre of the room, between two frantic, perspiring employees, attempting to affix a vast and unwieldy bustle to his buttocks. Next, a pair of short webbed legs was attached, and a sheet of emerald satin wrapped carefully over the whole affair. But Babu had begun fidgeting. 'Funga!' he yelled – the Swahili for 'Close it'. 'Fungaaa!'

The drenched young men continued to fumble and Babu continued to yell. There was little that a tipsy Muslim *moderne* could do to help, so I stood back and watched as they nervously hoisted up a full sized wire sculpture of a horse's head, chest and front legs onto Babu's urgently quivering form. They wrestled with straps and wires in a desperate bid to balance this over-scaled, top-heavy extravaganza, before the Emperor exploded.

Suddenly, we heard yells from the rooftop. Glasses, shrieks, cheering and celebration in moonlit sky. The Eid had begun and the New Year stood in the wings. The Emperor let out one last, thundering 'Fungaaaa!' And with his bewildered staff still attached frantically to his waist, he charged furiously for the doorway, where the vast emerald bustle firmly lodged itself. He whinnied like a demented stallion. We pushed and pulled, and heard an immense thud. I looked up and saw that vast, insane, green ass waggling frantically up the teak staircase. It is an image I shall never forget.

The night progressed to mayhem. The mad frog-horse and the Muslims *modernes* drank and frolicked in the moonlight. Come midnight, we tossed our underwear off the rooftop to hook on gutters and balconies, and ran naked through the streets. I last saw Babu lying on the street in the arms of one of his lovers, giggling insanely.

The following morning, I clambered up to the teahouse. He was in his usual spot, and evidently in a rather majestic mood. It was one of those mornings when an audience of one would suffice for a grand public address. And I was the audience of one. 'Dear Timothy,' he dictated, 'it is with great delight that I inform you that I have finally found the cure to dyslexia. Each morning I sit here and some dear soul transcribes my every utterance.'

I laughed. What a banal explanation for the curious task I had been performing all this time. And yet still, I realized, nothing here was ever as it seemed. Perhaps he had simply been enjoying my company. Perhaps, after all he had been through, he felt entitled to a little oral tradition with his morning coffee. Or perhaps what appeared as the most egotistical of exercises had actually been the most selfless. Perhaps it had all been for me.

I began to cry. I had walked so faithfully over the past weeks, tracing out the patterns of the labyrinth, feeling out the sweeping arabesques of the map with my heels. But gradually, in my exhaustion, I had sensed something hauntingly familiar about these patterns. Indeed, the maze played out the very same shapes as the conversations I'd been having. The sentences meandered into red herrings, ended abruptly, or forked off into double meanings, as they wove out their spider webs of truth and fable.

After living here all this time, Babu had skilfully incorporated these patterns into his personality. Warmth. Distance. Secrets. Revelations. Inventions. Embroideries. And all this time, he had been weaving this magnificent pattern into me – mentoring me in the fine arabesques of intrigue and infinite layers of truth of this extraordinary place. Directing me into the patterns of the maze. Instructing me in the language of the veils. Teaching by temperature. My God. I shuddered. Nothing is as it seems. Everything from the very evening of my arrival had been a game. And the game had been a method of instruction. And the instruction was a gift. And the gift was love.

When four months had passed and I had begun to tire of my apprentice-ship, the Emperor had embarked on a new project – an International Film Festival for the island. It was the most preposterous idea he'd had in years. Tanzania had scarcely made a film in the previous ten years. The cinemas that still worked, screened second-rate Bollywood epics that no-one understood. I'd attended screenings at the grand art deco Ciné Afrique at the port, where there was a hole in the screen and the audience spoke loudly throughout the film. Babu wanted to change this.

We had begun writing the documents, sketching out a plan for a fusion of African, Arab and Indian film and music, with women's, children's and village panoramas to boot. There were letters to funders, NGOs, embassies and film bodies to be written, printed and faxed. Given the unreliabilty of all the equipment, my morning hour of dictation had progressed to a full day's work. I had resisted, but he had insisted. Dictating more quickly. I felt manipulated, enslaved to the archaic fax machine. And so, I announced my departure. I would be moving to the nearby Zanzibar Hotel.

This, too, had been a palace in a previous life, but had been taken over by the government in the sixties, after which it had pretty much ground to a halt. A few, long-employed workers dozed in armchairs in the lobby. They were cheerful enough, but badly paid and less than energetic. As a result, the hotel was almost empty when I checked in. A couple of whores from the mainland lodged on the second floor, and I chose a room on the third. It was spartan enough, but its wooden shutters gave on to a vista of palm trees, which framed a small blue square of sea in the distance. In a maze like this, this was a rare luxury.

I went to the beach, stretching my body out on the fine white sand, dipping it into the warm, green sea. In the late afternoon I drank tin cups of tea on the seafront, their taste deep with ginger and cinnamon, and watched the silhouettes of the local kids as they flipped off the jetty into the sea, shrieking with delight. I nibbled on skewers of roast meat, *chapatis* and octopus and I made my way home. I opened my door to find Babu pacing up and down with a basket under his arm. 'Always my favourite room,' he said, placing the basket on the bed. He pulled out a few crumpled sheets of paper. 'Now, let's get to work ...'

I obliged with the first drafts of the festival information. For centuries, the wooden triangular-sailed *dhow* had served as the emblem of Indian Ocean trade. Laden not only with goods and spices, but also with songs and stories, these noble vessels had brought together the cultures of the Indian Ocean, creating a rich, cultural mélange that was at its most powerful here. But over the past decades, the mix had begun to thin out. A lack of trade had diminished the island's contact with the outside world. Cheap modern imitations were replacing old, exotic goods. But somehow, the Festival of the Dhow Countries, would change that, it was hoped. If Emerson's latest plan came to fruition, the festival could prove the catalyst for a full-scaled cultural renaissance in East Africa. And such fruition was most likely.

Over the next few days, I delivered fewer texts, and eventually I plucked up the courage to announce my departure. 'So soon?' he asked, surprisedly. 'Can't you stay a while longer?' I said I couldn't and he nodded, smiled courteously and made his way out along the dank hotel corridor.

In the previous four months, we'd spoken rarely about love or companionship, but I knew he was lonely at times. I had watched him clambering up the stairwell, off to watch another crummy Bollywood repeat that was available at the video store. I know he missed the luxuries of Western city living sometimes. And I know he wanted someone with him to share all this. He was surrounded and yet so very alone.

I knew he was running away from something. But he was also running towards something. Galloping, like some insane horse-frog-thing, out over the oceans, and into a world vast enough to accommodate his imagination. And in the absence of other, simpler things perhaps, this journey had become his reason for being alive.

The afternoon of my departure, we drank a fine southern bourbon in his teahouse. The coolness had become more sporadic over the past few weeks. Indeed, I was finally making the transition from subject to friend. I had persevered through my initiation and I was being rewarded with some consistency. But twisted as it may sound, I kinda missed the games. Their intrigues. The lessons they coughed up when you least expected it.

We drank to the festival. It was one of his more ambitious plans to date, but I had little doubt it would work. 'You do the best you can,' he said gravely. 'You employ the most insane methods you can think of. And you do the best you can.' He stubbed a Dunhill on the table-top. Slowly, the lines around his eyes scrunched up and he began shuddering with laughter at the resonance of that word – insane. He stuck out a palm for five. Laughed more.

His words carried with them an immense sense of possibility in the universe. A lesson in chutzpah, kindness and originality, and above all, a journey of gut-wrenching fun. It took a certain vision to come here and sway in the currents of a timeless town on a timeless continent. To absorb its traditions, and forge on through.

'You know Babu,' I said. 'I've been taking some notes like you said I should. I've been scribbling stuff down – making a story about this insane medieval apprenticeship I've been kickin' through at the court of this wayward African empire, circa 1998. A little written tradition doesn't harm anyone, you know. So I've been scribbling it all down – everything – like a good scribe.'

He sipped on his bourbon and contemplated the confession. And then, in a broad and courteous Virginia brogue, he said, 'I sure hoped you would.' He chuckled softly to himself, then louder. 'Yes,' he grinned. 'Wasn't that the whole idea?' And we both laughed. And beyond that moment, and beyond us, and beyond the edge of the rooftop, the veils of infinite meaning and possibility shimmered off forever in the golden tropic light.

The Mysteries
OF A TWINKLING STAR

At 85, Bi Kidude remains East Africa's greatest, living, musical legend. Spellbound by the raw, unforgettable emotion of her voice, we explore the tragedy and mystery of her brave, truly unconventional life.

Deep in the N'gambo slumlands of Zanzibar town, there is a broken path that takes you to the house of Bi Kidude. You might not call it a house, for weeds grow thick in the shell of a living-room, and an iridescent green carpet of mould has crept across the jutting coral walls, which hold neither doors, nor windows, nor a roof. Only the few small rooms at the back are anywhere near inhabitable.

Bi Kidude is sitting in the back alley with her sister's grandchildren when I arrive, chopping cassava and tossing it into a pan of sizzling oil. She is as haunting and androgynous as ever. The lime, floral frock hitched above her knees reveals the hard, thin legs, still supple and agile as a young boy's, and the woolly white hair, strapped into tidy braids along the scalp, frames the still-perfect oval of a face. The dark, almond eyes. The tiny puddles of deep brown flesh below them. The long, straight nose. The wide mouth. The thick lower lip, protruding in its show of steely, timeworn defiance.

She leaps up excitedly when she sees me. Stands just more than five feet tall. Waves long, thin arms as she leads me to the last dark little room. Outside, there are white doves, fussing in and out of a rusty coop of stacked oil cans; inside, there is a red light-bulb and the skeleton of a once grand Zanzibari bed, the tiles now gone from its headboard, the mosquito net missing too. It is her wedding bed – and now all that remains of that quick, loveless marriage arranged so many decades ago.

Bi Kidude digs under the mattress and pulls out a blue plastic packet, then sits cross-legged on the floor and begins rummaging through the past eight years. There are concert fliers; news clippings; a worn stub of a Kenya Airways ticket, a photograph of herself, on a spotlit stage, veiled modestly, chin raised, mouth half open, palms turned upwards. 'Gerumani,' she yells proudly. 'Hamburg. F'ransa. Finn. Japan.' And piece by piece, she passes me the treasured, crumpled proof of the brief, unlikely twist that has marked the end of a long, extraordinary life. A life as wild and fearless as the sea. As blue and mysterious as the moon. She smiles shyly, tilts and lowers her head, brushes a couple of warm tears off a still-high cheekbone.

Again, she is at the mattress. Digging, then snapping a backing cassette into a cheap new cassette player. Face, serene and silent, as a violin creaks open the song. Then the charge of the *dumbaks*, the eerie wail of the *oud*, and when she is ready, the slow, perfect release of breath, melting into that deep, raw, 85-year-old siren of a voice, unmistakable from the Congo to Lamu to Muscat. My heart must hear such a voice, for it carries all the wounded passion of a deep soul, and all the freedom and tragedy of a true but unrecognized artist. As many will swear, it is still the best voice in East Africa.

Ask anyone in Zanzibar if they know Bi Kidude, and they will giggle. Their eyes will sparkle with mischief, then shut bashfully. Prod them and they might spin you some strands of the legend that surrounds the star. She slept with the sultans, you know? Or wealthy Laatubi Arabs? Or fishermen? Or beautiful women? She steered a *dhow* and drank like a sailor; dressed like a man; rolled up her sleeves and curled her hands into tight fists; yelled obnoxiously; wrestled with anyone who crossed her drunken path. There are those who say the low, long-held notes invoked such wild passion, some took their lives rather than suffer the pain of her unrequited love.

Lies? Perhaps. Delicate embroideries, more likely. For this is Zanzibar where, as Livingstone remarked, 'Nothing is what it seems,' and the meandering arabesques of intrigue have always commanded more curiosity than dull, straight facts. On the three occasions I visit Bi Kidude, she contradicts herself often – sometimes forgetting, sometimes concealing, sometimes inventing the sort of details she imagines I'd want to hear. She remembers the life she'd hoped for rather than the one she had. Yet through the bewildering maze of secrets, paradoxes and ambiguities runs a single, unquestionable truth: Bi Kidude rattled the very bones of this society with her defiance, and no matter who shakes the head of convention or tut-tuts at her wild, drinking sprees, there are few in Zanzibar who do not secretly admire or envy her courage.

It is hard to perceive the weight of the constraints that shaped the early life of Fatuma Binti Baraka. Class divisions were strongly defined here in the twenties and thirties, and while most Zanzibaris lived in poverty, behind the heavy, brass-studded, wooden doors of the capital's gracious, coral mansions, their Arab colonists enjoyed among the highest standards of living in the world. Fatuma was born poor in N'gambo, with slave blood in her veins, but grew up in a household of wealthy Omanis, where her mother worked as a servant. Like all young girls, she attended Koranic school where, learning the melodic verses of the Koran by rote, she probably sang her first notes. It was her uncle, a violinist for the great early twentieth-century vocalist and feminist, Siti Binti Saad, who coined Fatuma's nickname: Little Thing, or Bi Kidude.

It was a time when women lived silent, cloistered lives in Zanzibar. Barred from the streets, they peeked at the world through windows, veils and latticed screens, and enjoyed little prospect of decision-making, let alone shaping a career. Yet, as Siti Binti Saad was demonstrating, music offered a rare, if remote, opportunity of empowerment for women. The romantic, musical form Arab authorities had brought to this coast in the nineteenth century was called Taarab – from the Arabic verb *tariba*: to move – and though singers were traditionally male, given sufficient talent and determination, a woman – even a poor woman – could open her mouth and move those in power, perhaps even command their allegiance.

Yet, while the lucky few could sing themselves into prestige and influence, wealth was a less likely prospect. Stars have a long history of exploitation in this part of the world, and to this day, rampant piracy and an absence of copyright legislation and enforcement deny artists their due respect and appreciation. So while Siti came many times to sing on the mint-green empire sofas of the Sultan's sitting room, she died a pauper. And so, in all probability, will Bi Kidude.

Some evenings, after Siti had finished her rehearsals, the musicians would step outside and find the young Bi Kidude curled up on the concrete step outside, fast asleep – too shy to come inside, yet magnetized by the powerful voice of the woman who was to become her role model. She would learn her craft like this. Never by formal training, but by listening and imitating, storing the words of the songs in her head, where most of them remain to this day. 'She always followed the sound of the drums,' Bi Kidude's promoter and agent, Mariam Hamdan, tells me. 'It was her escape.'

Hamdan receives me in her large office at Zanzibar's Ministry of Culture, Information, Youth and Tourism, where she is Deputy Principal Secretary. Helpful as she is in my research, she too, it appears, prefers to preserve the mystery around the star, and despite repeated promises, never produces the written material she has promised me, but feeds me instead on a few oral titbits of information each time I visit. 'Do come around again and we'll talk some more,' she smiles, gesturing at the pile of papers on her desk, 'Though just a little bit at a time.'

Hamdan is a powerful and attractive woman, who likes to think of herself as Bi Kidude's saviour. In many ways, this is accurate. 'You think that house is a slum?' she asks, horrified. 'You should have seen it a few years ago. It was a mud hut! Just mud and sticks, with holes in the walls. If you walked past, you could see Bi Kidude from the street! Now, she's rebuilding the house with the money she's earned in the past few years. Every trip abroad, we've put aside some money and bought bricks or corrugated iron. Sometimes she hates me for it. Once I remember, she'd been drinking a lot, and she lashed out at me for trying to help her. "You crocodile!" she screamed. "It's my money. How can you tell me how to spend it?" But I had to help her build something. You know, a lot of people say if it wasn't for me, Bi Kidude would be dead by now.'

The tale Hamdan tells about their meeting in the mid-eighties is a moving one. 'I was at the Bwawani Hotel,' she says, 'watching a Taarab show. Of course I knew of Bi Kidude. She was already very well-known for singing at weddings and *unyago* rituals – the young women's sex education ceremonies. Sometimes, people would postpone their weddings for months while they waited for her to return from her travels, but still she was exploited, most of the time. She'd sing for a bottle of local whisky and some cigarettes, or for a few shillings.

'She'd been performing with some of the Taarab groups at the time, but she was always a back-bencher. Never in the limelight. It was because of her character, you see. She was just too wild to be respectable. She'd get too drunk or too loud, or she'd sing without her veil. So no-one really took her seriously, and when she came out to sing that night, it was like some kind of a joke. They'd painted her up with weird make-up, like an old freak, and the audience was laughing while she sang.'

'Voices touch me,' she continues. 'Soul, you know? And this was a *great* voice. The tremendous vocal range. The breath control. No-one in East Africa could hold a note for that long. So it pained me to see this circus. Besides, my mother had just died, so it was awful for me to see an old woman suffering such ridicule. Old people also have a right to be happy, I thought.'

It was soon afterwards that Hamdan arranged for Bi Kidude to audition with a group of classical Taarab musicians called the Twinkling Stars – a move, not totally altruistic perhaps, given that Hamdan's husband, Mohammed Ilias, is its director. Around the same time, the mud hut finally collapsed and Bi Kidude moved in with Mariam Hamdan. It was then that she arranged for a British producer to hear Bi Kidude's voice. 'Bill Mendelsohn was so blown away,' she recalls, 'he came to Zanzibar.' And in her late seventies, for the first time in her life, Bi Kidude's voice was recorded.

'People changed their attitude to Bi Kidude after that,' Hamdan recalls. 'Somehow, because a European had recognized her talent, they did too. She was invited to sing in Germany and she went and toured. In Berlin, there was a large Arab audience who adored her so she sang for three-and-a-half hours without stopping. She even belly-danced for them. The sound engineers were so concerned they came and asked if they could put reverb onto her voice, but I told them not to worry. She had always sung without a microphone and I could see how happy she was that night; how relieved, at last, to be appreciated. She was so alive, I knew she wouldn't get tired.'

That kind of recognition is something Bi Kidude has craved all her life. And over the years the deep pain and loneliness of rejection has found its release on dark nights, in wild drunken brawls, or in the obnoxious tirades for which she has become so notorious. Yet, tragically, Bi Kidude cast herself as a pariah a long time ago in this conservative society, and sabotaged any real hope of respectability.

According to Fatma Aloo, a local film producer and feminist, Bi Kidude would have been thirteen or fourteen when her father procured a dowry for her, and spent it. Had he not been threatened with arrest, she might have resisted the marriage more fiercely; as it was, she had little choice but to comply and accompany her husband to the captivity of the countryside, where she recalls spending six unhappy months. And then, when she could bear it no longer, Bi Kidude did something quite unheard of: she fled, escaping as always to the ancient rhythm of hands slapping on stretched cowhide. She tracked the sound of the *dumbak* drums all the way to the port, where the Laatubi Arabs would moor their *dhows* before picking up the kas-kasi trade winds and making the long, difficult passage to the Arabian Gulf.

'It was then that she dressed as a man,' Aloo surmises. 'She had to, for you'd never see a woman near the *dhows* in those days. And of course, she sang and played the drums on the boats, but she was young and very beautiful, and because her skin was so black, she was a novelty for the Arabs. You don't need to be a genius to work out how she paid for her passage to Muscat. She'll deny this of course. She's ashamed of it now. She's old and tired and finally getting some of what she always wanted from this community, so she's not about to blow it again.' Aloo had first noticed Bi Kidude at an *unyago* ceremony. 'As I listened to her chanting and watched her beating the drums, I was struck by her remarkable power,' she recalls. 'It was rare to see a Zanzibari woman so fearless and autonomous.'

Unyago is an ancient, African ritual that has survived a millennium of Islamization on this coast. During the ceremony, the mother, the grandmother and the aunts of a pubescent girl initiate her into womanhood by crouching down on their haunches and demonstrating every possible sexual position, grinding and rolling their hips to the beating of traditional drums. In the deep trance that transpires, the *unyago* drummer taps a primordial source of sexual energy. Bi Kidude's reputation as the island's greatest *unyago* teacher supersedes her reputation as a Taarab singer, and it is perhaps this, as well as her work as a traditional healer, that accounts for the earthy, erotic charge of her voice.

One day, while I am visiting, a young woman arrives to see Bi Kidude, cradling an asthmatic child in her arms. Bi Kidude holds the baby, presses her still-strong hands against its chest like a stethoscope, sensing the nature of the child's problem as only a traditional healer can. 'Dawa,' she thunders, and one of her nieces fetches a plastic bottle of yucky, brown medicine. 'Keep it in the sun,' Bi Kidude yells. 'Take it, morning, noon and night.'

Bi Kidude has never borne any children of her own. One day, she tells me she remarried – though Hamdan suspects she simply lived with a man for some years. Yet to this day, she refers to all children as her own. And each young man she meets is her husband.

Perhaps, had she strayed further from African musical tradition into a more sophisticated Islamic one, Bi Kidude might have enjoyed more commercial success. As it is, her career peaked in the forties and fifties, when she lived in Dar es Salaam, established a group of musicians and travelled through the towns and villages of East Africa – to Mbeya, Mwanza, Mombasa, Kinshasa, Brazzaville – cupping her hand to her ear and setting those deep, wordless wails soaring into the African night. As is custom, those who were moved in the audience would approach the stage and tuck grubby shilling notes of appreciation into her veil – though never enough to make a difference. And by the sixties, when the Zanzibar revolution saw the flight of wealthy colonials, the possibility of moneyed patronage disappeared.

'It's a shame she was born here,' sighs Mariam Hamdan. 'If she'd been born somewhere else, I'm sure she'd have been world famous.' A Billie Holiday, perhaps. An Umm Kalthoum. But this is what it is to be a star in Africa. To carry your greatness like a burden unrealized. To never hear your voice on a record. To shine all the more brilliantly in the cobwebbed darkness of obscurity.

The day before I leave Zanzibar, I decide to pay one last visit to Bi Kidude, hoping to clarify some unsolved mysteries and fix some chronology into her sprawling life story. I have recently seen some rare, old footage of her on stage, and the fine, sculpted beauty of her face – even in her late sixties – affirms much of the Mata Hariesque legend she so cunningly erases from her living text.

'Is it true that people killed themselves over your voice?' I ask. She shakes her head, shuts her eyes and begins to sing, telling the haunting story of Kijiti who, according to legend, lured a stranger into the forest and killed her with a lethal glass of local whisky. But the truths of Bi Kidude's life are not so much contained in the cryptic message of the song's words, as in the ever-mesmerizing timbre of her voice. All the secrets, all the mystery expressed simultaneously in the endless, unforgettable wail of a bright star, twinkling in a dark, forgotten room.

I tell her I am leaving tomorrow and she thrusts out her bottom lip like an obstinate child for a few moments, then breaks into the gentlest little smile. 'Will you always sing?' I ask. '*Mpaka Kesho!*' she yells, slapping the dusty floor in front of her. *Until tomorrow.* 'How can I stop singing? When I sing I feel like a fourteen-year-old girl again.'

A fourteen-year-old girl, disguised as a young man, I imagine. Running as fast as she can to the frenetic thumping rhythm of drums; out, out, out, into the wild, crazy, blue sea – and coded somewhere in that image, is all the freedom and passion and despair that burns inside each and every one of us.

ABOVE: Fish-seller, Busua, Ghana.
NEXT PAGE (left): Voodoo priestess summons the masculine power
of Aklevete with a wooden phallus, Ouidah, Benin.
NEXT PAGE (right): Berber man smoking a pipe, Kasbah,
near Ouarzazate, Morocco.

PREVIOUS PAGE: Sunset at Forodhani Gardens, Stonetown, Zanzibar.
ABOVE: Bwejuu Village, Zanzibar.

PREVIOUS PAGE (left): Dinner-time, M'hammid, Morocco.
PREVIOUS PAGE (right): Berber guides, M'hammid, Morocco.
OPPOSITE: Modelling kanga cloths in Zanzibar.
ABOVE: Maman Hamisi and an adept, Cotonou, Benin.

PREVIOUS PAGE : The Blue Room, Emerson's House, Zanzibar.
ABOVE: Facade, Emerson & Green Hotel, Stonetown, Zanzibar.
OPPOSITE: Hadza and huts, near Chem-chem, Tanzania.

ABOVE: La Grande Mosquée at Djenne. I spotted a photographer shooting portraits through an antique camera in Djenne and asked him for a photograph of the mosque. He refused, stating that this camera was strictly for people, but he had another photograph for me, he said. We walked together for half an hour to his banco hut where, from a bottom drawer, he produced this photograph, shot in the early seventies. More buildings have been erected since then and it is now impossible to see the whole mosque in a single photograph. This photograph is one of my most treasured possessions.

TONIGHT THE
Elephants

This is a story about clothing and movies, and it stars a mysterious couturière called Oumou Sy and a wild, wonderful film-maker called Djibril Diop Mambety. While Djibril told his stories through symbolically charged actions and objects, Oumou speaks best in clothing. Together, they created a new, and magically African scope for cinema and fashion.

Friday night, Avenue Ponty, downtown Dakar. The street kids gnaw at your sleeves. From behind a cracked slab of white bathroom tiles, the stubbly Lebanese slices up greasy slabs of lamb and tosses *schwarmas* at a writhing queue. An old, grey man, in a filthy *boubou*, barks at the passing tourists and rolls out straps of souvenir snake skin. He has the blank, hungry, yellow eyes of a hyena. A few blocks away, on the upstairs patio of a place called Metissaccana, a great moment is passing: the Hyenas are making way for the Elephants.

Oumou

Metissaccana is a Bamabara word which means 'the mix is coming'. And the mix in this unassuming building in Rue Thiong is a rare one: West Africa's first cyber café; a restaurant; a twenty-four-hour open-door policy; regular cultural events and a stairwell, mosaiced with glass paintings of everything from *griot* minstrels to Tintin. But tonight, you cannot see the glass paintings – what with models in silver blue lipstick, tall men in box cut jackets and frantically fussing make-up artists.

Upstairs there are grey beards, left-bank berets and glorious ten-gallon head-wraps. The erudite hum of Dakar's intelligentsia is pierced with Baaba Maal's flame-thrower of a voice through the speakers and the anticipating rattle of over-scaled jewellery. Tonight marks the finale of SIMOD, Dakar's third international fashion week, conceived and facilitated by one of West Africa's most prolific artists, Oumou Sy.

I say artist – for though Oumou is best known as a Dakar couturière, she doesn't wear such narrow definition comfortably. Oumou produces theatre. She also co-owns and runs Metissaccana; SIMOD; and a fashion college, Leydi, in Dakar's medina. She has twelve children. Each February she stages a carnival in the city's streets, dressing a thousand people in a mad, characteristic mélange of ethnic costumes and fantasy-garb, and parading them round the city on trucks and donkey carts for the benefit of those who cannot afford a white, plastic seat at SIMOD. Oumou also designed costumes for the films of the late, great, Senegalese film-maker, Djibril Diop Mambety, which is why we are here this evening.

It takes a while to get to know Oumou. When we first met at the previous year's International Festival of African Fashion in the Nigerian Sahara, she offered few words and a single, polite smile to our conversation. But Oumou, as I had yet to learn, prefers another language to words. Oumou Sy speaks in clothes.

Born forty-five years ago into a strict Muslim family, in the small town of Podor on the banks of the Senegal River, Oumou was expected to live behind the veil. 'But because of what I have in my soul and my spirit,' she says, plainly, 'I knew I could never do that.'

Oumou wrote a play once, in which the entire stage was a dress. The play's title, *Life has Long Legs*, is an allegory for the unlikeliness of her life's path. 'Fashion was the only thing I could do,' she says, 'because my father would not allow me to go to school.'

Because this is Senegal, where family and caste have long controlled the right to learn particular crafts, a five-year-old Oumou had little choice but to sit quietly and pay attention to what the goldsmiths, leather-workers and tailors were doing. Already, she had begun collecting all sorts of objects and placing them on her body, contemplating their shapes, textures and meanings. And with each scrap of chiffon she fished out of a tailor's dustbin and stitched into a garment, Oumou, the artist, taught herself to speak.

Objects hold a rare power in Africa. Of course, for millennia, a myriad of animist ideologies have embodied them with a deep, symbolic charge. But denied the luxurious disposability of most modern societies, objects attain an unusual state of immortality round here. Electric fans, perfume bottles,

CDs – all are destined to live many lives on this continent, and the luckiest ones are reincarnated in Oumou Sy's ballgowns.

Djibril

Ten years ago, a man called Djibril Diop Mambety stepped into one of Oumou's design classes with a pile of paper under his arm. 'This,' he said, 'is a scenario, and it's our film, and we would like to collaborate with you.'

'Everyone stopped what they were doing and looked at Djibril,' Oumou recalls. 'It seemed quite forward to me, because he didn't know me and he didn't know my work and yet, from that day, Djibril was like a big brother to me. More than a big brother, really. A moral and spiritual guide. Everything.'

It is not unusual to hear Mambety referred to in such a reverential tone. As long ago as 1967, when his first film *Badou Boy* told the story of a Dakar bus boy, Mambety established himself as a subtle, challenging voice and eye in the spectrum of African cinema. While other African film-makers busied themselves with post-colonial revenge or Neo-Nationalist romance, Mambety gnawed at his audience's emotional core with stark, unconventional urban realism and brave honesty. As he would express later, in an interview at the Harare Film Festival, 'Hyenas are like you and me. Oh, and the Hyena is a terrible animal. He is able to follow a lion, a sick lion, through all seasons, and during the lion's last days he will jump on him and eat him. Hyenas are not the time. Elephants are the time. They follow the wind. They follow life. My last hope is that my children become elephants away from hyenas.'

In the handful of cinematic masterpieces Djibril made in his lifetime, this was to prove a recurrently haunting theme. Africa remains at the mercy of the World Bank, he believed, but the responsibility of rejecting such a simpering, obsequious existence and claiming a more dignified one lies wholly with Africans. Yet what made Djibril's work so convincing was its poetry. His stories revealed themselves as much through the symbolism of objects and actions as through dialogue. A pair of bull's horns strapped to the steering bar of a motorcycle. Settees sandblasted by desert winds. A herd of elephants shifting timelessly across a barren urban plain.

Among the celebrities gathered upstairs at Metissaccana, I spot Djibril's brother, Wassis Diop, talking playfully with one of the few professional actors Djibril ever worked with, Joe Ouakam. Ouakam has proved a nightmare to interview. When I call him, he says 'Hello' and then remains stubbornly silent. Frustrated, I pass the receiver to Oumou, with whom he chats most amicably. 'Joe will speak when it's time,' she assures me. And yet when we meet, he proves unnervingly Chaplinesque – ignoring me when I speak to him and interrupting rudely whenever I talk to someone else. Every now and then he grabs my hand, kisses me on the knuckles, then pushes me away.

What is this conspiracy? I wonder, forgetting that in this most evolved cultural clique, speech makes way for deeper, more subtle tongues. Wassis Diop employs no such tactics. Indeed, his baritone is as warm and gentle as it is on the ballads of his recent album *Soweto Daal,* which reached the Top Ten of the world music charts in the United States. Although much contemporary Senegalese music relies on frantic percussion for its rhythm, for Wassis, rhythm has an internal source and as he speaks, his words follow a very deep and personal metronome. 'Oumou and Djibril had a very mysterious relationship,' he remembers. 'A very cosmic one. Djibril was a spontaneous man, a turbulent man, a raging river in flood. Only Oumou could have contained a river like that.'

Whoever I ask delights in preserving a surreal aura around this relationship. There are resonances of Sartre and De Beauvoir, veils of mystery and hints of a supernatural intimacy. Then again, this is Senegal, the only place in the Islamic world where Holy Men, or marabouts, are believed to have magical powers. It is no accident that every buckled, yellow taxi I ride in is plastered with glittering silver images of such men. Here, among the harsh realities of poverty, thieves and barren, Sahelian soils, such magic provides a deep, collective sense of release.

And so, it was of little surprise to anyone that when Djibril lay dying of throat cancer in Paris in 1998, it was Oumou who appeared mysteriously at his deathbed. Wherever it was in the world that Oumou showed her collections, Djibril had always pitched up in her dressing room after the show. 'When we finished working on *Hyenas,* Djibril's critically acclaimed 1993 film,' she remembers, 'Djibril said to me, "We will be together until the end of time." And so we are.'

In some scratchy footage I see of Djibril being interviewed on set, I sense the wild, existential thrust of this raging river. A reporter corners him with questions but Djibril flees the lens, flinging his scarf around his neck and storming off along a Dakar pavement. 'Let them take me now,' he yells, slamming his fists on the doors of a police van. The more I learn, the more I understand that Mambety the man was inseparable from Mambety the artist.

'Djibril had his own notion of time,' Wassis expands. 'It was a notion quite different from the one we use in our society. Sometimes he'd sit for a whole day without moving or speaking; other times he was unstoppable. That was his freedom. He brought it with him, and he took responsibility for it, and I guess that's why we loved him. For Djibril, life in Africa is lived on the streets. For him, the Superstars of Life were the street people: the people selling cigarettes, the people in the gutter, the people who seemed so insignificant you could crush them. They were his universe and from the beginning, all his films were based on these people, and I think ...' he pauses, gazing out onto Avenue Ponty, ' ... he was right.'

I hide my half-eaten croissant as I step along the pavement, sheltering it from the filth, flies and pressing invitations to buy socks, underwear, yellowed *Paris Matches*, and peanuts in newspaper cones. The aging madame behind the iron grilles of the Café de Paris wears a tatty house-frock and counts worn notes of CFA francs in her cash box. A pair of Daschhunds, tied to a bistro table, yap at the Superstars of Life, should they hover in the door-way. Given enough time here, I too, I imagine, might take refuge in magic.

Speaking Clothes

Oumou doesn't look forty-five. The gold, Fulani-style drop-earrings and the dated, shoulder-padded cut of her long, gauzy frocks may hint at her rank in upper circles of West African couture, but her bright eyes and trademark pair of blue plastic flip-flops peeking beneath her hem, gives her a modest, almost girlish charm. As the days pass, she warms to me, holding my hand when we speak and dropping the odd clue as to her methods. 'One day, Djibril said to me, "I love it so much when you work. And the messages you offer in your work are so much stronger than when you speak." Since that day,' she states simply, 'I have spoken in clothes.'

'Once,' she recalls, 'I overheard some local couturiers discussing my work. "Oh, that Oumou Sy," they said. "She works too much with ethnic styles and traditions. She can't make clothes like the Europeans can." And so I responded: I made a dress out of calabashes, which was most beautiful and everyone adored it.'

Clothing has long carried specific messages in West Africa. Colour and exuberance are commonly understood languages here. Social rank has long been expressed in voluminous scale. And so, I am sure that when Metissaccana opened, Oumou's arch declaration struck a meaningful chord. A vast, coral, taffeta frock, festooned with masses of shiny compact discs. As often, wearability stakes were low, and the cut of the garment was way out of sync with seasonal fashion dictates. Yet, paraded as it was through the dirt roads of the medina, the dress signalled a new and most African scope for couture. When clothes are freed from fashion, they may become vessels for poetry, spirit and fantasy. Just as a hunter might hang a lion's-tooth talisman around his neck to access the powerful spirit of the beast, so the pressing of plastic discs to your breasts might lend you, the wearer, the objects' magical power.

In *Hyenas*, the bitter greed of Ramatou, the protagonist, is manifest as much in the gold metal body she reveals under her frilly dress, as through her words. When the antagonist, Draman Drameh, finally crumbles, he is literally squeezed into nothingness by an encroaching circle of sack-clad peers. Poetically, all that remains of him is a tattered blazer, flapping in fine orange sand.

The Elephants

Sneak into the dressing room at Metissaccana this evening and the mood is no less epic. One model squawks under a nest of gourds. Another disappears behind a crest of emerald satin and peacock feathers. Another straps what look like perspex peanut bowls to her chest. Renowned Senegalese choreographer Germaine Acogny sits patiently behind a leather stencil, as an artist dabs indigo on her cheeks. 'I have always been a great fan of both Djibril and Oumou's work,' she says. 'And when I heard she was mounting a tribute to Mambety, I wanted to participate to express the admiration I have for both of them.'

I return to the downstairs bar, where I meet a quiet young man in a cowboy hat and an embroidered Indian waistcoat. His name is Pape N'Dia, and he is a struggling young film-maker who came to Dakar with his younger brother when his father abandoned them and his mother for another wife. Pape came here with nothing. He slept on market tables down at the port and showered under a nearby tap. Nowadays, his brother is in jail and Pape is doing his best to make films. Pape knows all the Superstars Djibril used to hang out with: the hawkers; the beggar kids; the sock sellers; the Flag lager drinkers in backstreet bars. 'D'you wanna meet them?' he asks. Maybe later, I figure.

Now Oumou's voice is grave and heavy with sadness. 'Tonight is a very important night,' she announces, 'because tonight belongs to someone who was and always will be very dear. Djibril was somebody. He always will be somebody. Djibril and I spent ten years together. Ten years is something. But let us not cry, for we are not here to cry. We are here to pray for Djibril, to accompany him, and to keep him in our memory.'

A *griot* minstrel leaps on stage to wake the ancestors. The room blackens and the slow, heartfelt notes of Wassis' voice herald a most magical procession. Each garment tells a story. There is the sound of wind and sand, told in hessian and string. The heavenly flight of birds, in voile and sequins. The power of ancient kingdoms, in leather and brass. And a glistening cornucopia of bric-à-brac, fastened to white satin, tells of the love, reverence and admiration for one whose Arabic name, Djibril, means 'angel'.

I cannot hear the hyenas barking, but Tonight of the Elephants, the sure, slow gait of the models on the catwalk embodies all the dignity, magic and creativity Mambety could have hoped for. There are salty streaks of mascara all round. Goose bumps against tie-dyed silk. 'I think the angels were here tonight,' Germaine smiles. 'It was simple, strong and very human.' Oumou clutches a silk rose and curtseys into a flash-beam. She smiles shyly. 'Something marvellous has happened here,' Wassis grins. 'A rendezvous with the moon, with the stars, with the cosmos.' And Pape N'Dia and I set off along a cracked, yellow, barking Dakar pavement to meet with the Superstars of Life.

UNSTITCHING

Lamine

Lamine Kouyaté is an original. Born in Mali in 1962, two years after the country's independence, then raised in Senegal, he went to Paris in the late eighties to study architecture, but ended up shocking and seducing the city's elite fashion circles with his revolutionary couture range, XULY-Bët (pronounced Khuly-Bit). Since his first collection in 1990, Lamine has won accolades from Gaultier to Lacroix, and has gradually spawned a die-hard cult that stretches from New York to Tokyo and counts among its devotees singer Neneh Cherry and Almodóvar film star Rossy de Palma. But XULY-Bët is more than a clothing range: it is a kicking thesis on post-colonial Africa, stitched up sassily in crochet, PVC, synthetic jersey and a lot of old things you threw out.

It is a soggy morning outside the XULY-Bët headquarters in the grey, industrial suburb of Pantin on the edge of Paris, but inside, the creative energy is electric. A mural screams 'XULY-Bët's Funkin' Fashion Club' in bold red and white; and the shoppers poking among the rails of pricey, deconstructed faux fur coats and full-length, bronze anoraks are edgy and fashionable. There is a rack of vintage shirts, dyed into pastel modernity and screen-printed with a surrealist ode, and there are stacks of cardboard boxes stamped: Osaka, London, Denmark, Norway. Global? Well, sure. By 1998 XULY-Bët was turning over six million French francs annually. And yet, the cracked mannequins in crocheted dresses, the organic clutter of African wares on sale, the oversized rock posters, and a single, bare tree strung with a thousand slivers of fabric keep XULY-Bët's sub-cultural edge razor-sharp. Kinda neo-hippie. Kinda post-industrial.

Welcome to Paris. Ze fast, funky capital of the Francophone diaspora and *ze beegest* black city in Europe. Be it a Cesaria Evora concert, a tin of palm oil, an Afro wig or a post-modern Senegalese novel you're after, you're likely to find it here, in ze epicentre of ze African avant-garde. New York may be Hip-Hop's home town; but Paris, with its smug, classical traditions, brave modernism and grim migrant realities, somehow sustains a more progressive black aesthetic. And XULY-Bët, I imagine as I snoop around the Funkin' Fashion Club, is the future of African fashion.

Lamine, the man, is wrapped up enigmatically in a hoody and a padded waistcoat. He nods in greeting, screws up his already small eyes in concentration and slices a couple of squares of tie-dyed polyester: they will soon be incense pouches for a range of African cosmetics he's developing. Lelya Campbell, his assistant, rushes in late, but impeccably eclectic in a Cerruti scarf, blazer, XULY-Bët skirt and baseball shoes, her Afro pulled back into a neat chignon. These are indeed, as a colleague so archly observes later on, the hippest black people in the world.

Much of the audacious, winning panache of the early XULY-Bët ranges was rooted in Lamine's recycling ethic. While other couturiers pinned and fussed frantically with tomorrow's textiles, Lamine was making a more futuristic statement by buying up job-lots of second-hand clothing, pulling them apart mercilessly and reconstructing them as the season's most desirable chic.

'I like old clothes,' Lamine expresses in his habitually cool, street-slung drawl, 'because they carry the memory of a previous life.' This sort of transparency, I learn, is critical to his philosophy. And so trousers became coats, dresses became shirts, blankets became dresses and fishnet stockings became pockets – seams and labels always exposed in conspicuous, trademark red thread. Even the hems and necklines had that just-unpulled look.

'I wasn't trying to do a couture range,' Lamine recalls. 'I was just trying to express something through clothing. I wanted to unstitch the ideas one has of Africa, and Africans and our clothing, to get beyond the clichés.' Anywhere but Paris, this might have seemed an absurdly intellectual hypothesis for the ready-to-wear market. But here, where the depth and complexity of fashion is rivalled only by that of food, and where Africa's exoticism has, for centuries, compelled an intense gaze, Lamine's work marked an ironic dénouement in post-colonial dialogue. For how long had the First World been nursing its colonial guilt by sending off bales of graceless cast-offs to clothe the African poor? Now here was a wise young African, unstitching this well-intentioned charity, re-stitching it with wit, style and individuality, and flogging it back to Europe at couture prices.

I catch Lamine's reflection in a large, typically Senegalese, hand-painted wall of mirror. He is a fashion terrorist, armed with bundles of red thread and a mean overlocker. And he is by no means an easy interview. Blank-faced and media-wary, Lamine dishes dry, slangy bursts of explanation, punctuated with uncomfortably long pauses. 'I was born after Africa's independence,' he declares plainly, 'and so I found myself faced with the problems of the continent's emancipation. Logically this brought me to a certain state of revolt.' Are these logical clothes? I wonder. Well, perhaps. But they are also dark, angry, beautiful clothes. And from the hard, Jimi Hendrix-style bass guitar the man plays in his spare time, to the strange pair of copper, stiletto-heeled socks glaring, knock-kneed, at me from atop a glass mosaic table, I feel the thump of a most artful and heartfelt revolution.

A jeans label winks at me: 'Ninety-nine percent recycled. One percent waterproof'. For his Winter 1998 collections at the Paris Carousel, Lamine sent white girls marching down the runway to screaming rock tracks, eighties perms scrunched tackily beneath their hooded frocks. The feel was hard, urban and futuristic. The message: that thrifty, Third World pragma-tism could be elevated to apocalyptic glamour. 'Fashion is an illusion,' Lamine told New York's *Paper* magazine at the time. 'But perhaps it is something deeper.'

Initially, he recalls matter-of-factly, his work was shocking to the French fashion intelligentsia. 'Because I'm an African,' he remarks, 'they were expecting something much more postcard-ish – more Club Med.' But clearly such obsequious romance was not forthcoming. Not only were the fabrics unnerving, the usual tent-sized kaftans and loose wraps had been replaced with body-hugging stretch fabrics and strange retro cuts. Most shocking, perhaps, was the unashamed sexiness of the range. More Club Mod than Club Med.

One chilly Paris morning in late 1998, I joined Lamine on a pilgrimage back to his dry, sandy home region on the fringe of the Sahara, where he showed his work alongside the cream of Africa's couturiers at the first *Festival International de la Mode Africaine* (FIMA). Set outside the impoverished, dust-caked town of Agadez, on the dunes of Tiguidit, the evening recalled the most reliable of African couture clichés: mudcloths, cowrie shells, wax-prints, raffia, head-wraps – literally, for Africa. Yet, magnificent as the spectacle was, one couldn't help sensing that the event pandered to Western fantasies of the Dark Continent (a place where, if you hadn't noticed, most of the population moseys around in jeans and Taiwanese Nike rip-offs).

Lamine's collection marked a rare moment of realism in the evening. The range he showed was as significant in its process as in its results. Just chew on these trade routes for a moment: the man imports synthetic European textiles into Mali, where local women dye them using time-worn methods and traditional vegetable dyes. They then send the cloth back to Paris where Lamine cuts a tight range of coquettish, French cocktail dresses for Summer '98, which he brings back to Africa for a fashion show.

'Are these African clothes?' I make the faux pas of enquiring, as he fits one of them onto Sudanese-born supermodel Alek Wek. 'It's always the same question,' he yawns, tucking in his white turban. 'They're just clothes. The colours are African I guess, but anyone can wear them. Chinese, Aborigines. Why not? I don't wanna keep African designers in a ghetto.'

Lamine doesn't suffer foolish questions at the best of times, but when they touch on issues of identity and representation, he positively balks. I ask him if he identifies more strongly with the African or European designers here. 'That's a useless question,' he retorts. Indeed, Lamine will define himself. He is totally African, and 'African' will mean whatever he wants it to mean. Though he's careful not to diss the more traditional collections on show, he will concede later on: 'We're all doing the same work. I'm just trying to advance it a little.'

Despite the veneer of cynicism, when it comes to promoting Africa, Lamine's passion is tireless. The son of Seydou Kouyaté, a well-known West African writer and Mali's one-time Minister of Rural Development, Lamine has a laid-back street savvy, and is fiercely intelligent and highly complex. Even the name XULY-Bët (a Wolof saying, which I've seen translated differently in every piece I've read on Lamine), seems to echo the contradictions and ambiguities of his œuvre. 'XULY-Bët means: do you wanna take my photo?' he explains. 'But it also means: don't look at me with such big eyes. Be fascinated, but look beyond the end of your own nose. Enthusiasm, but also understanding.'

It's a fitting mantra for a range of clothing that pleases, but challenges; that blends fashion and conscience; fantasy and reality. When I prod Lamine on the ironies of showing couture in such an underdeveloped context, he is quick to the draw: 'Is it because I make clothes that they have nothing to eat, or does what I'm doing also have something to offer them, even economically?'

His recent project in Mali is a case in point. 'Just proving that they could work with synthetics has opened a door,' he says. It's a door that would be offensive to many cultural purists, but sitting here in the nothingness of the Sahara, rubbing the harmattan wind out of our eyes, it becomes clear that romantic notions are an unaffordable luxury. Having grown up in Bamako, Mali's graceful but forgotten capital, Lamine knows all too well that the tyranny of isolation is stagnating. Ultimately, he insists, Africa's cultural and economic development will hinge on its openness to innovation and outside influences. 'We have to open it up,' he says.

If bridging such gaps is the ultimate plan, it is ironic that XULY-Bët has long appealed to trendy, white professionals. But Lelya explains that gradually, despite the prices, the cult has earned its credibility in black street culture. And when Lamine opened his Petit Boutik for Xtra Funkin' Fashion in New York recently, he affirmed his sub-cultural commitments with a location on the Lower East side. For New York Fashion Week, he put on a show to rave reviews, at the Chelsea Piers. Yet, for XULY-Bët to achieve its full potential, the range should also be sold in Africa. While there are already some outlets in Senegal, there are plans for a more affordable range to be sold in Mali and throughout the continent. 'And of course,' Lelya says, grabbing my wrist, 'we want to go to South Africa.' It's a label that could make a difference in the African market. In the face of shameless American cultural imperialism, here is a clothing range that knows where it comes from, but has its gaze set firmly on the future.

The day after the FIMA event, we take a trip into Agadez and poke through the narrow, *banco* streets of the town's market. There is a lot of gawdy, sequinned women's wear; traditional blue *boubous* for men; straps of mudcloth dyed indigo; and, sure enough, strung up on washing lines, rows and rows of out-of-style Western hand-me-downs – lean fashion pickings for a young generation that wants nothing more than to feel new, young and sexy. And it strikes me that wherever you go in the world, everyone wants their photo taken, and everyone wants to be understood. But hey, Lamine could have told you that in a few stitches.

THE FINE PROLIFIC CULT
OF MADEMOISELLE

Were Were Liking

Were Were Liking strolls through her village. In one hand, she carries an antique Senufo cane, in the other, a small, but beautifully woven hand-broom. The cane, she quips, is a fitting accessory for the '*patriarche*' of such a village; the broom, she will expand on later. She stops to greet a child, then proceeds through the weeds, humming a soft but exotic harmony to herself. She is gentle, benevolent and yet quietly commanding. What with her black, leather pantsuit, matching fedora and jungle of dreadlocks knotted into a large ball on her forehead, Were makes for a most unlikely chief. But this ramshackle plot, here in a working-class suburb of Abidjan, is an unlikely location for a village. And besides, Were Were Liking is a most unlikely woman.

We approach her home, where a meal of fried plantains and spicy prawns has been prepared. The house is as homely as a hut, the walls thick with hand-woven textiles from Mali, Korhogo and Burkina Faso. On the table, there is a clutter of old trading beads, a perky, Baoule mask, some long-limbed Malian marionettes that Were has written books about, and a group of antique wooden safari-suited parodies of French colonials. Were seats herself on a batik cushion, sandwiched between her sister and her ever-competent assistant, Michel. She removes her fedora and begins unravelling the jungle which, I notice, has been accessorized with small bronze rings. And from behind this dense curtain of hair, Were Were Liking starts to speak.

'We all have a right to be creative,' she says. 'Even living is creativity. Cooking, eating, talking ... with each thing I do, I create myself.' Her eyes appear, and they are small, deep and focused. She lifts the broom, beholds it, then dusts the air around her, each stroke heavy with meaning. 'Even sweeping the house is creativity,' she says. 'Connect with yourself and this banal, mechanical activity becomes a dance.' Had this been anyone else expounding so intensely on the virtues of creative energy, I might have dismissed her as some pretentious Thespian evangelist. Given the context, I listen with all of myself.

In 1985, Mademoiselle Liking and four like-minded friends rented this land. Their resources were minimal; their objectives philosophical and idealistic. Their plan ran something along the lines of a Pan-African, multimedia artists' colony – a controlled environment where, as Were puts it, Africans could get in touch with the burning proactive energy they'd lost as lackeys to the colonies; where creativity, that most African of powers, could take up its rightful sacred place.

For Were, the dream had come a long way. She had spent decades researching African philosophies around the continent. She had journeyed through the Bassa region of Cameroon, the land of her birth, and gathered ancient oral histories. She'd finished a Fine Arts degree here in Côte d'Ivoire and sustained a prolific creative output: publishing plays, critiques and stories; researching, directing, painting, crafting, singing and dancing. But Were was ready to push the boundaries; to synthesize all these creative energies into a dynamic whole and put the philosophies to work. She would call the village Ki-Yi, borrowing the Bassa word for 'ultimate knowledge'. And twelve years later, when I rattle up its impossibly potholed driveway in a little, orange taxi, Village Ki-Yi is a legendary Abidjan institution, and home and workshop to some one hundred people.

Anywhere in the world, the creation of self-sustaining artists' communities is extraordinary. Given the levels of poverty, corruption and under-development in Africa, and the absence of arts funding, the success of Village Ki-Yi is astounding: it may not only offer lessons to apathetic coffee-gulping artistes in more bourgeois milieux, but also to those choosing social and economic models for today's still-dark Dark Continent.

At Ki-Yi this afternoon, the energy is palpable. A choreographer is grooving with a ghetto-blaster on a patio; a textile artist is carving printing blocks in a shed – the motifs borrowed from the ancient range of Ashanti gold weights. Next-door, a dreadlocked Beninois is hewing out logs and stretching cowhide over them for *djembe* drums. A Ghanaian acrobat somersaults through the courtyard. Toddlers shuffle over potholes, swaying their hips to the thick, central African rhythms pulsing from the theatre. To an outsider, strolling through this lively, low-tech jumble of Mohicans, lycra and cowrie shells, feels like stepping into an episode of *Fame*, set in the tropics.

I visit the village museum, where the eclectic jumble of African crafts is displayed; the sheer variety resonates with the title of one of Were's books: *The Tuareg Who Married the Pygmy*. A clothing range, Ki-Yi Lines, is the latest addition to Were's œuvre. Though closer to theatrical costumes than prêt-à-porter, the mix of textiles stays true to the Pan-African spirit. There are pieces of Congolese *shoowa* cloth woven from raffia, combined with shiny, regal, Malian *bazins*; murky, hand-dyed cottons and the bright, wax-printed *pagnes* that are ubiquitous on this coast. On the walls, there is a series of Were's paintings, but these naïve renderings of characters from African myths do not move me. Indeed, some have suggested that Mademoiselle Liking is too busy – that she'd benefit from focusing on one art form or another. But those who know Were know that the fluid dance of creativity through media is central to her philosophy.

There are pilgrims here from eight African countries; teenagers sent by their parents to learn to dance, sing or craft. Reformed delinquents. Couples. Kids born here, and christened by Were. Joining the village is straightforward: you audition or show your work to a democratic audience. If successful, you get a month's trial; after that, you can stay a few years, or permanently. Babanga Nyeek, a preppy Cameroonian who dropped out of medical school to study music here, has been around for two years and plans on staying another seven. 'It's a kind of cultural initiation period,' he says. 'I'll need to stay that long to get the most out of it.'

Initiation is another key feature of Ki-Yi philosophy. In *Le Girafe*, her reading of *Kaidara*, the seminal work of Malian-born Pan-African philosopher, Amadou Hampate Ba, Were writes, 'The main problem with our generation is a distortion in our ideas of initiation.' Conversely, by understanding and fully experiencing the process, Africans may again access their powers. In *Kaidara*, Hampate Ba draws on the belief systems of the Peul, or Fulani, people to make his point. He tells a story of three young companions and follows them as they travel through a world of symbols and significations in a quest for ultimate knowledge. 'The metaphor,' Ba explains, 'is the realization of the individual through an understanding of the mysteries of life.'

For the Peul, this quest is represented in a five-pointed star, the respective points corresponding to: thoughts, dignity, emotions, will and conscience. It is no accident that Were has appropriated this same symbol for her village. Were whisks the broom about. She offers a parable of realized creativity. Take a young girl who came here to cook, for instance. 'When she started, she only knew how to make one sauce,' Were recalls. 'Each day, she'd just make that same sauce and serve it to us. But gradually, as she became conscious of what she was doing, she grew more creative, more expressive, and eventually, each sauce became a symphony of flavours. Of feelings. Of spirit. So you see,' she says, smiling with conviction, 'connect with your power and you can change the world with a sauce!' She grins, then thinks for a while. 'We lost this power through colonization,' she whispers. 'We became consumers instead of creators, so we did things without consciousness. Without knowing why we were doing them, or for whom. And through all this degradation, we lost touch with our powers. We have to reclaim them.'

What strikes me, as Were speaks, is not the hackneyed, anti-imperialist stance I have grown uncomfortable with as a white African, but the thorough sense of responsibility implicit in her gospel. Often, Pan-African philosophies are loaded with blame and retribution, whereby Western governments, Aid agencies and white settlers are held to ransom for the sins of the past. Here, I sense none of that. 'Today's Africa, my Africa, is multifaceted,' says Were. 'There are whites who love this continent and have chosen to live here. We can't negate their presence. We need to be inclusive.' And rarely have I felt so sincerely welcome on this continent.

I stroll into the courtyard where Mohammadou Bombo, one of the village's co-founders, is parked quietly under the brim of a pork-pie hat. 'Pan-African unity is fundamental for us,' he expounds. 'As a united continent, Africa would be self-sufficient.'

Lofty as this ideal might seem, given contemporary African realities, it is realized daily in this microcosm. Indeed, this community functions like a real African village in many ways. Aside from a few tables and chairs, Ki-Yi has received no state support. Nobody pays cash to live here, but Ki-Yistes, as they call themselves, aren't here to laze around either. Some villagers earn more than others but the local economy adheres largely to

Pan-African principles of communal wealth. If you do any outside work, fifty percent of your earnings go to the village. Slack, and you'll be asked to leave. I ask Mohammadou to outline a typical day here. 'At half past five, we meet for meditation,' he says. 'Half past seven, we exercise. At nine, we go off to work: rehearse in the theatre, make clothes, dye fabrics, carve *djembe* drums, or whatever. Then at midday we go eat lunch with our families or friends. We work from three pm to six pm. Then, most nights we also put on a show here, which can run till midnight. We work six days a week. I suppose, as artists, we work harder than most people. But it isn't just work, of course.'

Though the communality of this creative organism would be echoed in artists' villages throughout the world, here in West Africa I am struck by its deep renaissance spirit. For centuries in this part of the world, where cultural traditions run deeper than the Atlantic, bloodlines have determined membership of elite, craft or performers' guilds. But amble through most West African cities today and the artists are curio-touting desperados or mindless pop musicians. In Mali, when I search for the legendary *griot* musicians, I come up with stoned buskers who squeeze me a melody for a cigarette. Here at Ki-Yi, they are making art with dignity and integrity, and it's working. 'Sure, I'm responsible for everyone here,' Were says, when I ask her. 'In many ways I am mother and grandmother to the village, but they're responsible for themselves as well. They aren't babies, you know. In the end, it boils down to a simple choice: you can be useless, or you can be useful. It's up to you.'

In the village theatre, an impressively grand but unfinished concrete shell where the walls are tattooed with stars and other symbols, I see the usefulness at work. The troupe is rehearsing for an upcoming US tour. Roughly translated, the title runs *Lullabies to Wake Up To* and expresses – in eight languages, through dance, marionettes, and a clutter of dazzling costumes – the Dark Continent's cultural awakening. Were stands centre-stage. As I watch her flex her stomach muscles to a Makossa beat, it's hard for me to believe she's almost fifty. Her voice ricochets through the auditorium like a flame-thrower. A couple of hours later, when the cast takes a break, I hear another voice: it is soft, clear and respectful. The room is silent as Were speaks, beseeching the cast to reach deeper into themselves. As often, the ideas are dense and somewhat enigmatic but the depth of her conviction alone is contagious. 'Sometimes you don't know what she's talking about because she's so deep and so focused,' says Pehoula Zereoue, a singer-dancer-comedienne in the show. 'But usually, if we trust her, it'll make sense in the end. It's a magic she has. Watching her ideas come together is like watching a flower opening.'

Pehoula came here nine years ago from Bouake in the centre of the country. She has married and is raising her family in the village. You can tell she's a Ki-Yi protégée when she speaks, for she too has that acute concentration when expressing herself. 'We need to always stay conscious,' she says. 'Even if we're performing at a festival, you can tell the Ki-Yistes from the others because we're always paying attention, staying open, learning. It's not an effort really, because we're working with a fixed objective. We're working for the cultural richness of Africa.'

Honkami Tape, another performer, echoes Pehoula's sentiments. She is quite beautiful, what with her strong features and shaven scalp, and when I ask her for five words to sum up her experience here, she answers without hesitation. Dignity. Responsibility. Engagement. Creativity. Conscience.

There are many misconceptions about contemporary Africa. For the most part, it appears to the outside world as a basket-case: war-ridden, economically disastrous and doomed to surrender its cultural heritage to cheap rip-offs of Western music, fashion and identity. Often, this gloomy picture is an accurate one and it is only occasionally, when trawling the continent, that one stumbles across small but potent challenges to such stereotypes. Village Ki-Yi is one such challenge.

One could hardly hope for a more relevant and encouraging response to post-colonial Africa. Bullets may be whizzing through neighbouring Liberia but here at Ki-Yi, Africa is reclaiming its dignity. This village works without borrowing money or ideology from its ex-colonizers. It defines itself: culturally, ideologically and politically. To steal an image, one might say Mademoiselle Liking and the members of her fine, prolific cult are scouring this diverse, ancient continent for ingredients, stirring them into a most delectable sauce, and changing the world with it.

THE GREAT WHITE
Chief

In the hills above Ghana's capital, Accra, Africa's only authentic white chief is polishing the memoirs of a remarkable life.

One rainy evening in 1991, the people of Nana Kofi Obonya hauled his heaving, septuagenarian body down the steep driveway of his house at Onyase, the place of the big Onya tree. The chief had survived malaria many times during his half-century in West Africa, by simply upping his daily prophylactic dosage whenever he felt a familiar headache coming on. But this time the virus was cerebral and Nana's people were frenzied with worry. They rushed him to hospital where, had he not been quite so well connected, he would probably have died within minutes.

Had this happened, there's little doubt that Nana's funeral would have been a major event in Ghana. Chiefs from all over the country would have attended, as would flight lieutenant Jerry Rawlings, the President of the Republic, and many of his ministers. Women from all around Onyase would have rushed to textile stores and paid dearly for bolts of mourning cloth, emblazoned with the chief's image, to sew into frilly, baroque dresses – not the standard red and black cloth, but the blue and white one reserved for older and more respected paramount chiefs. Only, as it happened, Nana Kofi Obonya was just the sort of no-nonsense, ox-stubborn Englishman to pull through.

Nana, as he is known, was born R. James Moxon in January 1920, in Shropshire, England. By the time I meet him at Onyase, some seventy-seven years later, he has lived such a full and most unconventional life, that I am anxious with awe. Thus reads his curriculum vitae: a decade as a district commissioner in the colonial service; another decade as Minister of Information under Ghana's – and independent Africa's – first president,

Kwame Nkrumah; author; publisher; entrepreneur; and since 1960, Ghana's – and Africa's – only true, white chief. 'Never a dull moment here,' he says, shuffling across his living-room floor in a pair of slippers. 'If there isn't something extraordinary going on, then you're writing about it.'

Nowadays, Nana concentrates on the latter and spends most of his time polishing his writings, at either Onyase or his house in Shropshire. Among them is an account of Baden-Powell's time with the Ashanti warriors – critical to his creation of the Boy Scout movement; a thesis on the nearby construction of the Volta Dam – the world's largest man-made lake; and an autobiographical trilogy detailing his successive decades as servant of the crown, minister to the nation and chief to his people. Due to squabbles with publishers, this remains in manuscript form.

At first it appears that Nana has little interest in an interview. 'Frankly, I am bored with publicity,' he remarks. 'They come, they take photographs and they sell them for a fortune. We don't see any of it,' he protests. He requests an interview fee of one hundred dollars, which I refuse. 'Well, never mind,' he says graciously. 'We shall do it in any case.'

The room is cool, homely and scholarly. One wall opens up like a garage door onto a perfectly green tropical garden, beyond which the misty Aburi hills seem to stretch out forever. The other walls are hung with a motley, unstyled array of African art and maps of the empire. In a corner, beneath an old Swissair calendar, Nana's nineteenth-century royal stool keeps itself warm under a patchwork cushion: no-one but the chief may sit on it. A goat strolls past the window. Nana yanks at a cowbell suspended from the ceiling and calls to his cook, 'Frank, I think we need a little whisky.' Frank arrives with a bottle of White Horse and, on instruction, pours a little onto the *slastoe* outside. 'We must offer our libations to the ancestors,' Nana explains. 'Otherwise no good will come of it.'

He is, indeed, the essence of incongruity. What with his swept-back, sandy hair, Cambridge grammar, grand, imperial tone, and Sir John Gielgud delivery, the thought of him in traditional Akan garb, weighed down with mountains of ceremonial gold and blubber, is preposterous. Yet each October, come the Durbar procession that follows the Odwira, or Great Yam Harvest, Nana is placed on his palanquin under an umbrella and paraded, along with his thirty or so fellow paramount chiefs, through the writhing, elated streets of Aburi, sword raised proudly above his head.

Indeed, there have been many honorary foreign chiefs on this continent: Isaac Hayes; Stevie Wonder; even Shirley Temple was ennobled during her time as ambassador to Ghana. But Nana's chieftaincy is anything but honorary. His powers, which are similar to those of a medieval king, have been gazetted by the government. He performs all the functions and enjoys full privileges befitting an Akan chief: sitting on a royal council, judging disputes, and addressing his people from time to time through a customary speaker who carries the royal Onyase staff. The latter has been accessorized with a pineapple, a chicken and a book, testifying to Nana's varied and prolific careers as farmer, restaurateur, publisher and author. 'Oh,' he quips, settling into his armchair, 'I also have an executioner, though he's been rather idle lately.'

Over the next five hours, Nana recounts his rare tale of chance and destiny, set in a long-forgotten time on this so-often-forgotten continent. He tells the tale with the skill of a great raconteur, peppering it with anecdotes of the rich and famous, and spiking the facts with just enough gin-soaked, colonial anecdotes to intoxicate me. As he speaks, he neither moves from his armchair, nor shows the remotest sign of fatigue. At one point, when I make the stupid faux pas of chipping in with some affirming observation of my own, he looks at me as if I'm completely mad, pauses and then simply proceeds. Hundred dollars or not, Nana likes to tell stories.

The son of an Anglican minister, Moxon studied History at Cambridge, then applied to the colonial service for a post in Malaysia just as the Second World War was breaking out. On his father's advice, he jotted the words 'Not West Africa' on his application, for the region was notorious as the 'White Man's Grave'. Ironically, in 1941 he was posted to the Gold Coast where, owing to a wartime shortage of colonial officers, he was appointed District Commissioner to the Korijuwah region a little north of the capital, Accra.

It is difficult enough imagining Moxon's remote existence here so long ago, but all the more so when he discusses it as if it were the most normal thing in the world. 'British Togoland,' he states. 'The forties. Of course there were no other whites in the region. There was my French counterpart, at Kpalime in French Togoland, but he was from Martinique. A Monsieur Hocht, if I recall.'

He proceeds to recount, with great relish, a lunch party given by Monsieur Hocht and his blonde, French wife. 'There were missionaries and clergymen there but it was always very open and amusing with the French, especially during the meal, when Madame Hocht stole the show. She was seated on one of these badly made African chairs, you see, and it gave way under her, sending her completely arse over tit, with her dress flying right over her head!'

At this point Nana's strong features collapse into laughter. 'And I'm very sorry to say that Madame Hocht was wearing absolutely nothing underneath!' As a good public schoolboy, Moxon did his best to look in the other direction, but the Frenchmen, he recalls, were ruthless. '"Oh-la-la!" they exclaimed. "*C'est si grand, Monsieur Hocht!*" and, "*Oh! Mais ce n'est pas la même couleur!*" And thus Madame Hocht was revealed as a bottle blonde.'

'The British would never have indulged such folly,' Nana laments. 'But the French approach delighted me down to the ground. I'm most thankful to them, for they taught me the humanity of it all and introduced me to a world full of fascinating people. They saw no colour bar, you see. If you were of the right class, it didn't matter to them. But the British were completely stuffy. They'd brought this stupid memsahib complex over from India. So they'd invite me to the club, making it clear that if I brought anyone of colour, I'd be crossed right off the list. Gradually, I came to despise the social mores down in Accra.'

For the first time today, through the upstanding, imperial pallor, I glimpse the colours of a true individual. If nothing else, this lends some welcome context to the perplexing incongruities of Nana's life. But still, his story remains riddled with paradoxes: while other nostalgic expats might be tempted to launch into a praise song for the natives at this stage, Nana remains restrained. 'They're very pleasant people, the Ghanaians,' he says, sipping his Scotch, 'and probably less hypocritical than people in more developed societies.'

Regardless of his distaste for colonial life in Accra, the precocious young man soon began displaying his leadership tendencies. At twenty-seven, he was mayor of the city. It was during this time that he received Queen Elizabeth II many times, and escorted General Montgomery on a motorcade tour through the streets. 'A frightful man, Monty,' he recalls. 'You know, he didn't even thank me afterwards.'

A decade later, when the Gold Coast attained its independence and became Ghana, Moxon saw no particular reason to leave. He had no wife to take home and no children to educate. 'Kwame Nkrumah, the new president, asked me to stay on and show them the ropes,' he recalls. 'And though I didn't approve of his politics, we were personal friends, so I agreed.'

Moxon bought a few acres of land in Aburi, ordered some trees and began farming. 'I had been friendly with the local chiefs for a while,' he says, 'but I was quite surprised when one of them approached me and explained that with the growth in population, they had begun to appoint new chiefs as well as hereditary ones.'

'And so,' Moxon asked, 'how does this concern me?'

'Well,' the chief replied, 'we'd like to make you a chief, Mr Moxon.'

'But I'm an Englishman.'

'Well, there's nothing in Akan tradition that forbids it.'

'But wouldn't it be awkward?'

'Well, in marking our independence, we thought we'd honour the British Empire by making one of their people a chief.'

It was perhaps his interest in history that had left Moxon with a deep and lasting reverence for tradition – despite his luminous African profile, he remains chairman of the Moxon Society and editor of a bi-annual clan newsletter in England. It was this same interest, I suspect, rather than any megalomaniac tendencies, eccentricity or delusions of exotic grandeur, that led him along his extraordinary life path. Moxon agreed to become an African chief, not because he desired to do so, but because it was the right thing to do. Indeed, when the great Akwapim chief Onana Osejan I proposed the honour in 1960, Moxon was simply too much of a gentleman to refuse.

He embarked on a crash course in tribal rule, after which animals were slaughtered and a suitable royal stool was found – its dust scrubbed off with some handy Vim. Then, in a nearby valley, in a ceremony that has altered little since the birth of the Akwapim dynasty during the Ashanti wars of the early eighteenth century, R. James Moxon became Nana Kofi Obonya. 'Of course there was some controversy at first,' he remembers. 'There was bound to be. The academics began muttering and eventually the matter was brought to The House of Chiefs.' The response was that there would be no second thoughts on the enstoolment, but that, to Nana's secret delight, they would not be encouraging any more such appointments.

For Nana, the implicit acceptance of traditional, animist, African values was of little consequence. 'I have never been an active Anglican, though I go along with it. Besides, as historian of my family, I have great regard for my ancestors. So yes, I suppose that more and more, my beliefs centre on ancestry rather than on some disembodied trinity.'

He admits that he did get cold feet the first time he was carried on his palanquin. 'But in those days we had ingenious little packets of whisky called Tot-a-Pack. I kept a bunch of them handy and passed them out to my people along the way. It worked wonders. Of course it was quite embarrassing getting all the attention of the photographers and such, but luckily a couple of years later a local woman was elected as a member of parliament, so they left me alone. They sort of got used to me after that.'

Nana got used to them too, taking most of the strict, royal customs in his stride and avoiding the others as discreetly as possible. 'The exchange of gifts, for example, is very important here,' he explains, 'and a little while after my enstoolment, I was invited to visit the old man I had bought my land from. We walked through the bush to his village. It's very sociable walking through the bush here,' he comments, 'almost like a ballet, with all the butterflies and animals and such. When we arrived, the old man presented me with a great spread of gifts: a sheep, some palm wine, eggs, poultry and, to my utter surprise, two of his daughters.

'Well, the sheep was okay,' he chuckles, 'as was the wine and the poultry. As for the nubile young ladies, I didn't have the slightest idea what to do with them, so I thanked him profusely and made some distant promises to come and get them at some stage, which of course I never did. But I have been collecting wives ever since.'

At present count, there exist five such ceremonial spouses. 'I've never put any restrictions on them,' he says. 'They've got on with their lives, and I've got on with mine. But they're there if necessary.'

Indeed, a few years ago, while a French television chain was making a film of Nana's life, they asked to interview his spouses. 'Bring me some of my wives,' he asked his linguist with a wink. 'It's no use having toothless old wives on the television,' he says. 'My linguist understood this. So he selected five of the most beautiful women in the village, who all played along perfectly. The producers interviewed them and were none the wiser.'

However, Nana effectively remains a bachelor. 'Many people might wonder what I'm doing here,' he remarks. 'What they don't realize, is that I can sit at a gathering of chiefs and really feel part of it all.' When I ask why he has never married, he responds without a glimmer of self-irony. 'Well, I've never had the time,' he says. 'Of course I like children, but I've always liked being alone. I suppose it's because I'm a writer.'

Indeed, Moxon's achievements inspire awe. As the Minister of Information, he stayed close to the workings of government and made some good friends. Among them was Louis Armstrong, for whom he organized a record-scale concert in Accra. 'Satchmo really enjoyed Ghana,' he recalls. 'He came back here many times and eventually bought the piece of land next to mine, hoping to retire here. However, before he got the chance, he died. A while afterwards, I happened to be in New Orleans and I went and sat in the park where there's a great bronze statue of him. We talked, you know, and something told me I should go to New York and see his wife. We remained great friends.'

It was soon afterwards that Nana opened Accra's first African restaurant, The Black Pot, which he ran for the next decade. Moxon's Bookshop followed, as did almost everything from managing a football team to publishing. He hands me a copy of his book on the Volta, one of the few works which have actually hit the presses. 'It seems the white ants have got to it,' he apologizes, gesturing towards the top left corner. 'But they haven't got to the good bits.'

'Oh by the way,' he asks, 'have you come across Jim Bailey?' I tell him that I've interviewed Bailey, South Africa's legendary liberal publisher. 'Oh he's a good man,' says Nana. 'But quite eccentric, you know.'

I'm tempted to offer the same observation about Nana in return. But I don't. For clearly, Nana finds nothing unusual about the extraordinary life he has lived. For him, it was simply a case of doing what was proper, regardless of the remoteness of circumstance. And for all his apparent obscurity, Nana Kofi Obonya remains an important and irreplaceable man for this continent, not just because of his proximity to the imperial and post-imperial administrations, but also because of his unique and unlikely experience as both colonial ruler and authentic African chief.

The taxi arrives and I wave goodbye to the chief, who is standing solidly at the entrance to his house. I know that according to Akan custom, succession to the throne is matrilineal, making the sons of Moxon's sister the successors to the Aburi stool. And while they could take up the honour, Nana has expressed the unlikelihood of them uprooting their lives in England and moving here. So somehow, as he disappears from view, I sense I'm bidding a larger farewell, for when the time finally comes for his body to be carried to the nearby mausoleum, it will not only mark the end of a short, exceptional episode in the Akwapim dynasty, but also a chapter in the grand, weathered tome of African history.

CHEZ

Mariette

Somewhere amid the ripe, exotic mysteries of Madagascar, Madame Mariette Andrianjaka has honed a unique culinary extravaganza.

High on a hilltop in Madagascar's mad, marvellous capital, Antananarivo, the mad, marvellous Madame Mariette Andrianjaka is cooking up a perfect storm. Her kitchen is ripe with ingredients: strange mafana blossoms that tingle in your mouth like electricity, silkworm pupae simmering in chicken stock, fresh algae, and a vast Royal Carp. Chef's hat slightly atilt, Madame ensures her eucalyptus-wood fires are keeping the food at a perfect twenty-seven degrees Centigrade – a hotter stove would amount to no less than a profanity. 'I'd never use gas,' she exclaims, visibly horrified. 'How could I? This is food. Nourishment.'

Back in the 1980s this imposing villa belonged to the country's prime minister. Today, it is one of Madagascar's best-kept secrets: a unique and exclusive *table d'hôte* run by one of the city's most cultured couples, Ludger and Mariette Andrianjaka. Ludger, with his bushy, greying beard, stuffy cravat and grey sports shoes, is the country's only baritone singer. For years, he ran restaurants in the port city of Tamatave. 'The first one burnt down when the Malagasy soccer team lost to Zambia,' he laments with a shrug of cheery resignation. When political riots saw a second restaurant go up in flames, Ludger and Mariette stopped tempting fate and moved to Tana.

Decades previously, Mariette had honed her craft in Nice under France's most distinguished chefs. On her dining-room wall, a smörgåsbord of certificates backs up her credentials: *La Société des Chefs de Quebec*, *Commanderie des Cordons Bleus de France*, and somewhere among them all, *Commandeur de la Chaîne des Rôtisseurs*. 'The only female Commandeur in the Indian Ocean,' she remarks, raising a slim eyebrow. 'Probably in Africa.'

Tonight, as usual, Madame has whipped up Madagascar's answer to *Babette's Feast*. Step outside the front door, and you could be in Provence or New Orleans: what with Madame's pet lemur scampering about the orchid garden and that dense thicket of cobwebs safeguarding the villa against mosquitoes and the ravages of vulgarity. Inside, the ambience is one of grand and wilted nostalgia. A stiff man in a stiff, white uniform pours me a Chivas. I can see my reflection on the polished parquet floor, and I could most probably hear a shrimp drop. Indeed, if it weren't for an obstinate scrap of beige, brocade wallpaper peeling away in the tropic heat, this could well be Paris.

Of course, that this is Antananarivo makes for intriguing contrasts. West of here, the city folds out into eight steep hills, most of them crawling with aging Citroëns running out of petrol. Tall, narrow villas cling to the hillsides, betraying a small, but persistent sliver of local aristocracy. Below, there are rice paddies and a vast gutter of a market, which brims with a fresher and broader variety of produce than you'd find in most African cities. So, despite a grim curtain of poverty, the rich strangeness of Madagascar's natural resources shines through. There are stacks of little red goat peppers, bundles of vanilla, and towers of grated carrots in rusty, enamel bowls. Then raffia hearts, baskets of green peppercorns or pale pink unpolished rice. There are lots of things without English names. Madame, of course, will have none but the very best of these. 'The very freshest,' she says. 'If a dish isn't perfect, I won't serve it. How could I? I'd rather waste money than waste the honour of serving a fine meal.'

Tonight's fine meal is an exquisite, silver-domed hotchpotch of fifteen exotic dishes, each the fruit of years of careful research. When Madame embarked on her quest, Madagascar was at the tail end of sixty years of French Colonial rule. French cooking had practically wiped out the traditional Malagasy table. 'We knew about our cuisine, but no-one was serving it,' she recalls. 'So you see, I was the first.'

And much as a shuffle of restaurants have subsequently followed suit, none has achieved quite the same level of intimacy, detail or sophistication. Here, the lines between food, culinary science and visual art blur with the likes of Zebu beef steaks, picked into painfully fine strands, then deep-fried in their own grease. The fresh carp has been rolled into *brochettes* and prepared with its own neon orange caviar. Even the *zanadandy*, or silkworm pupae, are beyond reproach. 'You should try one,' Madame tells me mischievously. 'They're an aphrodisiac.'

We eat and eat and eat. A goose arrives. It has been cooked overnight and is served with black pudding. Then a *romazava*, the clear soup on which most Malagasy subsist. Madame's *romazava*, however, is her own creation: a mix of fresh fish, prawns and langoustines, delicately flavoured with a rare algae found only off the Malagasy coast. Then a chicken stew, spiced with ginger and bitter vegetables. The fact that I'm running late for a key appointment with the editor of one of the country's dailies pales quickly under the warm thunder of Madame's hospitality. 'Pah, I know the man. He'll understand. He's an artist.' To be sure, she dials his number on her mobile phone and promptly explains where cuisine fits into the country's priorities. 'It is the vector of tourism,' she concludes, turning to me. 'I should come to South Africa some time. I should find your best local ingredients and prepare a meal of the highest French culinary standards. Ah, yes,' she says, distracted by the sight of the waiter, 'the *koba* ...'

I've already eaten *koba* on the streets here. And I'm not quite sold on this Cinderella of a cake the hawkers slice so finely and spear onto a scrap of newspaper for busy commuters. But Madame's *koba* has come to the ball. It is a song of wild honey and minced pistachios, served on a sweet, orange papaya *coulis*. Somehow the papaya tastes sweeter here than it would somewhere else. It could be the softness of the light or the warm, naïve smiles of the Malagasy. More likely, it's simply the thrill of this oddest of feasts, served here in this oddest of places, that tingles so in my throat. Coffee time, and Madame is happily oblivious to any sense of urgency. One glass of French red and she trades her pompous professionalism for a string of warm anecdotes and deliciously dry asides. My watch ticks as a box of photographs appears. This cooking demonstration in Canada. The time she cooked for President Mitterand. Then, 'Oh, I should never have sent my children to study in Europe. *Une grande erreur!* They've all become hypochondriacs, you understand. When they come here for their holidays, it's one little scratch and they're moaning for medicines.'

Through the sarcasm, there is warmth; and through it all, there is passion. Even in the slickest of Western establishments, this perfectionism would reach rare standards; and here in this bizarre, dilapidated paradise, it is all the more poignant. The richest of culinary traditions in the poorest of

African states. *Haute* uptightness, here, on the most laid-back of islands.

In a final plea to take my leave, I tell Madame I'm journeying to the east coast this evening, to the pretty pirate island of Sainte Marie. Any recommendations? Madame shrugs, turns her small, dark pupils up under her eyelids in despair, then reluctantly lets me in on a certain noteworthy dish. 'The resort is called La Crique,' she winks, 'and actually, I hear they do a chicken in coconut milk which is not all bad.'

VANISHING *Africans*

Fate or coincidence? It is six am on a bright Kenyan day. As our powerboat chops its way through the Pemba Channel, a wave sloshes over my paper-back. Irritated, I shift my attention to one of my fellow passengers. Wearing only a beret, batik-print shorts and a pair of sea-blue eyes, he motions with glee at a nearby school of tuna. Craggy, time-worn sea dog, I note mentally. Full of stories, no doubt.

Nomad, the now soggy paperback in question, is the tale of Mary Anne Fitzgerald, a British journalist, expelled from Kenya, whose consequent rovings on this continent fill me with wanderlust. The last dry paragraph I've read tells of a phone call Fitzgerald received from Mirella Ricciardi, a world-standard photographer whose seminal book, *Vanishing Africa*, I have relished since childhood. Next mental note: strange that so many of this continent's most passionate observers link up, like some sprawling, Pan-African soul-tribe.

Little do I realize at this stage that the old sea dog is figuratively and literally an integral member of this distinguished clan. He has travelled widely in Africa, writing and making films. He has sailed his *dhow* from the Arabian Gulf down to the Kenyan coast, and he has navigated some of the continent's most hostile and uncharted rivers *Heart of Darkness*-style, crossing from East- to West Africa by boat. He is also Mirella's husband, Lorenzo Ricciardi.

'I was born in jail,' Lorenzo says proudly when I visit him a few days later at Baobab Haven – the home in Kilifi, eighty kilometres north of Mombasa, where the Ricciardis have lived between journeys for the past twenty-five years. 'Ever since, my life has become more and more free.'

Indeed, the clinic of Milan's San Vittore prison was the nearest place to which Lorenzo's mother could be rushed when her birth pains started. He was raised near Genoa, 'a Catholic from my waist up', and then moved to Rome where he headed up the advertising agency Walter J. Thomson and worked as an assistant to directors Fellini and Rossellini. He even played a cameo as Christ, opposite Charlton Heston in *Ben Hur*.

Then, in 1957, he came to Africa. The hunting film that brought Lorenzo to Kenya, *Black God, White Devil*, was never completed, but it did lead him to some startling photographs in a Nairobi bar. 'Immediately, I arranged to meet the photographer to commission her to work on stills for the movie,' he recalls. 'I expected some ninety-year-old to pitch, but to my surprise, the most exquisite young girl arrived in a black MG – the only one of its kind in Africa. I was smitten. By the time she returned from meeting with my director, I had filled the cockpit of her car with flowers.'

Mirella had been born in Kenya. Her Italian father and French mother had completed a year-long foot safari through the Belgian Congo and had settled on the shores of Lake Naivasha when she was born. At eighteen, Mirella left Kenya, attended finishing school in England, studied photography in Paris under the great French fashion photographer Harry Meerson, and returned to Kenya. Shortly after she'd figured out where to sit in her MG, she married Lorenzo. It was the same set of prints from that Nairobi bar that Mirella slipped into an envelope a decade later and sent off to Collins Publishers. The result was an immediate book commission, *Vanishing Africa*, which was published in 1973. Internationally acclaimed, it is now in its eleventh reprint and has inspired a string of similar books by various authors. And indeed, as Mirella points out later on the phone from London – a little conceitedly, but correctly – no-one has ever captured the stark, sculptural quality of her original black-and-white prints.

The morning I arrive at Kilifi, Lorenzo is pacing the driveway, tailed by four noisy geese. He grumbles about the family's geography problem: their two daughters, Amina and Marina, live in San Francisco now and Mirella has one foot in Africa and one in Europe, as she has done for the past twenty years.

There are three houses on the eight-hectare property, which perches on a cliff at the entrance to Kilifi Creek. One of them was once the residence of the Sultan of Kilifi and the Ricciardis have dug up bits of Chinese *majolica* and Venetian glass from the sand nearby. The ambience here is a fertile brew of Africa and the Mediterranean, but most strikingly, it is witness to the passions, creativity and whimsy of its owners. Kind of like one of Picasso's villas, I'd imagine. Scattered about the garden are the stout, earthy pots Mirella has made in recent years – she recently finished a twenty thousand-dollar commission for Kenya's Nyali Beach Hotel. Helmets from the Ethiopian war perch irreverently on a row of fence-poles. Here a collection of toadstools; there a row of nasty beetles pinned to polystyrene. And testimony to Lorenzo's mischievous sense of humour, some silk flowers have been poked in between the tropical blooms. 'Look at this ancient African pot,' he beams, tossing it at me. 'Ha! Fibreglass. We cast a whole series.'

Despite their worldliness, the Ricciardis' tastes are simple and earthy. Mirella describes their London home, too, as an 'African' house which stirs a certain curiosity in Fulham, with its pair of buffalo horns placed above the gate. Here at Kilifi, some camping chairs and *kilims* tossed over a mattress make a sitting area. In a courtyard, Mirella's mother's austere, haunting paintings – she studied sculpture with Rodin in Paris – are the only ornamentation. 'I inherited my mother's eye,' Mirella recalls. 'From childhood, she had showed me the beauty of the Africans. So when I went out with a camera, I knew instinctively what I was looking for. I recognized it and photographed it.'

On a shelf at Kilifi, the humidity has been heartless with copies of Mirella's books: *African Saga*, the strange history of her family in Africa; a photographic book on Pavarotti; *Vanishing Africa*; and the more recent *Vanishing Amazon*. Then their joint book projects: *The Voyage of the Mir-El-Lah*; and *African Rainbow: Across Africa by Boat* – the first known crossing of its kind.

As an outsider, it's tempting to romanticize the relationship that has allowed such pursuits – be they joint or autonomous projects. Blissful, I imagine, to have the freedom to follow your passions with your spouse's support. Yet while that support is there, Mirella is frank that it has been hard-earned. 'For many years, I subjugated myself and helped Lorenzo as he followed his dreams,' she says. 'But there came a time when I had to follow mine. And when I work, I'm a one-man-band. Yet Lorenzo has grown to be very supportive. He is a great fan of my work.'

Indeed, when I remark on this autonomy to Lorenzo, his response is resolute: 'I think it's indispensable.'

'In the case of *African Rainbow*, I chose to subjugate myself,' Mirella says. 'Lorenzo led the expedition and I went along.' An epic undertaking, the voyage required nothing less than the mix of passion, fearlessness and lunacy the man so radiates. 'It seems like a rather ambitious project,' *National Geographic* responded when the Ricciardis proposed a feature on the trip. 'But yes, we are interested.' So, after a year of preparation and some trial runs up the Tana River to visit long-time friend George Adamson, the voyage commenced at the Rufiji Delta in Tanzania. Eighteen months of heaven and hell in inflatable boats lay ahead.

The six thousand-kilometre adventure took in everything from gorillas to crocodiles, volcanoes, smoked monkeys, villages floating on old steamers – even chimpanzee hunters. At times, the account is unromantic: 'We went to visit the island families [on the Zaïre River],' Mirella writes, 'living simple, monotonous lives which appeared quite intolerable to us.' At other times, it is deeply so. But throughout, it betrays the profound appreciation of Africa's people and places the Ricciardis share, and their sensitivity to conservation.

The tale ends with Lorenzo's momentous gesture of opening the gourd he had scooped up in the Indian Ocean and emptying it into the Atlantic. Mirella's photograph captures him, exhausted but satisfied, bobbing in the Atlantic holding up an Italian and Zaïrian flag. Subsequently, critics scoffed at Lorenzo for claiming to be an explorer – this was 1988 for God's sake. 'I am a traveller,' he says with reviewed modesty. 'Besides, people had been living where Livingstone stepped for centuries.' Yet his following expedition – a journey among the islands of Lake Victoria – was a case in point. 'Yes, it's 1995,' Lorenzo shrugs, 'but I can find no detailed maps of the area and I doubt that any exist.'

Between these voyages, Lorenzo spends much time at sea, chartering exclusive boat packages for the likes of Robert de Niro or sailing around the Indian Ocean on his own. 'Sometimes I'll moor at an island and stay there for a week,' he says. 'I bring nothing with me and take nothing away. I adore it.' His latest passion, *La Blanca Paloma*, a gleaming catamaran he bought on the French Riviera, is moored in Kilifi Creek. And he plans to charter exclusive but competitive packages around the Indian Ocean, which take in a week or two at Kilifi.

Mirella, who had been working on a book on the history of ceramics, hopes to retire soon to Kilifi. 'However, we'll each be on our own trip. Lorenzo will run his sea safaris. I plan to set up a ceramic studio, where I'll continue to facilitate this tremendous marriage of African and European styles.'

Why the shift from photography, I wonder. 'I'm tired of this hectic lifestyle,' she says. 'I want to be in one place. Besides, I have achieved what I wanted to with my photographs. In *Vanishing Africa* I looked at forms and shapes, but by the time I worked in the Amazon, I was looking deeper, more into the souls of its people – at their unpolluted simplicity. I think if I tried to shoot *Vanishing Africa* again today, I'd have great difficulty capturing those images. So yes, it is something that is truly ... vanishing.'

As, I'd wager, are the likes of the Ricciardis.

Traditions

THE SCISSORS OF
Abidjan

Pathe Ouedrago breaks a roasted corn cob in half and hands me a chunk. He is in the thick of a typically busy day. Wrapping a *foulard* around a client's head. Whipping up a *grand boubou* for an impeccably styled Cameroonian musician who must be in Paris tomorrow morning. The musician fiddles anxiously with the hem of his black *Comme des Garçons* suit but Pathe just keeps at it. He wanders into the sewing room. It rattles with old sewing machines and the snip-snip of scissors gliding through metre upon metre of *pagnes*, the busy, colourful wax-print cloths at the heart of West African couture.

Pathe O, as he's known, is West Africa's most prolific designer. His trouser suits, A-line dresses, waistcoats and palazzo pants emphasize quality and marketability, rather than trendiness or originality. Typical of local designers, Pathe runs his studio from a grimy working-class suburb of Abidjan, the cosmopolitan, commercial capital of the Ivory Coast, which bustles in glass and steel among the murky, snaking fingers of the Ebrie Lagoon.

Designers from all over the region come here to buy their fabrics from local textile houses like Uniwax, Woodin, Qualitex and ABC. Pathe hails from Burkina Faso; Alphadi, the slick-scissored genius from Niger, has a boutique downtown; and Chris Seydou, the late Malian-born darling of Paris couture circles, was regularly flown in by Abidjan's *grandes dames* to create, say, an elaborate mud-cloth ballgown.

Back in the seventies, Seydou revolutionized the Abidjan fashion scene by taking traditional *pagnes* and incorporating them into handbags and beachwear. He adorned his models with glittering gold-plated Baoule jewellery and, most shockingly, he borrowed the region's ancient textiles and reinvented them as contemporary haute couture.

Scour the planet, and you'd be pressed to find a textile tradition as rich as West Africa's. There are the coarse, hand-printed cottons of Korhogo; the striking, black and white *bogolans* of Burkina Faso; the shiny taffeta-like *bazins* of Mali, embroidered with the finest gold threads; and of course, the *pagnes* – a myriad of patterned cotton cloths, originally printed in Holland and now printed here and sold all along Abidjan's Rue de Commerce. The *pagnes'* motifs have kept up to date with the trends: while traditional designs featured beer bottles and fruit, lately one sees every covetable convenience from cellphones to computers and VCRs – so that if you don't have the object, you can at least have the head-wrap.

Buzz around Abidjan in one of its little orange taxis and behold the bold design ethic that permeates the urban fabric. La Pyramide, an office block in the CBD, is a monstrous triangle of glass and concrete. St Paul's Cathedral nearby is structured in the form of a kneeling pilgrim, whose robe flows backwards in a vast, fanciful concrete slab that forms the building's roof. On the edge of the lagoon, The Hôtel Ivoire is the ultimate in kitsch, African modernism, complete with gold and lavender ceilings, Op Art carpets and a mosaic lake (now empty).

Like many key buildings in the region, these monoliths were constructed soon after independence on big borrowed budgets. And while such fanciful designs would never have been passed in Europe, here they were celebrated as monuments to Neo-Nationalism, but because the expenses of maintenance were never considered, many have cracked in the heat or developed glistening carpets of tropic mould.

Up-country, in the political capital of Yamoussoukro, the country's long-time leader Félix Houphouet-Boigny erected a cathedral larger and more elaborate than St Peter's. The Basilica of Notre Dame de Paix rises surrealistically from the surrounding scrub. It cost four hundred million dollars, but what the hell, when impact here is everything.

After food and cathedrals, West Africans spend a fair whack of their income on clothing. One just has to flip through some old sepia photographs of Ashanti kings to see that adornment has a profound and important place in the country's culture. Much as the nightclubs of Treichville or The Plateau may be thick with denim and halter-necks, step into an exhibition opening at the Hôtel Ivoire – or any major ceremony – and the finery is strictly African. There are *foulards* the size of backpacks and ensembles that make opera costumes look like casual wear.

'The key word is baroque,' says Claudia Claudale, creative director at the Abidjan-based *Femme d'Afrique* magazine. Established in the eighties, the fashion monthly sells fifteen thousand copies, yet as Claudale laments, 'I feel like I've been running the same edition for the past five years. The same styles crop up again and again. You get your traditional African looks, the flowing Islamic styles and the tighter-fitting Western styles. That's it.'

While Claudale's comments are valid for commercial ranges, when it comes to haute couture, West Africa is anything but predictable. Fashion here is its own creative universe. Unbound from the constraints of Western trends, designers display immense freedom and creativity. Colour combinations range from lemon yellow, purple and orange to gold, pink and black. As with the architecture, shapes are often daringly bold or asymmetric and the combination of textures verges on astounding.

At around eight o'clock one evening, I meet with another well-known couturier, Etienne Marcel. He has his studio so deep in the side streets of Marcory, it takes my drunk Senegalese taxi driver a good half hour to find it. When he does, the place is still frenzied with activity.

Parked nonchalantly behind a pair of blue, mirrored sunglasses, Etienne is perfectly groomed. He wears a classic blue shirt, adorned with a rainbow of plastic alphabet letters, the sleeves inset with strips of *Zoulou*, Uniwax's recent rave take on traditional Ndebele wall motifs. I can tell Etienne studied design in Paris – not so much by his clothes, which ooze charisma and tropical energy, but more by the cool detachment with which he answers my questions. 'Wealthy Abidjanis used to shop in Europe,' he explains, 'but after the devaluation of our currency in 1994, they were forced to shop here. That did a lot for local couture. Because of the limited availability of materials,' he continues, 'one becomes more creative.'

To prove his point, he brings out a pile of multimedia garments from his back room. There is a lampshade of a blouse in sunshine yellow PVC, complete with matching miniskirt and a fifties-style handbag; a man's parka in grey denim, the back adorned with *kente* cloth, tiny mirrors and a small Baoule mask; then a woman's two-piece made from strips of newspaper, sandwiched in transparent plastic.

Finally, Etienne's latest coup – his and hers matching *boubous*, cut from *bazins* and detailed with rich co-ordinated prayer carpets – not quite the sort of thing in which you'd want to sashay through the streets of Teheran, but wrapped around a couple of models as they tip-toe barefoot along the Atlantic shoreline, the impact is quite spectacular. 'The times are changing,' muses Etienne. 'One has to adapt.'

Alpha Sidibe, another Abidjan-based designer, is as ingenious as Marcel when it comes to using materials. 'Upholstery fabrics,' he explains, running his fingers along the hem of a dress in his shoe-box of a studio in Treichville. 'Pom-poms, tassels, Japanese raffia, gold mesh, handbag fasteners.'

His influences run all the way from Peul milkmaids' dresses from the Sahel, to Louis XV tailcoats. A wedding dress, for instance, incorporates the traditional blue and white Baoule nuptial weaves with flowing kite-like strips of white crepe.

'I was born in the Odienne region near the Liberian border,' Alpha says in his soft, amicable manner. 'My father was a tailor there. He designed folk costumes, and his designs have had a strong influence on my work.' This influence is unmistakable – not only in the unusual contemporary folk-feel of his clothing, but in the pragmatism of his approach – just as one makes do with what's available in a small town in the Sahel, so Alpha scours his environment and incorporates whatevers around him.

Generally, such creativity is reserved for the likes of student fashion shows or theatre divas, but here nothing could be further from the truth. Indeed, as we speak, a young girl comes in for a fitting for a Peul-inspired wedding dress. Soon enough, Alpha is working, bundled in tassels and measuring tapes.

'Well, of course people wear his clothes,' comments Alain Biyack, a Cameroonian journalist at another fashion and culture based weekly *Top Visages.* 'Alpha is a name here in Abidjan, so his clothes carry a lot of status. Anyone can buy imported clothes, but if you step out in an Etienne, a Pathe, or a Nahode Okai, people will know it's an original.'

Of all Abidjan's couturiers, Okai is the least overtly African in her approach. Born in Ghana, Okai studied in Paris and then ran her *atelier* in Togo for seven years before moving to Abidjan and opening a few understated, up-market boutiques. Today, she also sells ranges in Ghana and the United States.

'There will always be some African element to my work,' she explains thoughtfully, fiddling with a *kente* covered hatbox on her desk. 'But it's usually just a touch – just enough to know where we are.'

The clothing in her stores reflects her philosophy. Although some of the fabrics and details are African, the styles are European. A navy crepe suit, for instance, is typically elegant Western evening wear – only the embroidery along the sleeves echoes the motifs of Ashanti gold weights. A silk *boubou* is best summed up in the phrase Muslim *moderne*.

In a nearby government office, I meet the woman known as West Africa's Chanel, Miss Angybell. Angy is not only a designer, but a mother, wife and Member of Parliament, and she quips, with a beautiful smile, 'I also find time to paint my nails.'

Angy takes me to her studio, where an ancient, painstaking process is in full swing. In her garden, a small group of labourers are stripping strands of raffia into tiny threads. From here, they are tied together and then woven into narrow strips on a loom, mixed in with glistening silk threads. The strips are then dyed and stitched together to form great shimmering pieces of raffia cloth, which Angy snips into great classic ballgowns. 'Traditionally, we have always made clothing like this for ceremonies,' Angy explains. 'I am simply modernizing the technique.'

The subtle sophistication of these designs marks a move toward a Western approach. However, for the most part, West African couture remains firmly rooted in this continent. Travel from Nairobi to Dakar or Cairo and every town market will be heaving with Nike or Levi's rip-offs. Yet here, in the face of such relentless cultural imperialism, the richness of African culture and tradition holds strong.

Step through the streets of Abidjan and there is as much African clothing as Western wear. Even the fake Chanel earrings one sees have been plated with the traditional yellow gold of Baoule jewellery. Indeed, the tailor's dummies in *pagne* shirts and the rattling machines of the embroidery studios tell a very positive fashion story: people do not buy clothes here so much as scurry to their tailor with a bolt of cloth and a photograph to custom design their own fanciful ensembles. Be these huge froufrou sleeves, tiny miniskirts or vintage safari suits, they are all individually crafted.

Little wonder the couturiers I meet here don't seem concerned about threats to African identity. West African styles are just simply too well-defined and the clothing too popular to disappear. In fact if you look at Paris fashion house Hermes' recent range, the Dark Continent has provided the theme for elite ranges of handbags and trademark silk scarves. 'Well, it's natural,' comments Etienne Marcel. 'You know how they are, the Europeans. They always come and steal our ideas. Africa has always been their inspiration.'

Alphadi's FOLLY

Alphadi, the so-called Prince of African Couture, mounts the podium. His trademark embroidered fez is askew as usual, and his blue robes rustle in the light desert breeze. He quivers with excitement. 'This,' he announces, wringing his hands passionately, 'is pure folly.'

All around us, the folly sprawls out across the orange dunes of Tiguidit. There are hundreds of grass igloos, borrowed from the local Tuareg pastoralists to house the visitors; neon beams to lead the way through the dunes; dust-caked 4x4s with 'mannequins' or 'models' plastered on their bonnets. There are portable toilets, plastic chairs and a grand podium shaped like a Tuareg cross and set off against a spotlit desert cliff.

In a few moments we are to witness an epic moment in African history: an extravaganza of fashion and music comprising Africa's twenty most important designers and the cream of European couture, set here, in a remote patch of Saharan sands in one of the world's poorest and least developed countries.

FIMA, or the *Festival International de la Mode Africaine*, has come a long way. For the past decade, Alphadi, Niger's only couturier of any significance, has been negotiating with sponsors, heads of state and couture houses to realize an extraordinary dream. But this dream is not simply about fashion; it is about bringing a chaotic clutch of around a thousand invited guests, news teams, fashion victims and desert specialists to the ends of the earth and, as Alphadi expands emotively, 'giving a chance to a country – and a continent – that has suffered so much.'

Until 1994, rebel Tuaregs who were seeking independence from the predominantly Hausa government, nine hundred kilometres south in the capital, Niamey, kept this region in a grip of long-knived terror. As recently as 1997, tourists were attacked in the region and today tour agencies in the nearby, faceless town of Agadez must pay protection money to the rebels. Given the desperate Saharan soils and lack of infrastructure, tourism is the only viable commodity in this area, and given the relative peace in the region, Niger has a lot riding on this evening's event.

It is hoped that FIMA will become Niger's fashion biennial, just as the MASA dance festival is for Côte d'Ivoire, or the FESPACO film festival is for Burkina Faso, but the benefits of *la haute couture du désert* have yet to be seen.

Our journey began two days ago, on a dark, freezing morning at Paris' Roissy Airport. Kenzo, the Paris-based Japanese designer is here, as are the representatives of Yves Saint Laurent, Thierry Mugler, Trussardi, Issey Miyake, Christian Lacroix and many more. Supermodel Alek Wek is hiding under a balaclava. I take fashion and hair notes, wondering just how well the ensembles will withstand the journey.

Six hours later, our plane clunks down onto Agadez's dust-bowl of a runway. There are Tuareg men, dancing and chanting, vintage sunglasses tucked neatly behind their *cheches*. Women, in gawdy, sequinned robes, yell and clap. Alek Wek mounts a camel for the photographers. The Absolut Vodka rep's blonde coiffure is suffering visibly in the sandy wind.

Predictably, it is a chaotic scene. Visas have been issued hurriedly on the aeroplane but Agadez airport is clearly ill-equipped for such numbers. We pile into 4x4s, borrowed from all over the country, and forge on to Tiguidit but it is not long before we are on our knees, digging sand out from under the tyres and pushing. The site is heavily guarded – to ensure against theft, I am told – though what precisely a group of Tuareg tribesmen would do with an Yves Saint Laurent frock, I cannot be sure.

Night falls in the desert. In the neon beams, tiny white mice and big black dung beetles scurry about, bewildered. But these are not the only confused locals. The following morning I sit at the edge of the site with a group of Tuaregs. Tea is brewing in a tiny pot as an old woman weaves a haunting, ancient melody on the *imzad*, or local violin. The Tuaregs are disgruntled. They have uprooted their lives, rented out their houses, and yet still cannot fathom what is going on.

As in much of Africa, fashion trends are a foreign concept around here. Haute couture is as remote as the sea. In the Agadez market, tailors rattle up traditional garb on antique sewing machines, and young people amble around in Taiwanese Nike T-shirts – that's about as trendy as it gets. 'We haven't sold many handicrafts,' Leyla Dawaka complains. 'So what's the point of all this? The people are messing up the dunes.'

Meanwhile, in a tent behind the podium, the designers are pinning up a frenzy. South Africa's Gavin Rajah is at his wits' end with the organization. 'They could put needles in my eyes rather than drag me here again,' he says. Namibia's Melanie Hartveld is pinning porcupine quills into place, while Senegal's Oumou Sy straps CDs to a vast, rainbow ballgown.

Satya, Kenzo's striking model, is shaving his famous bleached beard with the help of a bottle of Evian, while Lamine Kouyaté, the Malian-born Paris catwalk favourite, arranges a rail of tie-dyed lycra. He doesn't quite buy the romance of this African Renaissance. 'Perhaps they should have held this in Agadez with the locals,' he suggests wryly.

Yet, despite the ironies and lack of organization, the fantasy of Alphadi's coup is dazzling. Absolut Vodka has flown in ice sculptures from Scandinavia. I latch on to the Mugler people and Kenzo, who manages to wangle a few free bottles of vodka. There is a bar carved from a block of ice. Some local children finger it in amazement. Absolut Decadence, I'd say. We swig away at the vodka as a caravan of camels charges across the dunes. The mayor of Washington; the presidents of Chad, Niger and Gambia; UNESCO representatives shuffle into place on the leather pouffes and dromedary-wool carpets, and the show begins. Young Tuareg Muslims look on with embarrassment as a group of topless dancers from Abidjan begins to writhe and shake.

The richness and variety of the continent's couture offerings are wondrous. Oumou Sangare and Aicha Kone yell *griot* melodies into the sky, and Alphadi glows in the excitement. There is raffia, refined into slinky wedding dresses; bustiers encrusted with hand-painted cowrie shells; impossibly high head-wraps, and yet throughout, wearability gives way to cultural spectacle.

Whether African fashion can elevate itself from an exotic curiosity to a viable export industry is not yet apparent. And what this is achieving for Niger is uncertain. Does fashion have a place in a country where the levels of malnutrition and illiteracy remain alarming? Or should its luxury be reserved for developed societies? I guess not. For, even here in the desert, culture and creativity are as essential as water.

I stroll out onto the dunes as the European collections take the stage. There is a row of camels, transfixed by the Mugler range, chewing ponderously over the sequinned fetishwear. For me, it is a moment of rare surrealism and immense pride. For, in its extremes, its audacity and deep sense of hope, this event is a chilling metaphor for this continent. There is a group of young Tuareg men next to me, in long braids and blue cotton robes. One of them ambles up to me and wagers nervously, 'Excuse me, can I ask you something, Mister?'

'Sure, go ahead ...'

'Er, do they always dress like this in Europe?'

'Yes, quite often, I think.'

He can't help laughing. And neither can I.

WOMEN WHO MARRY *Fetishes*

In the tiny West African republic of Benin, the Priestesses of Voodoo drink French perfume, dust their fetishes with talcum powder and drip fresh blood and palm oil onto effigies of their ancestors.

Maman Hamisi's sweet, talcum scent arrives a few moments before she does. Wrapped, as always, in her holy white toga-and-turban set, she crosses the courtyard and enters the tiny, fetish-crammed temple at the back. But for the clinking of her antique glass beads, the space is reverent with silence. The four men who are her adepts have prepared for her arrival – lighting candles and poking a burning cigarette into the mouth of a clay fetish – so when Maman Hamisi seats herself, Hounnou is already tapping on the talking drum and Atiogbo is clanging a bell on the furry brown carpet. It is surely unusual to see a woman surrounded by male subordinates and playing the key role in a religious ceremony, but then again, voodoo is a most unusual religion.

Vadoun, as it is locally known, is as widespread today as any global faith. Thanks to the treacherous West African slave trade of the fourteenth to eighteenth centuries, it persists – in Brazil as *Candomble*, in Jamaica as *Obeayisne*; in Cuba and Miami as *Santeria*, and in Haiti as *Vodu*. But it was here, among the Fon, Ewe and Yoruba peoples of modern Benin, Togo and Eastern Ghana, that this most complex and sophisticated of animist belief systems was cradled. And on this cloudy morning, in the back streets of Benin's smoggy economic capital, Cotonou, it appears to have lost none of its potency.

'Ke-ke-ke-ke-ke,' Maman Hamisi shrieks, dusting her fetishes with a cloud of talc. 'Amen,' her adepts chorus. And when she is ready, our venerable voodoo priestess begins the deep, rhythmic chant that will invoke her deity – the capricious goddess of trade and travel, known throughout this region as Mamy Wata.

It's simple enough to see how voodoo earned its fearsome standing with visitors to these parts. Step into the sprawling fetish section of Dan Tokpa market on the edge of Cotonou's lagoon and the array of medicinal herbs and severed animal parts is vast and frightening. I have seen many such markets in Africa – though none quite so creepy or overwhelming as this one. Indeed, as one traipses through the menacing aisles of rats' carcasses, dogs' heads or baby pythons wrapped in elastic bands – all ready and waiting for ceremonial use – the horror of Catholic or Islamic zealots over the centuries is quite conceivable. Yes, of all religions, none has been so often misunderstood as voodoo – at best, exoticized on perfume bottles; at worst demonized as a savage cult.

Stripped of such fantasy, however, this morning's ritual is neither savage nor romantic. For as she probes the spirit world and calls up the voices of authority, Maman Hamisi is simply a powerful woman, maintaining order in the world around her.

Lately, voodoo has become something of a political pawn here in Benin. In the early 1990s, when President Nicephore Soglo came to power, he initiated a renaissance, prioritizing voodoo on Benin's cultural agenda and spearheading Ouidah '92 – a gathering of believers from all over the diaspora, held in the nearby coastal town. Yet when Mathieu Kerekou, the country's long-time Marxist leader was re-elected in 1995, he returned to power with a post-Cold War, Christian vehemence and again voodoo forfeited its prominence. Regardless, an estimated seventy-five percent of Beninois still practise the religion.

Maman Hamisi continues chanting, breaking her monologue with the deep peals of laughter synonymous with Mamy Wata's trance. Today she is seeking a blessing for a journey she must make. A thick blanket of clapping and drumbeats envelops us as she points her palms at the clutter of offerings on the altar. There are bottles of cheap perfume, a plastic kewpie doll, beads and some figurines bound together with string – all gifts to the goddess from those who know her powers. At the edge of the shelf, a statue of the Virgin Mary proclaims voodoo's ever-present syncretism.

No-one is quite sure where voodoo originally came from. Some believe it has Egyptian or Asian roots, for it incorporates the *fa*, a complex divination system not that different from the *kaballah*. Yet, over the centuries, voodoo has proved so fluid at incorporating elements of other faiths, its exact origins remain enigmatic. And many believers, even those who attend church or mosque regularly, return to their more mystical, primal belief system in times of distress.

For voodoo believers there exists one supreme god, Mawou, and an endless pantheon of lesser deities, or *vodu*, which correspond to every imaginable phenomenon: thunder, smallpox, iron and even plastic are represented. For each of these gods, there exist a series of intermediaries – voodoo priests or priestesses – who after many years of initiation, will have secured communication hotlines with their deities, most often to seek healing, good fortune or revenge.

That Mawou is considered female is significant, for of all religions, voodoo is perhaps the most egalitarian when it comes to gender. Here in the holy ranks of its hierarchies, there is no need for affirmative action, for women are as powerful – and often more so – as men. 'Though politics remains a man's world in modern Benin,' Monsieur Akala, a director in Benin's Ministry of Culture, expands, 'historically women have occupied an unconventional place in this society.' It was here in the eighteenth century, under King Ghezo, that an army of six thousand female soldiers was organized. Known as Amazon warriors, they were better armed than their male counterparts and reportedly cut off one of their breasts if it impaired their ability to shoot.

Today, however, the prevalence of aunties and grandmothers in voodoo's upper echelons comes down to practical considerations. 'Women live longer than men do,' Akala continues. 'Also, especially after menopause, women acquire a special degree of wisdom and neutrality which allows them to play a key role in the religious organization.'

Back at the temple, the intensity mounts as Hounnou reaches for the tellers of the *fa*: the four customary cowrie shells which, depending on how they fall, will communicate a message from Mamy Wata. Maman Hamisi nods as Hounnou clasps the cowries between his palms, shakes them and drops them onto the mat. The priestess shrieks with joy for the shells have fallen evenly – two facing upwards and two down. Mamy Wata, in other words, has heard her prayers and has responded with her blessing. Maman Hamisi whips open a bottle of French perfume, splashes a tot onto the carpet for Mamy, then takes a deep, ecstatic gulp.

For the uninitiated, it is hard to conceive the excitement in the fall of a few cowrie shells. Yet for voodoo believers, there is no distinction between the material and spiritual worlds. Here, holiness pervades everything. Toss in the intricacy and discipline of the relevant rituals and all sorts of every day objects become vested with meaning – so much so that as the priestess weaves her way through the courtyard, addressing the pantheon of gods on display, the afternoon evolves like a chapter from a magic realist novel.

She pours some more talc at the base of an iroko tree to appease the God of Lightning, then onto a dingy alleyway, where a couple more gods share space with the poultry. A duck waddles by angrily, leaving its eggs next to the pile of rusting Peugeot parts which has come to represent Ogun, the God of Iron and Creation.

To each god, his or her own tastes, and while Mamy Wata adores perfume and talc, Ogun, it appears, has a weakness for fizzy drinks. Furthermore, while Mamy Wata accepts only women as intermediaries, Ogun will accept only men. And thus it is Atiogbo who takes a deep gulp from a bottle of Fanta Orange and spits it onto the fetish – feeding Ogun, so to speak, from his own mouth. In the background, the duck quacks and Maman Hamisi chants, 'Amen'.

Though she may have some contact with other gods, it is critical that the priestess retains her distance, for the relationship she has fostered with her principal deity is a deep and long-term one, often referred to as a marriage. Mamy Wata, whose chuckling, mermaid likeness has been painted in fine, naïve brushstrokes on the temple walls, is Maman Hamisi's partner.

The following morning, in a larger temple, nestled between some shacks at the sea-front, another priestess, Madame Armande Houndjovi, greets Gnigblin the God of Thunder. She is a tall and commanding woman, but like Maman Hamisi's, her face glows with warmth, her eyes with wisdom. She has been 'married' to Gnigblin for some forty years, she explains. Having first heard her calling during a church service, she spent twenty years in initiation before becoming a priestess. Nowadays, she dedicates Mondays to prayer, and once a year she makes a pilgrimage to the town of Be in neighbouring Togo, where Gnigblin is most powerful. She saves for many months to make the trip.

Today being Saturday, others have come to worship the gods portrayed on the weathered temple walls. Some have even slept here for a few nights to strengthen their rapport with, say, Dangbe – the snake god, who represents eternity as he eats his rainbow tail; or Sakpata, the god of measles; or Gnigblin or Mamy Wata. But Madame Houndjovi is here to see a younger woman who has also heard Gnigblin calling. Together, they will consult the *fa* to see whether or not she will make a suitable adept.

Madame Houndjovi lowers her wrap and presses her vast, sagging breasts against a white sheet, already stained with the blood of animal sacrifices. She chants quickly, in a now familiar, measured tone, and an adept comes forward and dips a calabash into a mouldy, earthenware pot, scooping out some sweet, chalky water which the priestess and the novice must drink. They do so, and then gravely, Madame Houndjovi throws the *fa*. Again the shells fall evenly: Gnigblin has agreed. The priestess is delighted. She crushes some balls of kaolin and presses the dry powder into the young woman's mouth, along with a few fiery seeds from a Guinea Pepper. The ritual now complete, she pours a libation of Royal Stock Gin onto the concrete floor and takes a slow drag on a Marlboro. 'It's good to smoke in the temple,' she says. 'But I'd never dare smoke outside, you know. They'd think I was a prostitute.'

Despite this apparent Bohemian stance, beneath the surface, voodoo is a strict tangle of rules and sacred codes. 'Respect the gods and their wishes, and you'll have no reason to fear them,' the priestess states matter-of-factly, 'but cross them, and you're asking for trouble.' Depending on the circumstances, trouble could mean affliction, alienation or death. Yet to focus on this – voodoo's sinister edge – is to negate key facets of the religion, many of which attest to the powerful female energies in its upper ranks. The rich colours of its ceremonial garb; the bold, theatrical sweep of its rituals; and the vitality and creativity that suffuse the entire voodoo world, might all be less marked, given the constraints of a more patriarchal system.

A couple of hours east of here, near the Togolese border, the priestesses of Come and their adepts are about to substantiate this notion. Their costumes are as elaborate as a Broadway cast's, incorporating everything from raffia bodices to dreadlocked wigs, vintage seventies sunglasses, and silver tinsel. And this morning, as they sacrifice a chicken to their ancestors to seek blessing in the pending rainy season, the scene is as richly visual as a night at the opera.

There are sixteen women here this morning, representing various gods.

They form a long train, and sing softly as they meander to the centre of the courtyard, where the requisite fetishes are ready for ritual. There's a large calabash, cut through the centre; a series of padlocks chained together – each for a separate prayer – and a wooden figure, which somewhere under the gooey layers of dried blood, animal fat and red palm oil, represents the ancestors.

Presently, one of the women, the priestess of Avlekete, God of the Sea, steps forward. She wears a black smock and black pork-pie hat covered with sea shells. Expressionless, she glares at the fetish and begins thrusting her hips to and fro. Then suddenly, she lifts her smock to reveal a giant wooden phallus strapped around her waist. The few men present giggle with embarrassment but the women evidently see nothing strange in the priestess summoning up Avlekete's masculine power in this way.

The priestess calls for an adept, drowsily lifts her dress, and without further ado, begins thrusting the phallus between the adept's legs. Despite the now frantic giggling of the men, the other women just smile faintly. They know the difference between accessing sacred strength through a simulated sexual act and low-tech pornography.

After the giggling has died down, the priestess of Hebiosso, the Rain God, steps forward. She is a short woman, wrapped in black cotton and beads, and her expression is most grave, despite the singing and clapping of the others. One of her adepts steps out of a doorway. In her hands, a chicken, bound at the feet, is clucking for its life. The priestess kneels and begins chanting. She takes the chicken and plucks some feathers from its neck, which she scatters on the fetish. Then, in an instant, she silences the frantic clucking with a small knife, slitting the chicken's throat perfunctorily and showering scarlet droplets over the fetish – feeding the ancestors with the required fresh blood. She places the body in the calabash and retreats. The ritual is complete.

For anyone in search of a fleeting, Hollywood image of voodoo, this is it – a savage and bloody act, played out amid the chanting of exotic voices and the thumping of *djembe* drums. Yet in context, there is nothing savage about this sacrifice – the chicken will be shared out and eaten afterwards. The blood is simply a means of paying respect to the holy ones, little different from saying grace before a meal.

Indeed, strip away the exotic fanfare – the cats' heads sewn into cushions; the nauseating stench of old animal fat; or the talc-covered bodies slinking into midnight lagoons – and voodoo is simply an effective system for maintaining social order. If women's rights are anything to go by, it presents a far more civilized model than Christianity, Judaism or Islam.

Indeed, as Madame Houndjovi observes, 'There in the West, you are still fighting for women to be as powerful as men. But here in the *vadoun* world, we have always been powerful.'

LES NANAS

Benz

Though often illiterate, the millionaire businesswomen of Togo and Benin drive shiny, status wielding sedans; import shipfuls of car tyres or fertilizer at the flick of well-padded wrists; and wield considerable, though invisible, power.

Madame Aladja Apithy sips impatiently on a fizzy drink. Wrapped in her grand blue and orange *boubou*, white *hijab* slung modestly around her head, she is by no means a small woman. Yet, regardless of her ample presence, Madame Apithy is dwarfed by the scale of the surrounding comforts: the leather lounge suites, the gaudy ceramic lamps, the gargantuan television set and satellite dish.

It's hard to believe we are in Cotonou, the smoggy, economic heart of Benin, for beyond the landscaped gardens of this modernist villa, the mood of subsistence hangs heavy. Swarms of mopeds splutter along the dusty streets, scrawny chickens cluck through potholes and millions of Beninois scrape out an average annual salary of around three hundred and fifty dollars. Yet Madame Apithy is one of a most unlikely elite, a very wealthy clutch of self-made businesswomen, or *commerçantes*, known – for their favoured mode of transport – as Les Nanas Benz.

Anywhere in the world, the dominance of women in a country's top economic echelons would be unusual. In Africa, where the majority of women rank consistently lowest on social, health, and economic scales, it seems extraordinary. Yet scratch the surface, and the tradition of women in business goes back a long way in this part of the world.

For centuries, the Yoruba market women of southern Nigeria have been known for their cash savvy and bargaining skills. Yet it was only during this century that a few, smart *commerçantes* began reaping the profits of capitalist economies.

In Togo – where car duties are the lowest in the region – it became customary, in the eighties, for the most successful *commerçantes* to proclaim their newfound fortunes with the purchase of a certain shiny, German sedan, hence their regional nickname. Only lately, given the attendant pinch of Togolese Military rule, you're likely to come across Les Nanas Benz all along the West African coast.

Abidjan, in the Ivory Coast, is one of West Africa's largest, richest cities, and a major regional flight hub. Any day of the week, the city's Félix Houphouet-Boigny airport bustles with women from neighbouring countries hauling outrageously vast packages off the conveyor belts. They are here to take advantage of the country's lax position on migrant workers, but never without taking advantage of the region's cost discrepancies en route. Be it in the form of shoes, clothing, or tinned foods, money seems always to be changing hands here. 'We have an instinctive business sense,' *commerçante* Yta Gourias tells me. 'Far more so than in southern or East Africa.'

Gourias came to Abidjan from Togo twenty years ago and opened various shops selling textiles and household goods. A musician, Gourias now owns the Laguna nightclub, a large concrete landmark on the bank of Abidjan's Ebrie Lagoon. What makes Gourias unusual, however, is the way she's spent her money by setting up a home for one hundred and fifty of the city's street children. Her strong matriarchal presence hints at women's invisible, but irrefutable power, from here all the way east to Nigeria.

Back in Cotonou, Madame Apithy drives the latest Benz model. The car bears a Nigerian number plate, which saves her hassles on her frequent trips to Lagos, and is chauffeured by her eldest daughter who, in her ponytail, sweatshirt and brown gangsta-babe jeans, is a Nana Benz in training. 'My mother taught me,' Madame Apithy affirms. 'Now I'm teaching her.'

'While I was still at school,' she continues, 'I borrowed twenty thousand CFA francs from my father and bought some textiles to sell in the market. I was lucky. You never know when you'll be lucky. So you try.' She lifts a paper serviette from the table and dangles it loosely between her fingers. 'Maybe you try this ...' she shrugs. 'Maybe you're lucky.'

Lucky indeed. Since she shifted into full-time trading after quitting her job as a government secretary, Madame Apithy has netted an apartment in Paris, a house in London, and the house we're in. 'Plus one house for my husband,' she remembers. 'I bought it for him.' And while anywhere in the world, such a spin on traditional gender roles would be unusual, here in West Africa – where there are only token women in parliament and patriarchal Islam and Christianity have all but wiped out matriarchal animist systems – it is extraordinary.

A French fitness programme flashes across the TV screen. Madame Apithy sneaks a glance. The fizzy drink she is sipping is sugar free, for a Benz is not the only perceptible symbol of wealth in this society. Food, whether on the table or wrapped around one's waist, is a mean status symbol here, and sugar free drinks are a token caution in the name of cardiac health. 'I went to her house for dinner recently,' a colleague of hers confides. 'There were only four of us there, but there were twelve fish on the table. That's how much money she has!'

Madame Apithy's eyes keep wandering. She has little interest in this interview, it appears, but is happy at the chance to probe its commercial angle. 'What do you have in your country?' she snaps. 'Sugar? Rice? You tell me the price, I buy. One ship rice. One ship sugar. No problem!' I promise to enquire about prices and attempt to sway the interview towards lifestyle: 'Do you have any interests other than trading?' She thinks for a while. 'Yes,' she says, deadpan. 'Factories. Now, are we finished?'

She slips on her plastic shoes, heads for the Merc, and dishes me a business card; then she and her daughter cruise off along the crumpled streets in search of a deal, like a couple of serious Girlz 'n the Hood. 'But it's Saturday!' I gasp. 'What's the rush?'

'She's a Nana Benz,' my guide explains. 'So she's always busy. Always chasing money.'

The quicker and more fearless a *commerçante*, he expands, the more likely she is to make it. When neighbouring Nigeria banned certain imports, whatever the product was, within days, one *commerçante* or another would be shipping containers of the stuff into Cotonou harbour for sale. 'We saw a lot of new Benzes around during that time.'

Yet of course not all women in this part of the world are wealthy. In rural areas especially, women do most of the labour and reap little power or status. But this is also a region where divorce is rare and legalized polygyny allows men up to four wives. So for many women, the stamina and responsibility required to raise children, with little support from their men, has long been a part of life.

Indeed, step along the aisles of Nike rip-offs, glass beads and colourful wax-print cloths in Cotonou's vast Dan Tokpa market, and the majority of traders are women. Some shuffle so quickly through the wads of cash notes behind their tables, it's as though they're racing to Benzhood. And while some of those who make it learn to read and write along the way, what makes many of West Africa's millionairesses all the more extraordinary is that they're illiterate – and it is for fear that our interview will include the embarrassment of a written component that textile tycoon, Sabine Houessinon, sends a posse of agents to receive me in her apartment on Cotonou's Boulevard Saint Michel: her daughter, her accountant and her husband, Jules. 'Sabine doesn't do interviews,' Jules explains. 'Besides, she's already downstairs in her shop. And once she's in her shop, she won't come out.'

Like Apithy, Houessinon hails from a trading family. 'She started off selling tobacco,' Jules explains. She bought some stock from her grandmother and hawked it around the market. But her big break came in 1958, when she moved to the Ivory Coast and secured various textile contracts. 'Nowadays, she holds the licence for a range of Dutch, French and British brands in Benin, and owns and runs the Hotel Concorde downtown,' expands her daughter, who is currently grappling the commodity ropes with a few containers of car tyres.

No-one here acknowledges anything strange about Sabine being the family's chief breadwinner. 'Women are good with money,' Jules says, as he escorts me on a tour of his wife's wares. 'They get bank loans more easily and generally run better businesses.' Yet somehow, beneath this agreeable veneer, one senses the awkward rumbling of a power shift and its implicit threat to social order. 'A woman might be the boss of her business,' the accountant bristles. 'But in the home, her husband is still in charge.'

Because women have stayed out of politics here, their economic might remains largely invisible. It is a fact known by all, yet rarely acknowledged publicly. And though for Western feminists, the hypocrisy and inequality of the status quo might seem intolerable, this particular gender battle has been waged along different lines from Western ones: no suffragette banners, no affirmative action quotas, no ideological gibberish. These sisters have simply got down and done it for themselves. 'Let the men run the country,' as restaurateur and *commerçante* Aicha Alao puts it over the phone to me. 'We're busy making money.'

The moment I see Mademoiselle Alao's photograph on the wall of La Résidence – her well-known, up-market, Cotonou restaurant – the following evening, I know she is different from the others I've interviewed. Not only is she attractive and immaculately groomed, she is also sandwiched between President and Madame Mitterand in a figure-hugging, Afro-print dress. 'Sorry to disappoint you,' she says in perfect English when she arrives a few moments later. 'I don't quite have the figure for a Nana Benz. Got the car though. Want me to get it out the garage?'

Alao, it soon transpires, is a Nana Benz for the nineties. Direct, politically aware and fiercely independent, she embodies the aspirations of modern, Western womanhood, yet seems to suffer none of the neuroses. Twenty years ago, while working as a secretary for Nigerian Airways, she began bringing over American hair products to sell in Benin. Since then, she has raised two children; run this restaurant, a hair salon at the Benin Sheraton, and another similar restaurant in downtown Johannesburg; and imported shipfuls of wine or fertilizer at the flick of an elegant wrist, without ever seeing the point of a full-time man in her life.

'Ever been married?' I ask. 'Thank God, no!' she laughs. 'I'm friendly with the father of my children, but I never married him. Who needs a man all the time? If I want a man, I'll get a boyfriend for a couple of months, and whip him off to Paris and have some fun with him. But I certainly don't want to be dictated to by anyone.'

Her headstrong attitude, she concedes, has partly been shaped by her success. 'I don't know if it's an advantage or a curse – being successful. Often I land up wondering, "Does he want me or my money?" It always happens when a woman makes more money than a man. Either he leaves her out of humiliation, or sticks around to share the spoils and finds a mistress to restore his pride. Then you end up working to support the mistress!'

Given the grip of traditional African values, however, few *commerçantes* are as outspoken as Alao. 'I think a lot of women feel threatened by me,' Alao expresses. 'Especially the Nana Benzes. They might make far more money than their husbands do, but they still think they've got to have a man around, no matter how they're treated. He can beat her and she'll stay with him. So they stay in these empty marriages and gossip about me being single. Or they drive by when I'm jogging and have a little a snicker. But the truth is, they're stuck.'

Alao sips calmly on a mineral water. She might be a little extreme in her stance, but then again, so are the ironies of this situation. For though Les Nanas Benz hold the region's economic reins, they have yet to challenge the prevailing norms. And loaded as they may be, when it comes to social and political equality, many of them remain no better off than their impoverished village counterparts. 'It's a joke, isn't it?' Alao laughs. 'Everyone knows money is power and respect, but no-one has the courage to acknowledge it.'

'Never mind,' she adds confidently, tapping her nails on the table-top. 'I'm forty-six. When I'm fifty, I'm getting into politics. And somehow, I don't think those men are going to stop me. They've always known I was a fighter.'

A LANGUAGE IN
Cloth

In the warm, magic world of the East African coast,
the veils of Islam are never silent.

It is another blazing day on Unguja, the largest and most legendary island
of the Zanzibari Archipelago. Sada, one of the more beautiful women in
the village, wakes up and stretches. In the soft light of a tropical dawn,
her fine features divulge the rich, cosmopolitan history of the region – her
black, piercing eyes rimmed with kohl; her steep, elegant nose; her skin a
thick hue of brown, described somewhat deliciously in Swahili as *wa
kadbari*, or the colour of Cadbury's chocolate.

More than a millennium ago, Sada's ancestors came here by *dhow* from
the Arabian Peninsula, bringing to Africa some of the teachings and
customs of Islam's Sunni sects. Wherever you go in Zanzibar, there are
reminders of how deeply Islam has been woven into the African cultural
quilt. Should you stroll among the coconut palms at Kizimkazi, you may
well stumble across the moody, mildewed remains of a mosque bearing
Kufic plaques inscribed with the date 1107.

Yet of all the reminders of the teachings of the Prophet Mohammed,
none is more visible than the public veiling of women. Sada rises from the
grass mat where she has been sleeping. She washes, then steps into a corner
of her hut, where a cotton rainbow of kanga cloths is suspended from
nails, knocked into the pitted coral wall. She thinks for a moment, as you
might do, faced with a full rail of Donna Karan casuals. She chooses a
butter-soft pair of kangas from her selection. They are both vibrant orange
and tangled with webs of green squiggles. Sada ties one kanga around her
waist; the other she pulls tightly across her brow, tucking it behind her
ears, then drawing the leftover cloth loosely across her torso.

Drapery is a fine art here in Zanzibar; each cloth should hang just so,
wavering somewhere between allure and disguise. Sada steps out of her
hut. As she strolls through the village, the low-key glamour of her

two-piece would indeed cast a fair curtain of shade across the more extravagant ensembles of most Western label divas.

There are thousands of kanga designs. Each is printed for a limited period at a textile factory either on mainland Tanzania, in India or in Indonesia. While some bear astonishingly sophisticated patterns, others are naïvely tattooed with images of swans, paraffin lamps, roses, ships, brass teapots and pears. But no matter what the design, the rim of the cloth is always detailed with a short Swahili inscription. The words will have some of the allure the letters VERSACE might have, stitched into the hem of your T-shirt – only here, the message is all the more powerful.

KiSwahili is one of the world's more melodic tongues. Though it has its roots in the Bantu language tree, like almost everything on this coast, its vocabulary bears testimony to the diversity of the region's heritage: there are Arabic verbs, and English, Hindi, Farsi, even Portuguese nouns. Recently, by analyzing the structure of the language, linguistic historians have come a long way in substantiating the existence of a strong Swahili culture prior to Islamization in the ninth century, proving that Islam merely flavoured an already rich African tradition. However, the briefest glance at Sada as she flits exuberantly among the huts of her village could tell these historians the same primeval truth in far fewer words.

Partly because of illiteracy, a profound Swahili oral tradition has evolved over the centuries. It is a tradition of stories told at firesides; of wisdom, slipping from the lips of gnarled old men as they sip bitter coffee on village benches; of lessons passed from grandmothers to daughters to granddaughters; from wives to husbands to co-wives. And while the written literature of this coast would scarcely fill the library of an elementary school, the oral treasury of KiSwahili is far richer than its European counterparts. In particular, a diverse bank of *misemo*, or sayings, has evolved, which play a key role in ensuring the posterity of cultural wisdom.

The *misemo* is to KiSwahili what the *haiku* is to Japanese: tight, poetic, rarely translatable and generally bristling with erotic innuendo. Each day, new *misemo* are coined and passed around from lips to ears like telegrams, and over the past century, these cultural seeds have found another channel for their dispersal – broadcast via kanga. 'Don't pin your hopes on someone else's star,' one ripe yellow cloth exclaims. 'The sweetness of the sugar cane is in the tip,' another remarks huskily. And innocuous as such statements might ring in our virgin ears, in the gossipy thick of a small Zanzibari village, these hidden meanings are rarely missed.

As Sada makes her way to the marketplace, the words, 'My own bad deeds are better than those of my friends,' tattooed sassily on her behind, have little chance of escaping an intent public gaze. Mae West, eat your heart out.

Around here, deciphering the morning's riddle is as good as having last night's secrets dripped saucily into your ear. Perhaps Sada has been wronged by a neighbour? Perhaps she has discovered the infidelities of one of her co-wives? Or perhaps she is silently confessing to her own dangerous liaisons?

We have no way of knowing, for indeed, without context, meaning drifts like a silly cloud in a lost sky. And while the men of the village may or may not be able to decode Sada's proclamation, the other women undoubtedly will, for the encrypted poetry of kangas is known as *luga wa wanawake*, or the language of women. At around two US dollars a pair, kangas are within everyone's reach; the westernization of Zanzibari life has done little to diminish their cultural importance.

One evening a radiant office clerk named Turkia invites me to her apartment to talk kangas. The space is thick with aspirational trappings: a hi-fi, some plastic flowers, a carpet with the Taj Mahal on it. Yet the trunk in Turkia's bedroom holds more than a hundred kangas – some bought, others passed down from her mother or sister. Like all Zanzibaris, Turkia's life has been wrapped in kangas since birth. When a woman arrives at the nursing home, she explains, she brings with her three pairs of kangas. The first, she wears on the operating table; the second, she changes into after the birth; the third pair is wrapped around the newborn babe.

The vivid array of cloths scattered around us tells the story of Turkia's life. She shows me the pairs she wore as a toddler, knotted in a halter-neck. Then the traditional red and black geometric pair she wore on her wedding day. Then her favourite cloth. Scattered with dollar notes, it reads: *I love you.* 'The man or the money?' Turkia quips, mischievously.

Finally, we come across the plain red-and-white floral cloth she has chosen for her funeral. When she dies, it will be draped over her coffin and buried with her, completing its sinuous cycle from cradle to grave.

One sticky afternoon a few days later, I squeeze my way into the women's world of a kanga shop near the marketplace at Darajani. The smell of textile ink is heavy and the walls are quilted with cloths hanging neatly from their wire hangers. If you think the Macy's end-of-season sale is popular, think again: the store is liquid with excitement. Arms poke out of the human jungle like twigs; thousand shilling notes waving in the chaos like crumpled, green leaves. The event: the launch of a new kanga, announced just this morning on the local radio station.

Many have arrived with no idea what the kanga looks like, for it is generally the *misemo* that sells the cloth. Sales will boom should the message strike a chord. And should the saying lose its currency before the cloth wears thin, a black magic marker is said to come in handy. Of course, with little knowledge of Swahili, wrapping a kanga around your hips is a haphazard business. One foreigner I know was once seduced by a pretty design of yellow bananas in a sea of ultramarine. As she passed through the streets of Stonetown, a string of giggles followed her. She sought a translator: the *misemo*, it transpired, had been designed for the announcement of a new lover. 'Because I eat bananas,' it stated, 'I never get tired.'

In today's world, Islamic cultures remain among the most complex and enigmatic. Quick as Western feminists might be to decry Islam's oppression of women, few have begun to comprehend the power and seduction so profoundly scripted into the daily theatre of a veiled world. The ancient, pagan sensuality of Africa fares little better in our Western mindsets. At best it is romanticized; at worst it is dismissed as savage. The language of kangas combines the mysterious, complex codes of these two less-travelled worlds.

While I am no closer to fully understanding this dialogue than I am to grasping the meanings of a masked, tribal dance, I am both dazzled by its poetry, and convinced that its earthy intensity would do the neo-Amazonians proud. It does after all present a stunning paradox: in a world where women's voices are rarely heard publicly, the very veils which silence them have come to speak. Where, in our liberated world, do mischief, wit and sexuality enjoy such a sophisticated public profile? Where does fashion sustain such erotic sophistication? Indeed, while I remain impressed by the fall of a well-cut blouse from a woman's shoulder blades, after observing such rich codes woven into simple sheets of sun-bleached cotton, the status-hungry blare of a pair of golden Gs, interlocked on some five hundred-dollar lapel, does strike me as just a little crude.

UNTHREADING
History

Beads are still made by hand in West Africa, and they still pass from hand to hand as currency and keepers of history and cultural symbolism.

Wednesday nights at Chester's Place – that's why I love Ghana. For the suave, Sinatra-like baritones crooning High-Life classics on the green-lit linoleum stage. For the sensible volunteer workers blossoming into tropical dancing flowers. And for Afrika Mosquito, that unstoppable Nigerian lunatic from Labadi beach, who slaps up such a hurricane on the *djembe* drums, that Chester, the man, is rattling his hips into a liquid frenzy.

I'm with my friends Trish and Bushman, and we're trying to stop peeling the retro-styled Club Lager labels off sweaty, drunken bottles, because tomorrow is Thursday.

Thursdays at Koforudua. That's why I love Africa. Only here can you stagger out of a nightclub and into a minibus, crawl a couple of hours along a narrow, hilly road and traverse centuries. Koforudua is history for me, and geography too. On a continent where the past is so often forgotten, and where isolation is a lived tyranny, Koforudua should be compulsory viewing. But only on Thursday mornings.

The sun has not yet risen over the coconut palms when we park at the end of Market Street, but already the pavement is aflicker with cheap, Chinese torches. Their beams trace the haunched silhouettes of traders, digging in baskets and unwrapping curious bundles. There are flashes of agate; streaks of glistening ultramarine; shiny white plastic.

I step carefully along the pavement but for once there are no desperate hagglers. A young Hausa man sits gracefully, legs stretched out on a plastic mat. I admire the rough, brick-red patina of the bauxite slugs he's strung on a loop of raffia, but he will not budge on his price. This is no tourist sideshow; it is (and has been since 1928) West Africa's most extensive bead market – a weekly meeting of the region's bead producers and serious traders. I have visited twenty African countries, but never have I seen so many beads at once, and never in such astonishing variety.

Now, I begin to understand the insatiable fascination these objects inspire. Trish, a Canadian, who came here as an NGO worker, has gradually shifted to stringing beads and selling them to tourists for a living. Bushman, a local Rastafarian with a head full of cowries, exports small quantities. I am a new initiate but already the variety of materials, textures, shapes and colours carries the threat of a looming obsessive-compulsive disorder. And soon enough we are all tangled gleefully in rough glass ropes of pistachio, emerald, sea-blue and lemon.

Yet beneath the sheer aesthetic delight of these objects, there exists a deep, ancient magnetism. And watching as a young girl in a pink dress threads yellow, ceramic discs onto a piece of wire, I am overcome with the immense, haunting significance of the image. Not only is her gesture many centuries deep, there is something especially African about it.

The dawn sky is mauve and heavy, and sliced with turquoise streaks of day. Gradually, the light fills in the details: the busy wax-prints of the frilly, Victorian-styled dresses the market women wear; the hand-painted advertising billboards for soap and beer; the rows of small, scrawny vultures perched on the tattered tin roofs; the young girls stepping coyly among the adults, glass-and-wooden boxes balanced perfectly on their heads, the glass oily with the morning's doughnuts.

Already, many of the strings I've been haggling over have vanished. There remain black, snaky coils of coconut shell; cowrie shells; strange seed pods; polished cubes of agate and onyx. There are thick ceramic discs, finished skilfully to look like granite, and chunky, wax-cast, bronze beads – some filigreed, others tracing the geometric symbols of Ashanti gold weights.

Aside from the few recent additions of Taiwanese plastic and some glass European factory numbers, every bead at Koforudua is hand-made. 'That's the appeal, really, that it's not a machine that spits them out, but an individual who forms, and bakes and shapes each bead,' says Kati Torda Dagadu. She's a feisty Hungarian who has lived here for twenty years and co-founded the Ghana Bead Society. When Torda first arrived with her

Ghanaian husband, she was taken to his village, where each villager presented her with a single bead on a thong. 'Why beads?' she wondered. 'Why not cloth or flowers?' And like so many others, she was enchanted, and embarked on a lifelong investigation into the history and cultural importance of beads in this region.

Bluff a little knowledge on the pavement here at Koforudua, and you might convince a trader to dig in the bottom of his basket. Keep bluffing and he might unravel a piece of cloth and reveal the treasures that have been hidden from amateur eyes. These objects may be many centuries old and would trade in bead connoisseurs' circles for many hundred dollars apiece – though this town, as I unhappily discover, can barely afford a flushing toilet.

While often mistakenly described as old African beads, these objects were not originally made in Africa. Around four centuries ago, when the Portuguese first moored their ships on this blowy, palm-strewn coastline, the European bead industry was on the verge of an unprecedented boom. Italy, Holland and eastern Europe were all churning out glass and ceramic beads by the thousands. Little did they realize they were about to pull off one of the greatest coups in the history of world trade.

Africans had always made beads. Be it a lion's claw strung around a hunter's neck, a piece of wood or giant African snail shell on a leather thong, beads were already deeply threaded into local rituals and systems of social status and colour symbolism. The translucent hues of the beads that were packed in with the European trade offerings appeared so magical to Africans, that they were to effect a most tragic seduction.

I chew on a doughnut. A bead trader takes out a single, seven-layered chevron bead from his sack. It is about five centimetres thick and was crafted in Venice in the seventeenth century, in deep blue, red and white glass. As the slave trade boomed in this region, a bead like this would fetch seven human beings.

Though new beads are still being made in villages around West Africa, the abundance and variety of antique beads in the region are no accident. And wherever I go along this coast, from the muddy stalls of Dan Tokpa market in Benin to the cunning traders on Abidjan's Avenue 11, the quiet, ancient slipping of beads onto bits of string holds a memory of long journeys and deep pain.

The sun bakes down on Koforudua. The rattling of diesel engines and the quick, sharp yells of the market women fill the street. Plastic bowls and shoes fill in the gaps between the chunks of honey-coloured amber, and strings of chipped, but still splendid, old Venetian millefiori beads. Like all beads here, they have been renamed in various local languages, their histories creatively reinvented: these, I am told, originate not in Italy, but from the soil, where the rainbow meets the earth.

All over the world, beads have threaded their way into attire and rituals, but nowhere is their significance as deep as here. The Maasai and Somalis of the east, the Zulus in the south, the Berbers in the north and countless other tribes have evolved elaborate beading designs and significations. As units of currency, the value of old trade beads is defined not only by their origins, but by the number of times they have changed hands.

The trader hands me a string of camel bone beads, charred with Harlequin-style checks, and beautifully worn around the edges. They could be Nigerian or even East African. There is, of course, scarcely a road here from East Africa, let alone a flight. That these objects found their way here – in saddle bags, on camel-back, from hand to hand – is testament to the invisible spider web of trade routes this continent sustains. Here, where mud buildings crumble to dust, where wood rots, and where roads disintegrate as fast as they're built, these tiny objects are the keepers of history.

A few miles south of Koforudua, the minibus screeches to a halt at a junk yard and we traipse through to a coconut-thatched shack behind it, where Okleh Tete runs a small bead factory. There is no electricity here, only a small wood-kiln in which Okleh forms and bakes and shapes the ingenious, cheap, recycled glass beads still popular in rural Ghana.

Nowhere but Ghana would one come across someone as jolly and enthusiastic as Okleh, and yet, as he takes his visitors through the process, I am struck by the painstaking, pre-industrial tedium of his craft. He digs into some sacks of crushed beer bottles. The dark green is called 'green', he explains (Gee thanks, Okleh!). The dark brown, Guinness.

Carefully, Okleh places the tiny bits of glass into rough clay moulds, mixing some with a pinch of powdered pigment. He places the moulds in the kiln, and stokes it with long, twisted sticks. Half an hour later, he removes the moulds with an iron spatula, loosening each glowing glob of molten glass with a skewer and poking a hole through its centre. When the beads have cooled, he flips the mould and washes each bead, sanding down the rough edges in a shallow, stone bowl. Each mould will yield anything from one to five beads. And twenty or so will be threaded and sold as a string at Koforudua for one US dollar. Amazed as I am by the dedication of this craft, commercially this is a sad metaphor for African economics.

Even more worrisome is the absence of beads back in the capital, Accra. Snoop around the nightclubs at Nkrumah Circle, and there are nothing but kitsch gold-plated lockets around the necks of the young crowd. 'They won't wear them at all,' local fashion journalist Pa John Danford tells me. 'It's just too, um, African, for them.'

By and large, a young, urban generation of Africans is trying its damndest to distance itself from such symbols of traditionalism and clinging desperately to cheap imitations of Western status symbols. The pace of urbanization thus poses the greatest threat to a centuries-deep culture, leaving a dangerously polarized market with impoverished rural people at one end and rich expats or 'roots tourists' at the other.

At Accra's fanciest hotel, I have the pleasure of meeting Nana-Amu Fleischer-Djoleta, a Ghanaian school teacher who beads as a hobby. Having lived abroad, Nana-Amu is quite at ease with her identity, and looks the very essence of Afro-chic today in her close-cropped hair, and tailored mudcloth suit, bold red-and-black necklace strung around her neck. Her passion becomes evident as she takes me through her collection of strings, bead by bead. There is Indian Cerulean, Somali silver from a friend's collection, tiny black seed beads, bronze, stone, ebony. 'Sure, anyone can string some beads together,' Nana states, 'but the more involved one gets, the more sensitive one becomes to the juxtaposition of shapes, weights and textures.'

Nana exports small quantities of beads, but as Dagadu explains, the Ghanaian bead export market is at the whim of world trends in ethnic jewellery and consciousness of recycled materials. But as old trade beads become increasingly collectable, the challenges facing the Ghana Bead Society are considerable. 'We were robbed once because we overpaid for the beads in the first place,' Dagadu says drily. 'Now we are robbed again because we do not know their value. And so, we try our best to raise awareness of the history, value and myths associated with beads here. We cannot allow them to be siphoned out without a trace.'

In my Accra hotel room, I unpack the treasures I have bought at Koforudua. They are all new beads, there are far too many of them, and I spend hours selecting, examining and placing them side by side. If and when I return, I cannot be sure what will be left at Koforudua, for I know that the traditions of this continent are vanishing fast. But as I thread Okleh Tete's glass beads onto a grubby piece of string, I feel the immense legacy of unforgotten tragedy, cultural and mythological richness, and sheer aesthetic rapture passing click-click between my fingers.

Zanzibar
GOES TO THE MOVIES

In the tiny town of Wete, on the lush northern tip of Pemba, an island north of Zanzibar, a truck rattles along the potholed tarmac. From a loud-hailer comes the following Swahili screech, '*Leo leo leo! Filamu ipo Wete.*' Today, today, today. Film screening in Wete. This is a rare event for Wete: it happens only once a year.

As the sun dips into the warm Indian Ocean, a crowd gathers in the schoolyard. The classrooms have neither glass in their windows, nor doors. In the yard's centre, a few sticks support a dusty tarpaulin. Beneath it, a row of straight-backed faux-velvet chairs, a rickety table, a plastic flower arrangement and the town's most important people are all poised in anticipation. There is a small stage, festooned proudly with scraps of satin, a screen and a banner that reads, 'Zanzibar International Film Festival'. A generator purrs, and to roars of applause, an image flickers onto the screen.

The idea of a film festival in Tanzania is ridiculous. It is one of Africa's poorest countries, with no film industry to speak of, and television only arrived here in 1986. Local programming comprises basic news and the odd ghastly soap. There are no cinemas operating in Dar es Salaam, the country's capital, while in places like Zanzibar and Pemba, in peeling art deco shells, antiquated projectors rattle off B-Grade Bollywood epics and Japanese action flicks that no-one understands. They show these films because they are cheaply available and because, until recently, no-one has had a better idea.

It was back in 1997 that hotelier Emerson Skeens hatched an insane plan. Just a glimpse at the New York-native's opulent and eccentric *Arabian Nights*-style hotel betrays his penchant for turning wild fantasies into realities. 'I think mad is a good word for this project,' he chuckles, with some satisfaction, in a buttercup silk *kanzu* and embroidered *kofia* on his balcony at the end of the 2002 festival. For as Emerson knows, well-intentioned lunacy is a key development tool in a place like this.

Besides luring income-generating tourists to the island, the Zanzibar International Film Festival (ZIFF) has channelled major money into local cultural projects. Among them, the newly-opened Dhow Countries' Music Academy and an Institute of Contemporary Art. There is also hope of a Performing Arts School here. An East African cultural renaissance, if you like.

Since the fourteenth century, Zanzibar has been a crossroads in this region. Waves of Persian, Portuguese, Omani and British colonizers forged a rich, mystical cultural mix that is reflected in the island's cuisine, architecture, music, language and traditions. But with independence in the 1960s, wealthy Arab patrons fled Zanzibar, and the decades of African socialism that followed left the island increasingly poor and isolated. ZIFF's aim has been to restore Zanzibar's cultural significance. With a budget of four hundred thousand dollars, it has grown to span some hundred and forty films, forty music performances, workshops, seminars, and dynamic women's, children's and village panoramas.

This year's opening ceremony takes place, as always, in the seventeenth-century fortress on Zanzibar's seafront. From the balconies of the House of Wonders next door, flags appliquéd with sponsors' names flutter in the balmy tropical breeze. Zanzibaris are turned out gloriously, in their best, flowing, white *kanzus* and *bui-buis*. Gold jewellery sparks on ebony skin. Eric Ebouaney, the dashing French-Cameroonian star of *Lumumba*, and ZIFF's guest of honour, expresses his delight at being part of such a rare Pan-African cultural event. When a Mexican flamenco dancer bursts on stage and envelops ninety-year-old local Taarab diva Bi Kidude in her skirts, it is a high point for cultural fusion.

The mood is nothing if not cosmopolitan. While low ticket prices ensure the enthusiastic participation of locals, ZIFF has quickly amassed an eclectic group of fans and film fundis. Within hours, I have encountered perspiring British musicologists, Irish and Kenyan film teachers, Fulbright scholars, veteran hippie festival organizers, and film-makers from places you've never dreamed of. Their common passion for culture in the developing world makes them a radical and worldly crew.

British photojournalist Marion Kaplan is here to exhibit her *National Geographic* photo essay 'Life on the *Dhows*' – the distinctive lateen-rigged vessels that have ploughed the Indian Ocean for millennia. (The *dhow*, the symbol of cultural exchange in this region, is also ZIFF's logo.) Chatting to Kaplan makes the treacherous five-month sea journey she made to Arabia in 1973 seem the most normal thing in the world. 'It was just another story,' she says. As, I imagine, were Idi Amin and Bokassa's coronations, the last days of Haile Selassie and hitch-hiking solo across Africa in the 1960s.

Another amazing day at ZIFF takes in morning screenings in the House of Wonders; a glimpse at the music workshops, where Palestinian and Egyptian greats are giving master classes in Classical Arab Music; outdoor performances in the town's Forodhani Gardens; more screenings in the fortress, and finally, late-night dee-jay sessions, drenched in local Konyagi. Celebrated British-Ghanaian dee-jay Rita Ray is here for a second time. Like Apache Indian, Oliver Mtukudzi and other world music greats, Ray has agreed to cut her rates drastically to be part of the event.

Tonight there are African, Iranian and Indian features screening. *Circus Baobab* chronicles the journey of a travelling circus troupe in Guinea. *One Hundred Days*, is a tragic love story set amid the recent genocides in Rwanda. The haunting Senegalese folk tale *The Price of Pardon* wins the Golden Dhow for best feature film.

Yet ZIFF's documentaries are its most powerful offerings. Prizes in this category are awarded to Lindy Wilson's account of South Africa's Truth and Reconciliation Commission, *The Guguletu Seven*; *My Migrant Soul*, Yasmine Kabir's gut-wrenching account of Bangladeshi migrant workers, and Ziba Mir Hosseini's *Runaway*, which tells the tale of girls in Iran who run away from home because their situations have become unbearable.

The British-based Hosseini, aged fifty, is here to give a documentary workshop. Having waited for months for permission to shoot in Tehran, she simply allowed girls to tell their own harrowing stories, and the patience and deep respect of her process has resulted in a remarkable film. Hosseini's hope is that her work strikes a chord with Zanzibari women and inspires them to tell their own stories. 'Solidarity among Muslim women is a key part of our emancipation,' she says.

German Annette Wagner is here to present *Hadzabe*. When Wagner came across some 1930s footage of this East African hunter-gatherer tribe in a cellar of a German university, she restored it and brought it back to Tanzania. Her account of the Hadzabe's celluloid encounter with their ancestors is moving and beautifully shot. Thomas Allen Harris' *E Minha*

Cara tells the story of a black American searching for his identity in the Bronx, Tanzania and Brazil. Pieced together from Super Eight home movies, the film is powerfully personal and explores the yearning and confusion of the African diaspora. South Africa's *Steps for the Future* series is awarded a Special Jury Prize for four superb films about AIDS.

That *Lumumba* receives the People's Choice Award is of little surprise, as local kids have been quoting me lines from it all week. So, too, have they been humming the haunting melodies of Sudanese roots singer Salma el Assad, and acting out scenes from Egyptian storyteller, Sherin el Ansary's performance of the *Scheherazade*. As Yusuf Mahmoud, ZIFF's Music and Performing Arts Director says, 'You might say the roots of an East African Cultural Renaissance have been planted.'

LA ZONE
Francophone

It is three am outside Chez Ntemba nightclub in downtown Johannesburg. Mid 1998. A few black Frenchmen step out of a taxi, heads shaved clean as baseballs. They cut a bizarre contrast with the shabby pavement. I note their moustaches, like chic squares of Velcro beneath their noses, and their charcoal blazers styled carefully in homage to the thirties. It is a look that is currently *à la mode* in Francophone Africa and has been dubbed *Les Années Trentes*.

Thick *soukous* rhythms blare from the club upstairs as one of the men paces, gesticulates and rattles into a tortoiseshell cellphone in quick French patois. The sign above the door reads *Na Kusema Ni Kutaka*, Swahili for 'You are Welcome Here'.

Five years ago I used to hang out in this part of town, but with the gradual flight from Johannesburg's inner city, I stopped. In the meantime, the area has changed – reinventing itself, among other things, as home to some one hundred thousand French-speaking refugees, mostly from Zaïre, but also from Congo, Gabon, Cameroon, Benin, Rwanda and various states South Africans would have difficulty placing on a map. They have all trekked south, betting on a better future. Kind of like New York at the turn of the last century, I imagine.

South Africans first met these Francophone immigrants at fleamarkets. They were the faces behind piles of crude, captivating masks, the persuasive hands flogging squares of raffia velvets. By 1992 Ponte City, that grim concrete phallus of a tower downtown was already well known as Little Zaïre and, lately, Little Zaïre has been growing up.

Cautiously, the community has begun providing for itself. Kin Malebo, a diner in Yeoville, is as low-key and cosy as a plastic tablecloth. At ten o'clock on a Friday night, preppy Francophones are sitting down to bowls of pork, marinated in palm oil; gooey little sausages of steamed cassava or *maboke* and some gruesome goat heels in spicy soup. Nearby there are CD stores, church communities, boutiques full of bright wax-prints and hair salons, one of them christened Strasbourg St Denis in homage to Paris' famous African *arrondissement*. Prematurely perhaps, people are talking about Johannesburg's French Quarter and frankly, I'm thrilled.

Mine, of course, is not the prevailing view. If the prevailing view is anything to go by, Francophones have all walked here barefoot from Kinshasa or Abidjan, their sole purpose to spread disease, steal jobs or sell cocaine. Swept up as we are in a chummy smörgåsbord of Neo-Nationalism, few South Africans have bothered to authenticate that perception. And so the stereotypes persist. For white South Africans, Francophones are just more black faces joining the ranks of the masses, while to blacks they are just foreigners, or the dreaded *amakwerekwere*.

Today, I meet Samuel Maka in a makeshift chapel beneath Ponte City, the foreboding concrete monolith in the suburb of Berea. Samuel is writing a book about the evolving Zone Francophone. Samuel is friendly and quietly spoken, and is dressed in disguise. Rather than shave his hair at the sides in a Zaïrian style, he's grown it longer, like a local. As for the sporty, American-styled clothing he's wearing, Samuel can only shrug and laugh, 'It's not me.' But one of the realities of moving south, he explains, is that most of the time, one is better off hiding one's foreignness.

Back home, he tells me, women parade in their traditional finery, but here, wrapping your hips in a patterned *kikwende* is simply asking for trouble. For the most part, traditional, long, flowing braids have made way for shorter, dowdier South African styles. 'Locals think foreigners are rich,' Samuel says. 'So unless we dress down, we are moving targets for criminals.'

One shouldn't underestimate how downright undignified Francophones feel slopping about in preppy casual wear. Though their colonizers returned to Europe in the sixties, the restrained, somewhat stuffy dress codes they left behind remain critical to understanding these cultures. 'In the Congo, you could live in a shack and be starving,' a hairdresser tells me, 'but you'd never leave home without looking elegant.' Conversely, while the level of infrastructure in these countries may be zero, strut down the street in your new, two-piece Jean Paul Gaultier number and you'll immediately be recognized as a devotee of a clothing cult, Les Sapeurs.

The word *sapeur* comes from SAPE – an acronym for *Société des Ambianceurs et Personnes Elégantes*, or the Society of Ambience-makers and Elegant People. The cult became popular in Congo and Zaïre in the eighties. Famous musicians like Papa Wemba and Pepe Kalle led the way, styling in Yohji Yahamoto and *Comme des Garçons*. 'I am the *Grand Sape*,' Wemba would proclaim and young men emulated him with every last scrap of income they could muster.

Johannesburg has its own little clutch of *sapeurs*, whom I meet at Strasbourg St Denis. One of them carries a gold-handled walking stick. Others are having their heads shaved in styles named after Japanese designers or, shudder, Hitler. The suits they wear on this Thursday morning are a little dated, but impeccable.

The following evening I witness an even more extreme form of fashion slavery at a Pentacostal church nearby. '*Dieu*,' the charismatic preacher yells. The worshippers stream forth, arms outstretched, bellowing hallelujahs. Soon it transpires that many of these good Christians are members of another cult called *La Religion Kitendi*, and are largely here to show off their ensembles. 'Seriously,' an insider gabs, 'these people are here praying to the God of Chic. They are praying for style.' In his office later, the preacher confirms this. 'Yes it's true,' he laments. 'Many in my congregation spend all their money on clothes, before food even. It's so sad.'

Take Jose Essabe, a Congolese sign-writer I meet in Yeoville. Clad head-to-toe in seventies-vintage Yves Saint Laurent, Jose tells me he'd never wear Versace. 'Far too flashy,' he insists. Indeed, a request to photograph him with his hands in his blazer pockets meets with nothing short of horror. 'It's just not elegant,' he states, deadpan. So, what is elegant then?

A fashion tour of Yeoville holds some clues, and Emmanuel Mwamba, who tailors clothes from his flat nearby, makes an animated guide. In this relatively safe foreigner-zone, Emmanuel can spot Francophones a mile off. '*Bolit*,' he yells, singling out a suave, ebony giant in a baggy retro suit. Then, '*Bombas!*' – an even baggier look. 'He's probably wearing another pair of trousers underneath for bulk,' he explains. '*Les bombas* wear up to four pairs at a time.'

Like most immigrants, Emmanuel isn't doing what he set out to when he came here. In the early nineties, when opposition politics in Zaïre's universities prompted Mobutu Sese Seko's dictatorship to crack down upon and close these institutions, Emmanuel was only mid-way through a biology degree. In 1992, he headed south in the hope of completing his studies. Like so many young Africans, he was seduced by the sense of opportunity promised by the new Rainbow Nation, but he had little idea how exclusive that rainbow was to prove. After paying thousands of dollars in Kinshasa for his passage, when he finally arrived, his study permit was refused.

South Africa has not extended the warmest of welcomes to its new immigrants. As Libyan-born researcher Abdou-Maliq Simone says, it is difficult evaluating the legal status of these refugees. 'We don't have access to numbers,' he says, 'but based on my network, which comprises a few hundred people, I'd say around half the Francophones here are legal. Because many of these nationals don't need visas to enter the country, if they're here illegally, it's simply because they've overstayed their welcome. There are people who obtain illegal documents and others who go through the right channels. Ultimately, their fate will depend on South Africa's relationship with their home countries.'

Somehow, South Africa's current crime wave furthers the confusion. Under public pressure, police must be seen to be tackling crime. Immigrants, who are marginalized into ghettos and have few legal rights make for easy scapegoats. 'Sure, some immigrants are involved in crime rings,' adds Simone, 'but identifying criminality as a national trait is simply ridiculous.'

Many Francophones I meet are anxious to back this up. 'We're scared of blood, you know,' says Chayis Mobhe, a bright marketing student I meet. 'Where we come from there's a sense of community that provides a safety net against crime. I think if we were more aggressive, Mobutu wouldn't still be in power today.'

Despite this tendency to pacifism, most Francophones strike me as more industrious and pragmatic than South Africans are. Though generic immigrant zeal may account for some of this energy, it is also culturally rooted. 'We have an expression in Zaïre,' Chayis expands: '*Débrouillez-vouz.*' Roughly translated, it means "help yourself" and it sums up a certain enterprising spirit that took root in Zaïre in the wake of the government's total disregard for people's needs.

Although I have come across doctors, engineers and computer programmers in this milieu, most Zaïrians I meet are starting up businesses. Either they're exporting or freighting goods or they've found some way of servicing their community. One such entrepreneur is Sylvia Mwila, a smart Lubumbashi businesswoman, with the demure composure of a young Catherine Deneuve. 'Music is very important where we come from,' she says. 'Everyone listens to rumba and everyone dances, no matter what age they are.'

Last year, Sylvia and her family opened Cadence Tropicale, a CD store in Yeoville that stocks twelve-hundred World Music titles. Posters of Papa Wemba, Koffi Olomide and Angelique Kidjo pay homage to the stars of Francophone pop. Sylvie feels no urgency about returning home. 'I studied in South Africa,' she says. 'So, now I want to give something back.'

Others have similar sentiments. Jacques Kalambaie used to manage a factory in Zaïre's Shaba province, but here he has set up a taxi business, catering both to locals and newly landed immigrants. When I arrive at his suburban office, the place is buzzing like the Tower of Babel. Two operators take calls in French; one in Portuguese; one in Swahili. Others speak Zulu and Afrikaans. 'I was very frightened when I arrived here two years ago,' Kalambaie recalls. 'I couldn't speak English and I felt totally lost. The first person I met was a taxi driver; he showed me around and made me feel at home. In a way, through this business, I can offer the same hospitality.'

A friend of mine lives near Ponte City. Sometimes, through his window, he sees Francophones walking home at night. 'Only they don't walk,' he chuckles. 'They promenade – long purposeful strides down the hill. I watch the locals watching them from the pavement, transfixed, then trying to copy the walk after they've left.'

If this is one difference between French- and English-speaking Africans, it is one in a thousand. As the local manageress of a Francophone venue explains, 'They're very sophisticated, you know – posh actually'.

Monsieur Ganda, the new *chargé d'affaires* at the Zaïrian embassy, doesn't quite use the word 'posh' but he estimates that around eighty percent of the Zaïrians here have degrees. Indeed, while most of the Mozambican refugees in South Africa have simply climbed over a fence, when it comes to Francophones, distance and expense screen out poorer migrants. The latest wave of African refugees are its bourgeoisie.

Hence, a rather sad, new South African tale of suspicion, intolerance and miscommunication. As Chayis Mobhe explains, 'I thought I'd made some true South African black friends at university here,' he recalls, 'but as it turned out, they either had, say, a Malawian mother, or they'd been in exile. It's strange because when I go to Soweto, I feel right at home. In fact it's pretty much like Kinshasa. I see people eating *pap* and I identify. We eat *pap*. But I don't speak Zulu, so no-one's really interested in communicating.'

For some reason, I feel a need to apologize on the part of my compatriots. Here we sit in The Parrot, a bar in Yeoville, and I feel deeply embarrassed by my country. I'm sorry that we're so mean-spirited and ignorant. So rude and so prejudiced. And yet, beneath the shame, I am enjoying myself this evening. I'll savour the conversation I've had – partly for its intellectual and philosophical fluidity, but also because it seems so damn normal. We sit. We talk. No complexes. No race. No shit.

In time, we cover the usual beat of how South Africa needs to look after its own. We discuss how isolated we've been here and how rare it is that South Africans rub shoulders with other cultures. I express my excitement at discovering a little bit of Paris in my own backyard, but ultimately, my public relations exercise proves useless. 'I'm okay for now,' says Chayis. 'But as soon as I can, I'll go back to Zaïre. I just don't need this kind of attitude.'

The following day I meet Samuel Maka again. Still lost in his disguise, he is hoping I can help with publication of his manuscript. Entitled *The Underground Paradise of the South*, the book is aimed at dissuading more Francophones from heading south. Secretly, I can think of many xeno-phobic South Africans who would happily fund such an endeavour out of their own pockets, but why this title?

'People come here with capital and qualifications,' says Samuel. 'Because of what's going on at home, young people come here from Zaïre with their dreams on their sleeves. They have the best intentions of becoming part of this society. They want to study, to learn English and to build a new future in a new place.

'But when they get here, it's a different story. They're up against all sorts of hostility – legal, administrative and social. The way things are, they get pushed into an underground world. They're forced into an illegal existence in a ghetto, as they wait for Mobutu to die. I hope my book will convince some people to stay at home. We must work out our problems from within our country.'

Together with his motivation, Samuel has enclosed some photographs. They aren't quite your standard tourist brochure. There's a shot of some unemployed bums lounging in a park. A shot of educated immigrants driven to hawking goods on the pavement, and last in the pile, a shot I know all too well – Johannesburg's impressive metropolitan skyline, silhouetted against a golden Highveld sunset. 'And what about this one?' I ask. 'Oh that one,' Samuel muses ironically. 'That's paradise.'

FOOD FOR THE
Gods

Sometime in the late afternoons, the *baianas de acaraje* set up wooden tables in the shade of mango trees, on the steep cobblestoned streets of the Pelourinho – the pastel-hued, old quarter of Salvador de Bahia, in Brazil's poor and sweltering North East. The *baianas* dress as they have done for five centuries: in vast, layered, lace dresses that look like wedding cakes, white turbans and strings of bright, glass beads gleaming against their golden brown skin.

Their tables creak with the weight of ingredients: great Tupperwares of sour bean paste; packets of dried shrimp and chillies; bowls of slimy okra or peanut purée, varieties of garish pink confectionery, and somewhere in the midst of the feast, a wooden carving of a hand, middle finger raised to ward off the evil spirits.

As the tropic sun dips into a horizon of ornate, peeling church towers, the *baianas* drop balls of bean paste – or *acaraje* – into sizzling, red palm oil. Once crisp, these divine morsels are sliced, stuffed and wolfed down with such enthusism it's little wonder they are known as Bahia's hamburgers. Yet, in this spirit-soaked place, the *baianas* are not simply vending tropical Big Macs, they are fulfilling a daily obligation to their voodoo gods, or *orixas*. Indeed, the very word *acaraje* is Yoruba for 'Food of the Gods'

I have crossed the Atlantic with a riddle. For the past decade, I have poked through the grimiest corners of the motherland in a quest for answers, yet the riddle still perplexes me. What is Africa? I ask myself, ad nauseum. But perhaps the answers lie outside the continent. Perhaps, looking in, the diaspora can shed some light on the motherland.

Thus far, the riddle has led me on a great triangle of a journey. From Africa, I made my to way to Harlem, New York City, where I spent a year digging for resonances of home. Yet ultimately, my hand came up empty. Centuries of systematic oppression at the hands of their American masters has all but wiped out the traditional heritage of African Americans. And while many remember their blackness, subjected to remoteness, humiliation and economic misery for so long, they have forgotten their Africanness.

Indeed, it was not until the Civil Rights movement of the 1960s that a new African heritage was synthesized in the United States, complete with Afro Festivals, trinkets and beliefs. Yet for all the Ashanti names, cowrie-shell earrings and reams of fake *kente* cloth I've seen gleaming on One Hundred and Twenty-fifth Street, I can sense little genuine empathy with the African continent in America. It is simply too far away, its realities too far removed, or too different to matter.

At best, the Americans I've met have a fantasy vision of the continent. They may have made brief trips to Ghana or Senegal and returned braided, beaded and a little wiser, but most Americans have never been to Africa and know little of its geography, traditions or current affairs. Indeed, to many of the folk on my block in Harlem, Africa is just another backward Third World country, full of thieves and insects and malaria. 'Hey, when you going home?' an old woman barked at me on Lennox Avenue one afternoon.

'Soon.'

'Well,' she replied, gesturing out along a block full of scowling unemployed thugs, 'don't forget to take these animals back there with you.'

A few months later I continued my pilgrimage south to Lima in Peru. A few thousand African slaves were brought here in the 1500s. They had not come directly from Africa, but from the slave markets of Panama and Colombia. For fear of uprisings, their masters had not imported complete tribes, but rather a mix of people from different parts of the continent. Once in Peru, they were quickly Catholicized. With no common tribal authority or language, it was unlikely that they would retain any of their African traditions for very long. Even drums were banned.

But the African rhythms would not be so easily silenced. The slaves invented the *cajon*, a wooden box that you beat on, and the rhythms of the *cajon* have subsequently set the timbre for a whole beautiful genre of Afro-Peruvian music.

I make my journey south along the Pan-American highway from Lima to Chincha, where some of the country's remaining black population is based. We cut through the grey coastal desert. There is no vegetation, just dead dunes pouring into the sea. Just how anyone ekes out a living around here is beyond me.

From Chincha, I take a minibus to the village of El Carmen. The yellow Plaza de Armas is deserted when I arrive, but for a single old man pulling up weeds. I scour the town, but find no-one who can tell me anything of its black heritage. Go to the house of Amador Bellambrosia, I am told. I do, only Bellambrosia has unfortunately had a stroke and I can scarcely understand a word he says.

Nearby, in a singularly hideous copper and glass hotel, a few kids are beating away on the cajon. They shake their arms wildly, wriggle, leap and yell in Spanish. Only their bodies have remembered the ancient rhythms of their origins. Rhythm is the sole keeper of history.

I return to Lima and make my pilgrimage to the home of the great, Grammy-winning Afro-Peruvian singer, Susana Baca. It is a large, sparsely furnished mansion in the seaside suburb of Barranco. Susana and her boyfriend, Ricardo Perriera, have long been passionate about Afro-Peruvian culture and have a small library of literature on the subject. They have also travelled Peru to record rhythms, which Susana has reworked in her beautiful songs. 'It's true,' she says. 'This culture is very much invisible in Peru. Even at school, I was taught nothing about black Peru. It was as though we never existed, and since then we have assimilated even further. 'And so the culture is disappearing?' I ask. 'Yes,' she laments. 'Only the rhythms remain.'

I cannot hide my disappointment. Indeed, only the sublime power of Susana's voice set against the haunting thump of the cajon can console me. Yet beyond this small but dedicated intellectual clique in Lima, African culture has all but disappeared in Peru.

Alas, thus far I have not found Africa in America. And while I am no closer to understanding what the continent is, my sense of what it isn't is growing clearer. Africa isn't Harlem. Neither is it Paris or Brussels or Lima. God, half the time it isn't Dakar or Nairobi or Johannesburg either. But perhaps – just perhaps – it is Bahia. Perhaps here, in the warm waters of the Baia de Todos Santos, I might find what I'm looking for.

I stand out on the edge of the Peninsula. The stretch across the Atlantic to Angola and the Gulf of Guinea is relatively narrow at this point, the climate is similar, and yes, the circumstances of colonization here were unique. Of course the slaves brought Africa with them, but cultural survival is unlikely under oppressive political and religious regimes. Has Africa remembered itself in Brazil? Has it blossomed or has it shrivelled to nothing? And, either way, can this teach me something about the motherland? I gaze out over the Bay of All Saints and hope.

The Colour of Mondays

Throughout Brazil, Salvador has a reputation for its sense of primal, pulsating mystery. Once the country's capital, this languid hilly port, scattered with colourful high-rises is now Brazil's fourth-largest city. According to UNESCO, it also houses the most important collection of colonial buildings in the Americas. Step inside one of the city's three hundred and sixty-five churches (yes, one for each day of the year, it is said) and acres of gold leaf will attest to a glorious but forgotten colonial past. Yet lately, thanks to a tropical climate and blonde beaches strewn with palms and bronzed, athletic bodies, Salvador is being reborn as a tourist destination.

Although the religion of *Candomble* is practised throughout Brazil, it is at its most powerful here. Based loosely on voodoo – the deep animist belief code practised in West Africa – *Candomble* made its way here in the sixteenth century with the African slaves. To the Catholics of the new colony, however, the cult presented a savage threat to civilization and its practice was banned; slaves were forced to attend church services.

But the slaves were not so easily fooled out here in the Bay of All Saints. One by one, they identified Catholic saints and twinned them with their pantheon of voodoo deities, placing icons of them in the altars of their temples. They wove the traditions so closely together it became impossible to distinguish one from the other. For indeed, if Africa was to survive in Brazil, it would need to come up with some extraordinarily clever disguises.

I step over to a mango tree and seat myself next to Senhora Ana Sueli Rodriguez. She seems wary of me at first, but I purchase an *acaraje* from her stock and she chats more easily. Today is Monday, she observes. Mondays are the days of Nana, the God of Calm Waters, so the beads she's strung around her neck are white and her great cake of a dress is trimmed in shiny white ribbon. White is the colour of Nana, she explains. The colour of Mondays.

Though the gods have different names from those I've encountered in West Africa, their functions and attributes are similar. Indeed, for each *orixa*, there are favourite colours, foods, rhythms and days of the week. But on all days, as Sueli explains, believers are obliged to make some small offerings to the gods to appease them of any hostility.

Luckily, the gods are wise. They know that their followers are poor women who need to help provide for their families and cannot afford to waste any food, and so, centuries ago, it was agreed that they prepare the *acaraje* the gods required and sell them to make a little money on the side. And so, as often in Bahia, a single act has come to carry multiple meanings.

I step into an open-air restaurant in the city's grime-stained CBD. I drink a large beer and nibble on fresh fish and *farofa* – Brazil's answer to couscous – and, as Monday winds to a close, I make my way back to my *pensão*. The whole city – the carved baroque facades, the palms, even the tourist touts – seems bathed in a faint white light. Tomorrow, the day of Iroko, will be greener.

The Terreiro

Tuesdays are not only the day of Iroko in Salvador, but also the slaves' day of rest. While they toiled in sugar plantations all week, come Tuesday afternoons, the Pelhourinho was reborn as a vast and joyous street party. Half a millennium later, the tradition is as vibrant as ever.

I step over to the *Terreiro de Jesus*, the grand, palm-lined square at the entrance to the Pelhourinho. In its centre, a large stage is being erected against a backdrop of exquisite carved stone churches. Already, around the edge of the square, duos of athletic young men in loose patchwork pants are kicking their way through rhythmic *capoiera* routines.

Said to have originated in Angola as a martial art, *capoiera* too was forbidden by the Portuguese, and so the slaves embarked on yet another master plan of disguise, twisting their fight into a sensuous dance. The men flip cartwheels into the sky, kicking and leaping to the sound of the one-stringed *berimbau*, a perfect mix of energy and grace.

I walk on through the Pelourinho, following the melodies of sambas and maxixes. I spot Senhora Rodriguez, pretty today in pale blue lace and deep indigo beads. I buy an *acaraje* and I walk as I eat.

Music, too, was subject to a process of disguise here for its survival. To make the frantic African rhythms acceptable to their masters, the slaves adopted Portuguese lyrics and themes and wove them over the African beats. I gaze in at narrow, wooden bars, their doorways a-dangle with green coconuts. Inside, old men in straw hats and white leather shoes are strumming out tunes on old, four-stringed guitars – some melancholic, some celebratory or romantic. Meanwhile, the rest of us tap in time with matchboxes, sticks or our palms – on paint tins, wooden crates and table tops.

Once sufficient cane has been poured over chunks of lime, we spill out into the narrow streets and dance. Every couple of blocks, a flood of people indicates yet another music school displaying its talents. At Dida, an all-girl school, the clear pitch of a robed and braided soloist rings triumphant over the thunder of some thirty drums. A few blocks away, at Oludum, the world-renowned troupe that backed Paul Simon beats thunder through the town. Even the sun-bleached roof tiles seem to clatter in celebration. The light is blue and sacred.

Oba

On Wednesday, the day of Oba, the God of the Seas, I find myself in a neon-lit suburban shed, privy to a secret *Candomble* ceremony. In many ways, this looks and feels like those I've attended in West Africa. In a corner, a small, thatched altar holds a telling mix of saints and fetishes. Each house is led by a priest or priestess, and often – as the century of faded snapshots in the local Afro-Brazilian museum reflects – they become revered public figures.

In this house, the priestess, or *Mae de Santo*, is an imposing old woman, with few teeth, a gold turban and a large bronze bell that she clangs with the rhythm of the drums. She rests on a cowrie-encrusted throne, eyebrows raised, as her adepts prostrate themselves before her. Each dance speaks to a different god. Oba. Oxum. Iemanjah. Xango. The frenzied Yoruba chants would be perfectly understood in Nigeria.

'This is so much more than a religion for me,' explains Ana Claudia, an advertising executive who's parked her station wagon outside and changed into white cotton for the ceremony. 'It's folklore and history and tradition. I can feel the experience of the slaves so many centuries ago. After six years,

I am just a beginner here; there is still so much to learn.'

While, officially, ninety-five percent of Brazilians are Catholics, many belong to a house of *Candomble*. While some needs are best served in the church, when it comes to more pressing problems, they will consult their *Mae* or *Pae de Santo*. And indeed, while the belief systems seem opposed to us, in the hearts of Brazilians, there is space for both. Syncretism runs deep in the veins of this nation. It has had to.

After hours of dancing, two adepts fall into a trance, slipping backwards, eyes shut, amid the slamming of the drums. The *ekeji*, or assistants, whisk them off to another room and return with them wrapped in floral fabric. In turn, they hold each of us to their chests. The *Mae de Santo* breaks into a cavernous grin, waves her arms, and clangs her bell frantically.

'This was always a simple religion,' explains Otavio, a chemical engineer who was raised Catholic but has been coming here for fifteen years. 'Because its devotees were poor, food was all they had to offer to the gods. And so it was woven deeply into our rituals.'

Presently, a trail of adepts usher in a range of dishes for tonight's celebration. Cross-legged on a straw mat, the *Mae de Santo* scoops out individual platters from large wooden bowls. There is *caruru*, a gooey, okra paste, served with crunchy, yellow *farofa* – roasted manioc flour; then spicy chicken and a range of beans. We eat with our hands, communing with the gods and thanking them for their protection. The light is red tonight. Oba is delighted.

Thursday

For the past few mornings, I have been making my way down the steep cliffs by bus to Salvador's favourite beach, Porto de Barro, and already, some of the faces nestled under umbrellas are familiar to me. 'We are here every day,' explains a leathery, old man. 'It is our paradise.'

Hawkers stroll lazily among the sun worshippers, their wares dangling from great sticks they've hoisted over their shoulders. There are small sachets of suntan oil, cheap sunglasses, beads and surf shorts. Others sell icy drinks or roast chunks of sweaty white cheese over little fires. The *baianas* at the roadside are yellow today.

I gaze at the bodies on the beach, and at the various hues of brown glistening in the sunlight. The mix of Africans, Europeans and indigenous Indians produced what is known locally as *mistura fina* – the exquisite mix of races that is modern Brazil. In yet another act of disguise, Portuguese men buried their genes in African and Indian women, and their children mixed and their children's children mixed more. Today, in Bahia, the Brazilian *mistura* is at its richest.

Yet still, Brazil is full of paradoxes. While inter-breeding was encouraged to help populate this vast land, the black population of modern Brazil remains socially and economically disadvantaged. There are few blacks at the country's universities and fewer still in parliament, and the country's economic elite remains almost exclusively white. Bahia, the country's blackest state, is also one of its poorest. Only culturally has Africa triumphed in Brazil.

Yemenjah

It is Friday 2 February, the holy day of Yemenjah – the vain, but fertile Goddess of the Sea. As always on this day, a vast procession of white-clad devotees are making their way to the water's edge to pay homage to their goddess. If Yemenjah's vanity is sufficiently indulged, she will bless the fishermen with calm waters, and so the procession makes its way to the beachfront, laden with gifts.

There are baskets and little polystyrene boats, laden with special trinkets for our vain lady of the oceans: make-up, mirrors, hairbrushes, nail files, cheap bottles of perfume and bouquets of white flowers. One by one, the devotees kneel at a grand statue of the mermaid goddess and then slowly make their way out to sea, boats and baskets raised above their heads. Entranced as they are by the power of the act, they seem not to notice the water deepening around them.

The waves wash the little boats out into the bay. A carpet of pink and white plastic flowers floats on the water. I stroll down the beach and back. By now, the tide is coming in and the sands are strewn with little mirrors and broken bits of boat.

Dada

Come Saturday, I make my way to the local cooking school, where chef Nivaldo Galdino runs me through the culinary *mistura*. Though certain foods – like palm hearts, manioc, aipim and other roots – were already used by indigenous Indians, the quintessential culinary elements of palm oil, fiery malaguenta chillies, ginger, coconut milk and dried shrimp all arrived from Africa with the slaves. The Portuguese introduced sugar, salt and some preparations, like salting meat and fish, along with a range of sticky desserts, which came to include roasted coconut, candied guava, banana, pineapple, jackfruit and *quindim*, a sticky egg and coconut concoction, sold everywhere.

'Now,' says Nivaldo. 'You need to go and see Dada.' He draws me a map and I follow a steep winding street in the suburb of Rio Vermelho. Set in a back yard and strung with washing lines, this cheerful, low-key eatery is the work of one of Salvador's most celebrated daughters.

Dada began cooking aged five. By twelve, she was already a *baiana de acaraje*. Gradually, she expanded her culinary range to include prepared dishes like *moqueca* – fish or mixed seafood, swimming in a warm sea of coconut, ginger, chillies and palm oil – and *vatapa* – a yummy paste of dried shrimp, ground peanuts and green pepper. Today, these same dishes sizzle in earthenware bowls on a buffet table, in what has become a favourite haunt of famous local musicians like Caetano Veloso and Carlinhos Brown.

Dada has refined the local palate, diluting the pungent palm oil with olive, and toning down the *malaguentas*. Today, the buxom and energetic hostess, in a yellow turban and equally bright smile, spoons me through her Bahaian feast. There is a piquant green clam and ginger soup, accompanied with baby *acaraje*; *acara*, a bean and onion paste, wrapped in banana leaves and steamed solid; *bobo*, a yam and seafood stew. There are also some delicious improvisations explained only as *mistura de Dada*. One of them is a coconut risotto, with juicy chunks of pineapple, dusted with chilli and crowned with large fresh lobsters.

We suck on home-made *cachaca* – a rainbow of unrecognizable tropical fruits steeped in a wicked, sugar-cane brew, and then a fiery little liqueur Dada has dreamed up with cinnamon, cloves and honey. She glances at her steaming table. 'I think the *orixas* will be satisfied,' she nods.

Domingo

A week has passed since my arrival – green, blue, red, white, yellow, orange, black. And how many such rainbows have passed here since the sixteenth century?

I make my way back down to Porto de Barro. The beach is so packed, you can see no sand, only a multi-coloured jigsaw of oily bodies. The sunglasses touts clamber among us, the air heavy with the smell of roast cheese. The scene is so very African. In a blink, I could be hanging out on Labadi beach in Ghana or nibbling *atjeke* in a lagoon-side *maquis* in Abidjan. Yet ultimately, it is neither the balmy, tropical setting nor the robust flavours that transports me home so much as the tome of meaning that shadows the rituals of daily life. The deep animism of the African continent imbues everything with spirit, and creates a fertile and magical universe. That magic is everywhere in Bahia – in its songs, its feasts, its dances, its cults, its people.

As with genetics, the mixing of cultures has made them more robust. Faced with cultural oppression, Brazil's African slaves mastered a most wily series of disguises and so ensured the survival of their ancient beliefs and traditions. Nowhere have I seen African culture preserved with such dignity. Yes indeed, the *orixas* would be most proud.

Glossary

AKAN: tribal group, West Africa
ALPHA BLONDY: Ivorian reggae star
AMAKWEREKWERE: South African slang for 'foreigner'
ASHANTI: West African tribe
ATJEKE: ground vegetable paste, Côte d'Ivoire

BACHEQUE: Dance from central Africa
BALAFON: West African xylophone
BANCO: mud-brick building technique similar to adobe
BAOULE: tribe in central Côte d'Ivoire
BAZIN: damask cotton, popular in the Sahel
BERBERS: pre-Arab inhabitants of Morocco
BILTONG: dried meat, South Africa
BOGOLAN: or mud-cloth, hand-woven cotton from Mali
BOUBOU: West African men's robe
BOZO: Malian tribe, often fishermen
BROCHETTES: kebabs
BUYI-BUYI: concealing women's garment, East Africa
BWANA: Swahili for 'mister'

CAR RAPIDE: communal vehicle found in Senegal
CHECH: fine cloth worn as headgear by Berber men
CFA: Currency shared by member-states of the African Financial Community

DHOW: wooden trading vessel with lateen rig

DIESEL: luxury clothing brand
DJEMBE: West African drum
DOGON: animist tribe in Mali's South East
DUMBAK: type of East African drum
DURBAR: parade

FA: voodoo divination system
FOULARD: women's head-wrap, West Africa

GANJA: dagga, marijuana
GRIOTS: the Sahel's legendary praise singers or troubadours

HAIK: women's head scarf, sometimes trimmed with coins
HAUSA: Sahelian tribe
HIGH-LIFE: Up-beat Ghanaian music style
HIJAB: women's head-scarf

KABBALAH: Jewish holy book
KANGA: cotton cloth, East Africa
KANZU: long men's shirt, East Africa
KASBAH: walled banco palaces in Morocco
KENKEY: sticky Ghanaian porridge
KENTE: hand-woven royal cloth of the Ashanti tribe
KHALAM: one- to three-stringed Senegalese violin
KIKWENDE: Cloth from central Africa
KOFIA: embroidered men's skullcap
KONYAGI: cheap East African cane liquor

KORA: seventeen-stringed
West African harp
KURTA: men's two-piece suit, India

MAASAI: East African pastoralists
MAXIXE: melancholic Brazilian
musical form
MBALAX: percussion-heavy popular
Senegalese music
MEDINA: central residential district
of Dakar
MUEZZIN: He who calls the morning
prayer from the mosque
NDEBELE: South African tribe
NKRUMAH, KWAME: Ghana and
independent Africa's first president
NGO: Non-governmental organization

OUD: Middle-Eastern lute

PADRI: Swahili for Padre, or Father
PAGNE: wax-printed cloth
PANGA: large knife
PAP: cornmeal porridge, staple
in South Africa
PENSÃO: small, cheap hotel
PEUL: or Fulani, nomadic Saharan
tribe thought to have originated
in Egypt
PIROGUE: flat-bottomed wooden boat

RAI: protest music from Algeria
and Morocco
RENAMO: Mozambique National
Resistance
RICKSHA: hand-pulled vehicle

SAHEL: strip of savannah south of
the Sahara
SERENGETI: vast game reserve in
East Africa
SKABANGA: South African slang for
ruffian
SOUKOUS: Zaïrian rumba music,
popular throughout sub-Saharan Africa
SWAHILI: or KiSwahili, language
spoken along East African coast
SLASTOE: slate flooring

TAARAB: East African musical form
based on classical Arab music
TANA: short for Antananarivo,
Madagascar's capital
TOUBABS: Wolof for 'foreigner'
TUAREGS: blue-robed nomadic
Saharan tribe
TRO-TRO: communal vehicle, Ghana
TRETCHIKOFF: Russian/South African
artist famous for his idealized
exotic beauties

UMM KHALTOUM: great Egyptian
vocalist
UNESCO: United Nations Educational,
Scientific and Cultural Organization

VALIHA: Malagasy string instrument
VIM: household scouring powder

WOOLIES: Woolworths department store
WOLOF: tribe and dominant language
in Senegal
YORUBA: Nigerian tribe

About the Author

Adam Levin was born in January 1969 into a suburban Johannesburg household, where he was surrounded with books and African art. He was moved to Singapore at an early age. Then to Hong Kong. Then London. Then home to South Africa, where he ploughed through seven schools before finding himself at the University of Cape Town, reading French and Anthropology, and entertaining thoughts of sabbaticals with remote nomadic tribes, *s'il vous plaît*.

He took his first writing job on *Style* magazine, under the sharp, dry tutelage of editor Marilyn Hattingh. Within a couple years, Levin had wormed his way through most of West and East Africa. Though he initially wrote travel features on these trips, he shifted gradually to profiles, documentaries and ultimately first-person narratives. Hattingh published the results as a series in *Style*.

In 1996, Levin left *Style* and worked as freelancer. His work was published in many international publications, including *Vogue* (UK); and *Conde Nast Traveler* (US), as well as most South African magazines. He was twice awarded a Mondi Gold Award for pieces published in *Style*.

In 1998, Levin was employed by Times Media Television to produce *Afro 2000*, a series on African couture for the South African Broadcasting Corporation series *Elegance*. In the same year, he began trading in African goods and set up Soul Trading, dealing in hand-made craft and textiles.

In 2000, Levin moved to New York, where he worked as a correspondent and freelance writer. In 2002, he returned to South Africa and in 2003, was employed to set up the South African Fashion Week's Pan-African events. He's currently working as a features writer for South Africa's new daily newspaper, *This Day*. He has recently been wandering and writing in Brazil and Peru.